Bird Magic

About the Author

Sandra Kynes is a yoga instructor, a Reiki practitioner, and a member of the Bards, Ovates and Druids. She likes developing creative ways to explore the world and integrating them with her spiritual path, which serves as the basis for her books. She has lived in New York City, Europe, England, and now coastal New England. She loves connecting with nature through gardening, hiking, bird watching, and ocean kayaking. Sandra is a member of the Cornell Lab of Ornithology and Maine Audubon. Visit her website at www.kynes.net.

Bird Magic

Wisdom of the Ancient Goddess
for Pagans & Wiccans

SANDRA KYNES

Llewellyn Publications
Woodbury, Minnesota

FIRST EDITION
Third Printing, 2021

Book design: Donna Burch-Brown
Cover art: iStockphoto.com/26706378©Ricardo Reitmeyer
           iStockphoto.com/33661646©ilyianne
           iStockphoto.com/7159729©touring
Cover design: Lisa Novak
Editing: Stephanie Finne
Interior art on pages 9, 23, 35, 46, 59–60, 65, 88 and 120: Llewellyn Art Department
Interior Bird illustrations and art on pages 39 and 41: Wen Hsu

Llewellyn Publications is a registered trademark of Llewellyn Worldwide Ltd.

Library of Congress Cataloging-in-Publication Data
Names: Kynes, Sandra,
Title: Bird magic : wisdom of the ancient goddess for pagans and wiccans / by
   Sandra Kynes.
Description: First Edition. | Woodbury : Llewellyn Worldwide, Ltd, 2016. |
   Includes bibliographical references and index.
Identifiers: LCCN 2015037456 (print) | LCCN 2016006256 (ebook) | ISBN
   9780738748641 | ISBN 9780738749310 ()
Subjects: LCSH: Goddess religion. | Birds. | Witchcraft. | Wiccans. |
   Neopaganism. | Magic.
Classification: LCC BL473.5 .K96 2016 (print) | LCC BL473.5 (ebook) | DDC
   299/.94--dc23
LC record available at http://lccn.loc.gov/2015037456

Llewellyn Publications
A Division of Llewellyn Worldwide Ltd.
2143 Wooddale Drive
Woodbury, MN 55125-2989
www.llewellyn.com

Printed in the United States of America

Other Books by Sandra Kynes

Herb Gardener's Essential Guide

Star Magic

Mixing Essential Oils for Magic

Llewellyn's Complete Book of Correspondences

Change at Hand

Sea Magic

Your Altar

Whispers from the Woods

A Year of Ritual

Gemstone Feng Shui

Forthcoming Books by Sandra Kynes

Plant Magic

Contents

"There is nothing separate from her;
All things come from her, return to her, and are her." [1]

1. Wendy Doniger, ed., "Earth Mother," *Merriam-Webster's Encyclopedia of World Religions* (Springfield, MA: Merriam-Webster, 1999), 308.

Introduction

The ancient goddess-worshipping cultures of Europe have fascinated me for a long time, and I have spent more than twenty years researching them because they speak to the root of my beliefs as a Pagan. Throughout the years, the intention of my reading and research has been to personalize the essence of the Great Goddess for my own spiritual practice. Books about the Goddess by archaeologist and professor Marija Gimbutas sparked a major shift in how many of us regard the Divine. Even though scholars debate about the civilization of Old Europe as portrayed by Gimbutas, her work is far from romantic mysticism. She brought to light the fact that civilization started long before the time of the Greeks and the Egyptians, and that it was centered on the concept of a Great Mother Goddess.

Part of this book actually started out as a workshop that I presented in the late 1990s that was based on the work of Gimbutas. Although I had wanted to turn the workshop material into a book then, I felt something was missing. I had a sense that there was a basic, important connection that I had not made.

Over the years, the idea of putting my research into a book kept calling me back. As I continued to look at the material I had collected, the consistent note that resonated with me was the Bird Goddess. At first I thought that this was a reflection of my backyard birding and connecting with the natural world at our local Audubon preserves. But then about five years ago I went back to the works of Marija Gimbutas, Riane Eisler, Merlin Stone, and others who have influenced me, and I found what I had been missing. It was the Bird Goddess after all.

Many creatures served as symbols of the Great Goddess, but one of the earliest and most pervasive was the bird. For a span of almost twenty-five thousand years, the Divine was portrayed as a woman/bird fusion, the Bird Goddess.[2] According to author and artist Buffie Johnson, "Avian symbolism is found all over the world" and the bird was "sacred above all other creatures" to goddess worshippers.[3]

Animals depicted with the Great Goddess were not just her totems; they embodied her and represented her power. Of course, the other highly important creature associated with the Great Goddess was the snake. However, while religious zealots bent on extinguishing goddess worship made the snake into something abhorrent, the power of the bird was too strong and appealing. These creatures of the air were adopted as representatives, messengers, and the ultimate emblem of the Divine. Associating birds with spirit is something that people of many faiths have done for millennia.

The Great Goddess was and is considered to be immanent, her presence felt everywhere: sky, earth, and sea. Her most fundamental and long-standing icon, birds, are everywhere, too. They exist in every type of ecosystem and have been present through all of the civilizations that have come and gone. For thousands of years birds have been a sign of freedom, the immortal soul, messengers of gods and goddesses, and shaman's helpers. Although the emblematic roles of birds have evolved over time, they have been consistently associated with spirit and divinity.

We humans have a special affinity with birds. Like us they are bipeds, they sing, they can be showy, and they build homes. While birds are so common in our lives, they remain mysterious. They are highly visible but elusive. Birds live amongst us and do not hide from us, yet they easily avoid capture. We may feel close to them because we can observe most of their activities, yet they remain wild. They are familiar but still hold an

---

2. Anne Baring and Jules Cashford, *The Myth of the Goddess: Evolution of an Image* (New York: Penguin Putnam, 1993), 58.

3. Buffie Johnson, *Lady of the Beasts: The Goddess and Her Sacred Animals* (Rochester, VT: Inner Traditions, 1994), 8.

air of mystery because they have mastered the air while we must rely on machines to lift us from the bonds of Earth. Even today when we understand and can explain a great deal about the natural world, birds hold enough mystique to inspire us.

My purpose in finally writing this book is twofold. First, I want to share the wonder and meaning I find between the Great Goddess and birds. After all, the Bird Goddess was the form by which she was known for so many millennia. My second reason is that birds provide us with a simple yet powerful way to stay in tune with the natural world. We spend so much time indoors or in cars that we lose the intimate connection with nature and seasonal markers. Birds help us maintain this connection. In addition, they can help us access different levels of energy and awareness no matter where we are, even in the concrete canyons of Manhattan.

I chose the quote from *Merriam-Webster's Encyclopedia of World Religions* to begin this book because it sums up three major aspects of the Goddess as highlighted by Gimbutas. While the concept of maiden, mother, crone is a nice way to relate the Goddess to a woman's life stages (or son, father, sage for men), it does not encompass the profound and interwoven mysteries of life, death, and spirituality.

All things come from her, return to her, and are her. "Come from her" is the life-giving/nurturing aspect of the mother, the creatrix. "Return to her" is the death-wielder/regeneratrix aspect. "Are her" is the aspect that Gimbutas referred to as transformation, energy, and unfolding. To me, in this aspect she is transformer and eternal spirit. These three interwoven aspects of the Goddess encompass the profound mysteries of life, death, and spirit and create the dynamic energy of cyclical time that turns the great wheel of life.

In this book, we will explore the Great Goddess through these aspects and discover how closely birds are associated with them. We will also see how her association with birds echoed through millennia to later goddesses. We will learn how birds can deepen our celebrations of nature's cycles as we move through the wheel of the year. We will also learn about some of the spiritual symbols used by the people of Old Europe, which Gimbutas called "an alphabet of the metaphysical." [4] We will discover the deeper meanings of these symbols and how to incorporate them into our magic, rituals, and spiritual paths.

This book is divided into two parts. The first I have called the Practices. Chapters 1 and 2 provide historical information about the Bird Goddess and about birds in reli-

---

4. Marija Gimbutas, *The Language of the Goddess* (San Francisco: HarperSanFrancisco, 1991), xv.

gion, shamanism, and divination. Chapters 3, 5, and 7 each focus on an aspect of the Great Goddess as life-giver/nurturer, death-wielder/regeneratrix, and transformer/eternal spirit. Each of these chapters is followed by an associated one containing practices, activities, and a ritual to help you connect with these aspects. Chapters 8 and 9 present additional practices to connect with the energy and power of birds.

Part 2 is called the Profiles and includes history, myths, folklore, and magical information as well as how to connect with the energy of more than one hundred species of birds. Also included is a physical description for identifying these birds and information on where to find them.

Working with birds helps us awaken intuition and psychic abilities, and it aids in tapping into the subtle energies around us. Birds help strengthen our connection with the natural world and bring us closer to the Goddess. And now, let us start with a flight back in time to begin our journey to the Bird Goddess.

Part One

THE PRACTICES

Chapter 1

Birds and Divinity

Birds exist everywhere and are so common that we take them for granted, often considering them part of the landscape. In ancient times, birds were regarded as mysterious creatures. They seemed to suddenly appear and disappear into the clouds as though they held the power of the sky. Birds were recognized as radically different from other creatures. They could go where humans could not, travel to unknown regions, return with the morning sun, or make their presence known when darkness fell. In addition, the migrations of some birds gave rise to their reputation as heralds of particular seasons and keepers of the rhythms of nature.

In the Beginning

The Bird Goddess is believed to be the earliest and best-documented deity. During the Paleolithic period (Old Stone Age), carved figurines and cave paintings began to appear in a vast area that stretched from the Pyrenees of France to Lake Baikal in Siberia, just north of Mongolia. A commonality of imagery existed throughout this area that stretched through seven modern time zones. Figurines of the Goddess were carved from stone, bone, and ivory, and they were small enough that people could take them along on their seasonal journeys for hunting and gathering food.

One such figurine, known as the Lespugue goddess, was found on a hearth stone in a cave in France. Carved of mammoth ivory and only about six inches tall, she has a bird-like head, long neck, and upper arms that appear winglike. Her breasts, thighs, and buttocks are exaggerated and egg-shaped. Other similar figurines and cave paintings depict women with egg-shaped buttocks or buttocks that were exceedingly rounded as though holding an egg. This human/avian fusion of the Bird Goddess as creatrix represented the source of life, which contained the cosmic/world egg. Millennia later, the egg would be a central component in creation myths worldwide.

Archaeological evidence shows that the caves of southern France were occupied for about twenty thousand years.[5] While this was not always continuous, as people needed to follow their food sources, the caves were used year after year. For these people, the caves were sanctuaries of the Goddess in two ways: as a safe place in which to live and as a sacred site for ritual and worship. While living quarters were usually situated just inside a cave, rituals took place in the deeper caverns, often a mile or two from the entrance. Although a few are well known, such as Lascaux and Chauvet, more than one hundred painted caves have been discovered. As the climate warmed and people moved out of caves, their use for ritual often continued.

Beginning in approximately 10,000 BCE, Neolithic (New Stone Age) culture blossomed in isolated centers at different times in eastern Europe, southern Turkey, Egypt, Palestine, Mesopotamia, and India.[6] This change from Paleolithic culture was a gradual process that took several thousand years. The hallmark that distinguished this change was the development of agriculture and settled life; no longer did people have to follow food sources. This big revolution is believed to have also occurred in people's minds. Being settled meant that people had a more controlling hand in directing their lives. However, they did not lose touch with the Goddess. If anything, agriculture tied them more intimately to the cycles of nature and to her.

This more stable life enabled the development of crafts such as spinning, weaving, cloth dyeing, metallurgy, and pottery. These crafts reflected people's connection with the Goddess. And just as in the Paleolithic era, when commonalities stretched across a large area, so too did Neolithic images and symbols that would have been recognized and un-

---

5. Baring and Cashford, *The Myth of the Goddess*, 16.

6. Ibid., 47.

derstood by people from Europe to India. This imagery revealed that a single deity—the Bird Goddess—presided over life, death, and rebirth, providing a cyclical continuity to their spirituality.

The civilization that Marija Gimbutas referred to as Old Europe existed for approximately four thousand years and encompassed an area that stretched roughly from Vienna to Kiev, through Central Europe, the Balkans and Greece, southern Italy, Sicily, Malta, Crete, and the Aegean islands.[7] Occupying the western area of Turkey, the Anatolian region had a distinctive culture of its own, but like Old Europe it was centered on a Mother Goddess. In both Old Europe and Anatolia, people used spiritual symbols and had "a religion focused on the wheel of life and its cyclical turning."[8] The Goddess was also the spiritual focus of the slightly later megalithic culture of western Europe and the British Isles where great stone tombs and mounds were constructed to represent the womb of the Goddess.

Figure 1.1: Map of Old Europe

7. Marija Gimbutas, *The Goddesses and Gods of Old Europe: Myths and Cult Images* (Berkeley, CA: University of California Press, 2001), 16.

8. Marija Gimbutas, *The Living Goddess* (Berkeley, CA: University of California Press, 2001), 3.

From the beginning of pottery making, figurines were part of the creative inventory, and approximately thirty thousand of them have been excavated from about three thousand Neolithic sites.[9] Many of them depict the Bird Goddess as a woman/bird fusion with a beak or ducklike bill. In addition, some of these figurines had small holes in the shoulders where feathers may have been inserted. These and other types of pottery were incised or painted with symbols associated with the Bird Goddess.

In addition to typical pottery, clay temple models and miniature shrines have been found, and they are thought to have served as votive gifts. Marked with symbols of the Bird Goddess, many were discovered near altars and in temple courtyards. Some resembled human dwellings and were topped with a bird's head, while others were entirely shaped like birds.

Dating to around 4000 BCE, Egyptian figurines that have come to be known as Nile goddesses had beaked faces and upraised arms suggesting flight.[10] In later times, Isis carried some of the power of the Bird Goddess, and she was often portrayed with wings on her upraised arms. In addition, she was said to have the ability to turn into a bird. Isis was one of the great mother goddesses of Egypt who also had the power of regeneration. According to legend, it was in the form of a bird that she breathed life into her dead husband Osiris.

The Sumerian Inanna was another goddess who retained some of the Bird Goddess's powers. As Queen of Heaven and Earth she was associated with the creatures of the sky.

The Bird Goddess was important to the Minoans of Crete and Mycenaeans of Greece. In both of these civilizations, the Goddess's wings evolved into upraised arms like the Nile goddess, a gesture that we will explore in the next chapter. On Crete, the Goddess continued to hold the power of life, death, and regeneration. Because the dove was one of her principal emblems, clay doves found in many caves in Europe are believed to have been offerings. In the building complex at Knossos, doves atop pillars are believed to have represented the presence of the Goddess.

As we have seen, vestiges of the Bird Goddess can be found in later goddesses. However, where the Bird Goddess had offered continuity in the cycle of life, death, and regeneration, these aspects became separated into different deities. Without the promise of rebirth, death became a dark and fearsome aspect. Although not directly associated with birds, Lilith was depicted with wings and was greatly feared. Her roots go back to

---

9. Baring and Cashford, *The Myth of the Goddess*, 54.

10. Cassandra Eason, *Fabulous Creatures, Mythical Monsters, and Animal Power Symbols: A Handbook* (Westport, CT: Greenwood Press, 2008), 52.

Mesopotamia, where she was considered a demon whose name meant "air." In Hebrew her name meant "night," which is when she was said to bring death.[11] Despite the fear of night-flying creatures, the owl was later allied with the Greek Athena and Roman Minerva. While these goddesses were associated with war, they also carried the owl's attributes of protection and wisdom.

Due to outside cultural upheaval and invasion, the concept of deity changed radically in Old Europe and Anatolia. As the Goddess's power was compartmentalized and diminished, male deities took center stage. Although the snake, the Goddess's other important creature, was vilified and subverted, the mystery and power of the bird was too great to discard and so it was usurped as a symbol of many gods.

The New Gods and Birds

Despite the Goddess's title of Queen of Heaven throughout the Middle East, a major shift occurred. The Sumerian word for divinity was also the name of their sky god Anu, who for a while became the supreme god of the Babylonians.[12] Although the very early Greek goddess Gaia held the power of the Great Mother, later mythology provided her with a husband, Ouranos. Gaia personified the earth while Ouranos held the power of the sky. And thus, the sky gods took over the symbolism and power of the mightiest birds.

Hindu, Sumerian, and Egyptian sky gods became associated with high-flying birds such as hawks, eagles, and vultures. These birds were considered exceptional because they seemed able to approach the sun, which was now considered the source of life instead of the life-giving moisture of the Goddess. In turn, the sun itself also became associated with birds. In India, the sun was often depicted as a large bird, usually an eagle or swan. The Egyptians portrayed it as a winged disc. In addition to their association with the sun, flying high in the sky where weather originated linked these birds with the power to control these formidable forces.

The attribute of mighty, weather-ruling power was adopted for gods of many pantheons. Zeus, Thor, and others were associated with storms, thunder, and lightning. The Babylonian storm god Zu was represented as a large bird. The Hindu Garuda, a wind deity in the form of an eagle, was believed to stoke the power of storms by flapping his wings.

---

11. Geoffrey W. Dennis, *The Encyclopedia of Jewish Myth, Magic, and Mysticism* (Woodbury, MN: Llewellyn Publications, 2007), 67.

12. Anthony Stevens, *Ariadne's Clue: A Guide to the Symbols of Humankind* (Princeton, NJ: Princeton University Press, 1998), 178.

Also in India, the fire god Agni was called the Eagle of the Sky, and the god Indra was said to take the form of an eagle. Birds served the Indian gods in various capacities. The eagle deity Garuda served as a vehicle for Vishnu, and a swan or goose carried Brahma. In Egypt, the falcon became a symbol of high power as expressed in the gods Horus and Ra, who were depicted as having falcon heads.

While Aquila the eagle carried Zeus's thunderbolts, the wily god used the guise of a swan or a cuckoo for seduction. The Celtic solar god Lugh was also associated with the eagle as well as the raven and crow. The Hebrews employed bird imagery and noted that Yahweh's presence was known by the sound of wings. This was carried over to the Holy Spirit of Christianity, which is represented as a dove.

Many of these gods were associated with high places, especially mountaintops. These were places that only birds could easily transverse, giving them the role of emissaries of gods. Myths about birds serving as messengers come from cultures around the world. However, the avian highway was a two-way thoroughfare: birds brought messages and blessings from on high and were believed to carry human wishes and prayers to deities. In addition to their association with deities, birds were integral to a number of metaphysical and spiritual practices, which we shall explore in the next chapter.

Chapter 2
Birds in Spiritual Practices and Symbolism

In addition to representing or lending their power to a plethora of gods and goddesses, birds were integral to certain practices, such as shamanism and divination, especially as guides and messengers. Their ability to fly linked them with supernatural forces that humans wanted to harness and master. In addition, birds continued to serve as powerful symbols.

Shamanism

Throughout the world, birds figured largely in shamanism as a symbol of magical flight. They also served as guides and guardians to help navigate between the worlds. In some traditions, shamans were believed to shape-shift into birds. Widely used as clothing and tools, feathers provided the shaman with the transformative power needed to enter the spirit world. Even a single feather was believed to hold significant power. As a substitute, coats with feather-like fringes were occasionally worn.

In addition to feathers, wings and beaks were incorporated into ritual garb in the belief that these items could transmit the bird's power to a human. Eating a bird was regarded as another way in which the power of a bird could be acquired. Bones also held magical power. In many cultures it was believed that bones contained some of the animal's (in this case a bird's) life-force energy. It was also believed that from the bones, the spirit of the creature could be rejuvenated. Bones were carved and worn as amulets, incorporated into ritual clothing, or used as prophecy devices. In addition, bird bones were often carved and fashioned into flutes, which have been found at a number of ancient sites.

In Irish lore, the druid Mag Ruith was referred to as a bird-man, dressing in bird costume like a shaman. Druids and priestesses were said to have worn robes of feathers for magical power and for aid in contacting other realms. In addition to being goose-footed, Norse goddess Freya possessed a feathered cloak that enabled the wearer to fly.

Bird garb and tools provided one way to summon the power of a bird. Dancing or imitating a bird's movements was also used to summon and merge with its energy. Imitating a bird was a method for drawing out and assuming particular qualities. In addition, bird postures were used for sympathetic magic. According to Celtic myth, a crane posture was used for general spellwork as well as for a form of retributive magic known as crane wounding.

Augury and Bird Divination

While many animals were linked with divination practices, birds were very closely associated with it. Augury encompassed several methods including observing birds in flight, listening for their songs or other noises, and the study of entrails. The word *augury* comes from either the Old French *augurie* or the Latin *augurium*, both meaning "the interpretation of omens." According to Don Stap, professor, author, and a leading expert on birdsong, the word *augury* was also interpreted as meaning "bird talk." [13]

Watching birds for prophecy was practiced by the Hittites who lived in the Anatolian region of present-day Turkey from approximately 1700 to 1200 BCE. [14] Clay tablets written by Hittite officials mention their observation of eagles and falcons. Closely linked with birds, the Sumerian goddess Nanse was associated with divination and dream interpretation.

---

13. Don Stap, *Birdsong* (New York: Scribner, 2005), 139.

14. Jackson J. Spielvogel, *Western Civilization, Sixth Edition* (Independence, KY: Cengage Learning, 2005), 28.

The Etruscans of northern Italy became famous practitioners of augury. Their augurs were regarded as intermediaries who received divine messages through birds. Most often, Etruscan augurs observed crows, ravens, eagles, owls, and woodpeckers. In Rome, an augur was an official who interpreted general nature signs, which included the behavior of birds. Omens gleaned from birds were called "Etruscan teachings." [15] According to myth, the location for the city of Rome was determined by observing the flight of birds.

Ravens and doves were highly regarded for their oracular powers. According to one Greek myth, a black dove that flew from Thebes in Egypt landed in one of the oak trees at Dodona. It was said to have the power of human speech, and the prophetesses at Dodona came to be called *peleiades*, "doves." [16] This important oracle site was later dedicated to Zeus. The Greeks also built towers from which they could observe and listen to birds because the animals were believed to bring messages directly from the gods.

Bird divination continued through the centuries, especially for predicting the weather. The direction of a birdcall, its location, or certain behaviors in flight held specific meanings. In southern Germany, the breastbone of a goose eaten for the feast of St. Martin's day (November 11) was used to tell the weather of the approaching winter. More familiar is the breaking of the Thanksgiving turkey wishbone, which is a holdover from bird divination practices.

Symbolism

Although we may not be aware of them, symbols are an integral part of daily life in the form of road signs, laundering instructions, and other types of notation. While these symbols communicate information, they do not hold significant meaning. However, in art, myth, and religion, symbols convey nonverbal clues that reach into our psyches. These symbols work because without explanation they hold the essence of a concept. Throughout time, people have used a wide range of symbols to explain the world and connect with deity as well as to express abstract ideas.

The earliest use of symbols dates to the Paleolithic. These were found in Lascaux Cave in France, Altamira Cave in Spain, and numerous other sites. Because symbols evolve over time or lose their significance, the ones that are most powerful are often the oldest. Since

---

15. Daniel C. Snell, *Religions of the Ancient Near East* (New York: Cambridge University Press, 2011), 144.

16. Marguerite Rigoglioso, *The Cult of Divine Birth in Ancient Greece* (New York: Palgrave Macmillan, 2009), 139.

most symbols are multilayered, operating on the emotional, intellectual, and spiritual levels, they awaken a response from our inner worlds.

It has been argued that the symbols portrayed by Gimbutas were nothing more than "designs" because it was believed that people of the Paleolithic and Neolithic were not capable of abstract thought. However, Alexander Marshack, American scholar and Paleolithic anthropologist, noted that "as far back as 30,000 BCE the ice-age hunter of western Europe was using a system of notation that was already evolved, complex, and sophisticated."[17]

Symbols from the ancient Goddess-worshipping cultures of Old Europe were rarely used on their own. Multiple symbols graced pottery, figurines, and a plethora of other objects. Many symbols relating to the different aspects of the Goddess overlap, showing that life, death, and spirit were interwoven parts of the whole.

The power of the Goddess could be felt in a bird or a plant as well as in her symbols. Some of the symbols that we will explore were used for many thousands of years. We will see how we can use these symbols and birds to draw the Goddess into our rituals, magic, and everyday lives. When we incorporate these symbols into our practices, they become sacred to us and connect us with those amazing people from so very long ago.

The Epiphany of the Bird Goddess

Often used as a secular word, *epiphany* means "sudden inspiration." When used in a religious sense, it is usually associated with Christianity, meaning "the presence of God or the Holy Spirit," which is most often represented as a dove. However, the word *epiphany* actually has Pagan origins drawn from the Greek word *epiphaneia*, meaning "appearance" or "manifestation."[18] In the Greco-Roman world it signified a deity visiting devotees in a sacred place as well as revealing him/herself in order to aid humans.

According to Jungian analyst Anne Baring, the bird was "the supreme image of epiphany" in a number of ancient cultures.[19] Wings raised out to the sides became the gesture of epiphany and signified the manifestation of deity. Over time as depictions of the Bird Goddess evolved to more woman than bird, raised arms replaced wings in the

17. Alexander Marshack, *The Roots of Civilization: The Cognitive Beginnings of Man's First Art, Symbol and Notation* (Wakefield, RI: Moyer Bell, 1991), 57.

18. A. G. Martimort, I. H. Dalmais, and P. Jounel, eds., *The Liturgy and Time: The Church at Prayer: An Introduction to the Liturgy* Vol. IV (Collegeville, MN: Liturgical Press, 1986), 80.

19. Baring and Cashford, *The Myth of the Goddess*, 124.

gesture. The Minoans of Crete and Mycenaeans of Greece often depicted the Goddess with arms raised in epiphany.

In this gesture, the arms are out to the sides at about shoulder height, elbows bent, and hands raised with palms facing forward. It was used to indicate the presence of the Goddess. The epiphany gesture has roots in the Paleolithic and extends through the Neolithic into historical times. It is seen in a terra-cotta figurine from 5200 BCE Romania, in the depiction of a Sumerian goddess from 1800 BCE, and in portrayals of the Greek goddess Hera in 700 BCE.[20]

The ancient Egyptians perceived a person's soul as a bird called the *ba*. However, another component of the soul was called the *ka*. This represented a person's greater soul that merged with the *ba* after death. The hieroglyph for the *ka* was the gesture of raised arms. Associated with the Bird Goddess, the graceful Nile goddess figurine exhibits the gesture of epiphany with raised arms/wings.

Although the Mycenaeans depicted the Great Goddess in the epiphany gesture, an eighth-century Greek figurine from Olympia shows a male believed to be Zeus using the gesture.[21] This gesture also appears throughout the ancient sculptures of India. And speaking of India, anyone who does yoga will recognize the epiphany gesture as the arm position for the posture called the Goddess.

Over the millennia, the epiphany gesture came to represent expressive prayer and was adopted into Christian art and practice. In addition, a variation on this gesture is used by some modern Pagans as the Goddess-invoking posture in ritual.

Today's World

We have seen how birds have been integral to spiritual belief and expression since very ancient times. This leaves us with the question of how they fit into our twenty-first-century lives. Exploring how birds have touched humans spiritually gives us a perspective on the pervasive power that these creatures possess.

Once you begin to connect with birds on a spiritual level, you may begin to feel an energy shift when working with certain ones. Is this the presence of the Goddess? Only your intuition and heart-of-hearts can answer that. Whether or not you experience this, birds can open a whole new world for you in nature and within yourself. The following chapters will help you discover what happens when you listen as the Bird Goddess speaks.

---

20. Gimbutas, *The Living Goddess*, 45.

21. A. M. Snodgrass, *Dark Age of Greece* (Edinburgh, Scotland: Edinburgh University Press, 2000), 418.

Chapter 3

Come from Her:
Life-Giver and Creatrix

The first aspect of the Goddess is her role as life-giver. However, this encompasses more than giving birth; it includes nurturing, sustaining, and protecting life. Following the nurturing and protective ways of the Great Mother Goddess, Neolithic people tended their crops and domestic animals, acts that tied them more closely with her and with the cycles of nature. Because of this, I think it is no accident that we refer to our planet as Mother Earth.

However, the Goddess was more than a mother deity of fertility who gave birth to creatures and fostered plant life. She was the cosmic creatrix who manifested everything, from the smallest thing on the earth to the vast heavens. The Goddess brought everything into existence and taught skills and crafts.

The Goddess as Waterbird

The Bird Goddess created, nourished, and charged the earth and its creatures with energy through the power of the life-giving element of water. She was regarded as the source of water that fell from the heavens, flowed on the surface of the earth, and welled up from underneath the ground. At home in the sky or in a river, waterbirds were considered the life of the waters. Waterbirds were an important source of food, and the annual migration was a major event. The return of ducks and geese to northern waters in the spring was an event for celebration because it ensured survival. Waterbirds brought abundance as food and as comfort through the use of their feathers. Cranes and other waterbirds also represented nourishment and abundance.

Millennia later the Egyptians and Babylonians regarded water as the source of life-giving forces as they witnessed fertile, new land being created from river silt, which would bring abundance. As the mother goddess of Egypt, Isis was associated with the annual flooding of the Nile. Like many rivers and marshy areas, the Nile is teeming with waterbirds.

Greek, Roman, Celtic, and Baltic legends linked goddesses to the magical potency of water in the form of streams, rivers, and sacred wells. In Ireland, the Boyne and Shannon Rivers were named after the goddesses Boann and Sinann, and the River Seine in France for Sequana. Sequana had a waterbird as her emblem and was often depicted in a duck-shaped boat. In addition, the name of the Gaulish goddess Nantosuelta means "winding river" and her pre-Celtic origins date back to Old Europe.[22] In one depiction of her, Nantosuelta was shown with wings.

Born from water, Aphrodite has been portrayed sitting on a swan throne, standing on the back of a flying goose, and with doves. Her mythology has been traced back to Cyprus and even earlier to Mesopotamia. Although Artemis/Diana came to be regarded as a goddess of the hunt, she inherited the role of Mistress of the Animals. As such, swans and other waterbirds were closely associated with her.

While the character Mother Goose is but a small remnant of the mother-provider, the stork is still a symbol of the bringer of life. In mythology, not only did storks bring babies, they helped birth the new year and were considered the bringers of spring on their return to Europe. Like other migratory birds, their arrivals and departures were markers of cyclic time.

---

22. Anne Ross, *Pagan Celtic Britain: Studies in Iconography and Tradition* (London: Constable and Company, 1992), 313.

Although the mother/life-giving aspect of the Goddess is mainly associated with waterfowl, and odd as it may seem to us today, the vulture had a place here, too. With her name coming from the same root as the Egyptian word for *mother*, Mut was the archetypal mother goddess of Egypt and her symbol was a vulture. Worshipped with her husband Amun at Thebes, called Waset by Egyptians, Mut was regarded as the mother of the pharaohs. In addition, Isis was occasionally depicted as a vulture.

Nests: The Bird Goddess as Weaver and Giver of Crafts

It has been suggested that making baskets was an idea gleaned from birds, especially as it was an obvious way to carry off more eggs than could be held only in the hands. As cultures evolved from hunting and gathering and people became settled, depictions of the Bird Goddess changed, too. She became a spinner and a weaver, and the giver of crafts. Neolithic temples were not grand structures, instead they were house-like with connecting workshops that integrated daily craft activities with spiritual practice.

Weaving became a metaphor for creating life, perhaps because the Bird Goddess was portrayed as a spinner and a weaver who spun and wove the threads of life. Regarded as magical practices, spinning and weaving are methods for creating something from practically nothing. Simple threads become clothing and twigs become baskets.

As the giver of crafts, which included spinning, weaving, cloth dyeing, metallurgy, pottery, and music, Bird Goddess symbols were incised on spindle whorls, loom weights, crucibles, and musical instruments. Spindle whorls and loom weights are small, round or oblong discs that steady the movement of a spindle or prevent the threads on a loom from getting tangled. Inscriptions on these objects are thought to be dedications to the Goddess.

The practice of using Goddess symbols on spindle whorls and on figurines of people spinning continued into the classical period of Greece. However, in Greek mythology Athena was the giver of the crafts of pottery, spinning, and weaving. Her Roman counterpart, Minerva, was also associated with spinning and weaving. In addition, Norse goddess Freya was a spinner and a weaver, too, and she was often described as wearing a feather headdress.

Eggs: The Bird Goddess as Creatrix

To most of us, an egg is just a simple everyday item of food. However, throughout cultures worldwide and through time, the egg has had strong symbolic meanings. It represented new life and nourishment. The ability to hold life within was part of the mystery of the egg, as was the fact that it is fragile yet strong. Metaphorically, the egg is very grounding, providing balance to wings that liberate from the bonds of Earth.

With egg-shaped thighs, buttocks, and breasts, the Lespugue goddess and other similar figurines present a trinity of woman, bird, and egg. In addition to figurines, bird- and egg-shaped vessels and vases have been found in numerous places. Some of these depicted birds carrying eggs within their bodies.

In countless mythologies from later civilizations, a cosmic egg was the womb of the world and the source of all that existed. In some myths, a creator spirit took the form of an egg floating in primordial waters. According to Egyptian myth, the world egg was laid by a great goose. The Greeks believed the primordial egg was laid by a large black-winged bird. In many creation stories, the egg cracking open was equated with the breaking of the water, which was a sign of imminent birth. When this happened, the world and cosmos came into being and time began. The cosmic egg gave birth to the sun as symbolized by the yellow yolk. It also divided the sky and land as symbolized by the shell broken in half.

Life-Giving and Nurturing Symbols

Migrating ducks, geese, and swans are well known for flying in the classic V-shape formation. It was a natural suggestion for the V to become associated with the Goddess as a symbol of fertility and abundance. The V and chevron (two or more Vs nested in each other) were the insignia of the Bird Goddess. Actually, the use of the V and chevron dates back to the Paleolithic period.

Found in a cave in Spain and dating to around 13,000–10,000 BCE, the shape of a crane or heron was engraved on bones that were also marked with chevrons.[23] Use of the chevron continued throughout the Neolithic period and into later cultures. Resembling the markings of many birds, the V and chevron were used to represent a bird's or woman/bird's beak, wings, or feathers as well as to mark the pubic area. In addition to figurines, the V and chevron were used on vases, votive vessels, lamps, altars, plaques, and ritual objects.

Chevrons were commonly used to mark musical instruments. Bird-bone flutes marked with chevrons were found in France and other locations. In addition, a cache of flutes and rattles engraved with rows of chevrons was found in the Ukraine. Although the combination of birds and chevrons lingered into the eighth century BCE as a common Greek motif, their use lacked the sacredness they once held.

---

23. Gimbutas, *The Language of the Goddess*, 4.

The cross-band or X, which can be considered as two juxtaposed Vs, is another important symbol of the Bird Goddess. The V, chevron, and X appeared on their own as well as in combination. According to Gimbutas, a chevron or X alone seemed to have marked an object as belonging to the Goddess, and the V, chevron, and X in combination served as a blessing or invocation. Chevrons placed sideways between the arms of Xs were a common configuration of these symbols.

Figure 1.2: The life-giving symbols of V, chevron, and cross-band (top row); M, double M, and zigzag (middle row); Goddess face and meander (bottom row)

The meander is another fundamental symbol of the Bird Goddess. Looking like a squared spiral, the meander is a rhythmic pattern that was often used in association with the V and the chevron. It was sometimes emphasized by being framed like a cartouche. According to Anne Baring's interpretation, the meander was a symbol of water running beneath the earth and through caves, giving access to the otherworld.[24] Like the spiral, it is thought to have represented a path between the worlds of the seen and unseen. The

---

24. Baring and Cashford, *The Myth of the Goddess*, 135.

meander, like water from underground springs, represented the waters of birth bursting forth.

The meander was commonly used on beaked or winged figurines, altar pieces, and temple models. In later times, abbreviated meanders laid out in a straight line became known as the Greek key, a design that was frequently used on pottery and in temples.

An M-shaped symbol was used with chevrons and zigzags on pottery, pendants, and loom weights. The M and double M (one above the other) served as a primary symbol on vases and marked them as sacred objects. The M was positioned below the breasts on Goddess figurines to emphasize life-sustaining milk. The M symbol was also placed above birdlike faces, and frequently a double M was positioned underneath a face on large vases. The double M marked a face as that of the Goddess to imply that the vessel and its contents were sacred. While the Egyptians used an M-shaped hieroglyph (*mu*) to signify water, to the Phoenicians the same glyph meant running water.[25] On Egyptian dishes, the *mu* hieroglyph often appeared with chevrons.

A row of connected Ms creates another symbol called the zigzag. Alternatively, it could be said that the M is an abbreviated zigzag. Throughout the world, the zigzag has been used to represent water. As early as 30,000 BCE, the M and zigzag were used to mark birdlike figures.[26]

Bird-shaped pottery was some of the earliest made during the Neolithic period and continued through the Bronze Age. Marked with the Goddess's symbols, these vessels integrated sacred and mundane functions, as implements that served an ordinary purpose were used to pour sacred offerings. A vessel holding water or milk served as a representation of the Goddess, allowing her nourishment and blessings to be symbolically poured. A variation of the waterbird vessel with a spout shaped like a bird's head and beak was found in northern Greece. On Crete, a Minoan pitcher in the shape of a waterbird with a long neck also had human breasts.

The overarching theme of these symbols and aspect of the Goddess encompasses creation/procreation, nurturing, and protection. In the next chapter, we will see how we can incorporate these symbols into our practices as we connect with this aspect of the Goddess and her birds.

---

25. Johnson, *Lady of the Beasts*, 36.
26. Gimbutas, *The Language of the Goddess*, 19.

Chapter 4

Connecting with the Life-Giver and Creatrix

The basic themes of this aspect of the Goddess are creation/procreation, nurturing, and protection. While the Goddess was regarded as the creatrix of the world and bringer of fertility, she was also the giver of crafts, encouraging creative expression. Nurturing is especially important in today's fast-paced world. By nurturing ourselves and those we love, we bring strength and fullness to our lives. In addition, being mindful of the impact we have on the environment helps us nurture and protect the earth and all her creatures.

Life-giving and Nurturing Ritual

For this ritual you will need a red candle, a bowl, and a pitcher of water. Using a large sewing needle or a fine-point marker, draw some of the symbols associated with this aspect of the Goddess on the candle. Other objects to use on your altar include a small open or nest-like basket, a clean eggshell or an egg-shaped crystal, and spindles or other small things used in spinning or weaving. Pieces of yarn or thread can be laid out to form some of the Goddess symbols. Also include pictures of birds or figurines, especially waterbirds. The ritual is written as a solo practice that can easily be adapted for a group.

Once your altar is set up, light the red candle. Raise your hands in the epiphany gesture with arms out to the sides at shoulder height, elbows bent, and hands raised with palms facing forward. As you do this say: *"Red is the color of life. It represents the life-giving blood of the Goddess and the pulse of life. Bird Goddess, bringer of life, provider, sustainer, I call on your presence, be with me this day."*

Create sacred space through breath and toning. Slowly inhale and exhale three times and then chant "*mmmm*" for as long as you can with a single breath. Afterward, stand in silence for a moment or two and then say: *"Now in sacred space, I bring that sacredness within me as I enter the realm of the Bird Goddess."*

Water is one of the most precious things on Earth. We use water to receive the blessings of the Goddess and to acknowledge ourselves as creators and nurtures. Creation includes procreation and creativity. Pour a little bit of water from the pitcher into the bowl as you say aloud the nurturing things you do. It could be that you are raising children, you tend a garden, you do something artistic or musical (not necessarily as a profession), or you are caring for an elderly parent, teaching a class, tending animals, or you clean up the woods when you go for a walk. It is not often that we proudly acknowledge ourselves as nurturers. As you say aloud all of the nurturing things you do pour a little water into the bowl for each one.

Chanting is a way to honor the Goddess. It is also a way to send the energy raised in ritual out to the universe. Let it be known that you proudly carry on the ways of the Goddess by being a creator and nurturer. Say: *"May the birds of the Goddess be messengers to carry my intention and energy forth."*

And then chant:

> *Listen to the voice; the voice of the water,*
> *The voice of the Mother; calling you and me.*

When it feels appropriate, end the chant. Stand in the epiphany gesture in silence as you ground and center your energy. Extinguish the candle and then say: *"I thank the Goddess for her gift of life and her presence this day. May I continue to seek and affirm the nurturing and creative aspects within me and around me. Blessed be."*

Invite Birds to Your Yard

If you have a backyard or any outdoor space, put out a birdhouse, a feeder, and/or a birdbath to nurture your local birds. Paint or mark these items with some of the life-giving symbols. Use zigzags on a birdbath to associate the water with her life-giving moisture. Also use Vs, chevrons, or meanders on bird feeders and houses to mark them as special and belonging to the Goddess.

Make your yard a sanctuary, as a place of security for birds and as a sacred place for you where you can connect with the Goddess. Designate a special place to set up a small altar. This can be made simply with several bricks or flat stones that you mark with some of her symbols, or it can be more elaborate. When you set these things in place take a moment and say: *"Mother Goddess, Bird Goddess, may your creatures of the air find protection and nourishment in this yard. Great Mother, I dedicate these things and this space to honor you. Blessed be."*

Attracting birds to our backyards provides a way to observe and get to know them. While we might think of putting out a bird feeder only in the winter, birds can use help all year because of diminishing habitats. While the food in the feeder will attract birds, most of them eat a combination of insects, berries, and seeds, so after dining on what you provide they usually stick around to see what else they can find. Year-round residents such as chickadees, sparrows, or cardinals that stake out your yard as a food source will also attract migrating birds.

Feeding in the spring is especially important for birds returning to your area until they reestablish the lay of the land for multiple feeding sites. While summer offers abundant natural sources for food, extra help filling the mouths of hatchlings is a big attraction for busy parent birds. In the autumn, migrating birds need to get ready for their long journeys, and of course, winter is most important when natural sources dwindle substantially.

In addition to food, providing water for birds is another good way to attract them to your yard. It also represents the life-giving moisture of the Goddess. A birdbath can function as a decorative feature and a focal point for your garden. As an alternative to a birdbath, use a large flowerpot saucer on the ground or on an upended flowerpot in the garden. If your porch is your garden, place a saucer amongst the flowerpots.

Feeders and birdbaths should be located near vegetation, which provides a safe place for birds to wait their turn at the feeder or to take cover from a predator. Also, it is important to keep feeders and baths clean to avoid diseases.

The availability of nesting sites also attracts birds. Trees and shrubs offer natural places but we can foster their interest by providing nest boxes or birdhouses. Ideally, these should be at least five feet above the ground, out of direct sunlight, and sheltered from heavy rain. Locating these near trees or shrubs is helpful. There are two excellent websites for more information about attracting birds to your backyard: The Cornell Lab of Ornithology at www.allaboutbirds.org and the Audubon Society at www.audubon.org.

Whether or not you have outdoor space, designate a windowsill as your special Bird Goddess area. Place figurines, feathers (see chapter 10 before gathering feathers), or anything that helps you connect with birds as well as the Goddess. Paint a few small stones or crystals with Vs or chevrons and place them on the windowsill. In addition, make or purchase a birdhouse to use as a Bird Goddess shrine that you can hang on a wall.

Decorate Eggs

Don't wait until Ostara to color and decorate eggs. The next time you make scrambled eggs, carefully poke holes in each end and blow them out so you can keep the shells intact. Rinse them thoroughly and allow them to dry. Using colored markers or paint, decorate the eggs with Bird Goddess symbols or paint them to resemble the eggs of birds with which you want to work. If you have a small basket, arrange the eggs in it or simply place them on your altar or in your Bird Goddess shrine. As you do this say: *"Ancient and beautiful Bird Goddess, I ask you to touch these eggs with your energy. May they represent your wondrous blessings."*

In the spring, place a few eggs with life-giving symbols in your garden or indoor flowerpots with the intention of encouraging growth. Hanging decorated eggs makes them more visible. For this you will need a large darning needle, crochet yarn or embroidery thread, and a couple of decorative beads for each egg. Make the strand of thread long enough so it is at least three or four times as long as the egg, which will make it easier to work with.

Thread the needle and then carefully insert it through the hole in the top of the egg. You may need to gently wiggle the egg to get the needle to come through the other hole at the bottom. When it does, insert the needle through a bead. Carefully insert the needle back into the egg, and then turn it upside down to coax the needle through the hole at the other end. Now you will have two strands coming out of the top hole. Thread both of them through a second bead and then tie a knot so it rests against the top of the egg. Decide how long you want the loop for hanging the egg, cut off any excess, and then tie the strands together to finish the loop.

The people of the Ukraine have a long tradition of decorating eggs with elaborate designs. This stems from a folk belief that birds spent the winter in heaven and returned in the spring with blessings. Decorating eggs at Easter represented these blessings. However, at other times of the year eggs were decorated and used as talismans. Different designs were painted on them for different purposes; for example, placing an egg in the attic protected a house from lightning.

To attract abundance, paint an egg with Goddess symbols or anything that represents this to you. Hang the egg in your kitchen to attract abundance to your home. Decorate an egg with symbols of wealth and hang it near your desk to engender success, or use the life-giving symbols of the Goddess to stimulate creativity. If you have small children, make a project with them to paint their names and symbols on an egg (one for each child). Include the Goddess face on the eggs, and then hang them above the children's beds to invite the blessings and protection of the Goddess.

Additional Activities

Get outdoors and look for birds, especially waterbirds. If it is early spring or late autumn look for migrating birds flying in V formations. Although some birds have been mentioned as being closely associated with this aspect of the Goddess, you may feel that others hold this association for you. Use the profiles in part 2 for ways of connecting with the energy of certain birds, or simply go out and observe them. Take along a notebook or use a smartphone app to record your thoughts or anything you may experience.

Another way to honor the Bird Goddess is to place an open, nest-shaped basket on your altar or someplace where you will frequently see it. Place a decorated egg, a crystal egg, or a bird figurine inside it. Let this serve as a reminder of her life-giving and nurturing aspect. The basket can also serve as a focal point when working with the energy of birds.

Chapter 5

Return to Her: Death-Wielder and Regeneratrix

To the Goddess worshippers of Old Europe, life and death were not considered conflicting opposites, and death was not regarded as the absolute end. Symbols relating to death were accompanied by life-giving signs of regeneration and renewal. The Goddess as death-wielder was not so much the bringer of death as she was the mother who waited to accept her children home and then prepare them for the next life. Gimbutas believed that death was not regarded as "mournful triumph over life." [27] Instead, death was inseparably linked with rebirth and considered an integral part of the ongoing cycle.

The Goddess As Bird of Prey

Mostly birds of prey were associated with this aspect of the Goddess, not so much because they kill for food but for their role in excarnation, which is sometimes referred to

27. Gimbutas, *The Language of the Goddess*, 19.

as sky burial. Scavengers and other birds were also important because removing the flesh from bones was regarded as completing the death process. Although exposing the dead in this way was not universally practiced in Neolithic cultures, birds were acknowledged as having a role in finalizing death before rebirth could occur.

One of the earliest types of objects found in graves, and dating to approximately 16,000 BCE, were the figurines that came to be called stiff white ladies.[28] Long and slender, they were rigid like bones and represented the stillness of death. Made of bone, ivory, or stone, these figurines were the white or pale yellow color of bare bone. Their placement in the grave represented opening the way to the subterranean womb in preparation for rebirth. Although the style of the stiff white ladies changed over time and differed slightly among regions, they were consistently found with red ochre, which symbolized life-giving blood. While these figurines often had pronounced pubic triangles, the only facial feature was usually a beak. Occasionally they were incised with owl faces.

In addition to human-made artifacts, bird bones and wings were common grave offerings. Ninety percent of these came from vultures, eagles, hawks, owls, black-backed gulls, rooks, crows, and ravens. A tomb on the Orkney Islands off the northern coast of Scotland held the remains of 342 people and 35 sea eagles.[29] Symbolizing life as well as mourning, birds were placed in graves, especially those of children, well into the classical period of Greece. Centuries later, a common Gallo-Roman funerary motif portrayed the deceased holding a raven or other bird against his or her chest. However, of all the birds connected with this aspect of the Goddess, the owl and the vulture were most prominent throughout Old Europe and beyond.

Representations of owls and owl goddesses have been found on pottery, on standing stones, and in tombs. Depictions of owl eyes representing the eyes of the Goddess were commonly used on a range of ritual and funerary objects. In addition to protecting the departed on his or her journey into the next world, the owl also had the role of comforting the bereaved who were left behind.

A famous terra-cotta plaque from Mesopotamia known as the Burney Relief depicts a woman with wings flanked by two owls. Her feet are the talons of a bird of prey. The image is most commonly considered to represent Inanna/Ishtar or Lilith. Inanna was

---

28. Gimbutas, *The Language of the Goddess*, 198.

29. Caroline Arnold, *Stone Age Farmers Beside the Sea: Scotland's Prehistoric Village of Skara Brae* (New York: Clarion Books, 1997), 35.

called the "Divine Lady Owl" and her story of descent and return from the underworld symbolized death and rebirth.[30]

The association of owl and goddess survived into Greek culture in the form of Athena. While Greek writer Homer (c. 800–701 BCE) described her as having the eyes of an owl, this bird was not a minor attribute. The owl was continually depicted with her, sometimes on her altar, and occasionally even representing her. With Athena regarded as the giver of crafts, the owl maintained its ancient association with spinning. Marked with Bird Goddess symbols, spindle whorls were used as funerary offerings to symbolize rebirth.

As mentioned in chapter 3, the vulture had an association with the life-giving aspect of the Goddess in Egypt. Our present-day view of this bird links it only with death; however, in Old Europe the emphasis was on regeneration. In fact, the vulture is not equipped to kill and does not bring death. It is a scavenger; it waits and then rids the world of dead flesh. Through this act of cleansing, it initiates the cycle of renewal and transformation.

Dating to 7000–5000 BCE, Çatalhüyük is especially famous for its vulture shrine.[31] Located in the Anatolian region of Turkey, it is the largest Neolithic site in the Near East. Like the culture of Old Europe, worship in Çatalhüyük was centered on a mother goddess. The wall paintings in one of the shrines depicted large vultures hovering over headless human figures whose arms were raised in the epiphany gesture. The Bird Goddess received them into death to be readied for rebirth. Significantly, the vultures in the shrine room were not black or dark like actual birds but red, the color of life-giving blood.

Eggs: Twice Born

As previously mentioned, eggs represented new life; however, they also symbolized rebirth or twofold birth. The egg being laid was considered first birth, and the hatchling emerging from the shell was second birth or rebirth. In fact, in many places worldwide, burial tombs were rounded and egg-shaped. The tombs of Corsica, Sardinia, Sicily, and Malta were constructed with egg-shaped chambers and symbolized the womb of the Goddess from which life would re-emerge. Like tombs, Neolithic burial jars were often

---

30. Paula Marvelly, *Women of Wisdom: A Journey of Enlightenment by Women of Vision Through the Ages* (London: Watkins Publishing, 2005), 15.

31. Baring and Cashford, *The Myth of the Goddess*, 83.

egg-shaped, symbolizing the regenerative powers of the womb. Egg designs were painted or incised on funerary pottery along with whirls and spirals, symbols of vitality and energy.

The domed tombs of Dowth, Knowth, and Newgrange in Ireland are believed to have been completely covered with white quartz in the past, giving them an egg-like appearance. In addition, rounded pieces of quartz and other white, egg-shaped pebbles were often placed within graves.

In northern Europe, egg replicas made of clay were buried with the dead as a promise of the rebirth to come. Well into the Middle Ages, eggs played a role in feasts of the dead and were placed as offerings in graves to prompt regeneration. Into modern times in Russia, it was an Easter tradition to place eggs that had been colored red on graves as a charm for resurrection.

Death and Regeneration Symbols

Depictions of the Goddess's eyes represented her presence and her powers of regeneration. These were most often round, owlish eyes, which have been found in a wide area from Spain and Portugal through France and Great Britain. They have also been found in the tombs of Malta and Sicily. Additionally, owl eyes were marked on figurines and amulets. On megalithic tombs, a beak sometimes accompanied the eyes. Owl eyes have also been found on bones with parallel markings that suggest feathers. In Ireland, owl eyes have been found in the megalithic tomb of Dowth, the name of which means "darkness." [32]

The owl face with round head and eyes and a beak was depicted on standing stones as well as on the stones of passage graves, which consisted of a narrow passageway and separate burial chambers. The representation of an owl face was often accompanied by V and chevron markings, which as we have seen, were associated with the Goddess's life-giving forces.

According to Gimbutas, "the magic regenerating eyes" of the Goddess were sometimes regarded as "radiant divine eyes."[33] This symbol resembles a sun motif and has been found on megalithic tomb shrines in Ireland, funerary vases in Denmark, and ceramics in Spain. Odd as it may seem to depict a night bird with sun-like eyes, the combination portrays the closely intertwined aspects of life and death, light and dark.

---

32. Patricia Monaghan, *The Encyclopedia of Celtic Mythology and Folklore* (New York: Facts on File, 2004), 63.

33. Gimbutas, *The Language of the Goddess*, 56, 59.

Another symbol, the brush/comb, consists of parallel lines joined by a perpendicular line at one end. It was used to represent the energy of life and rebirth as well as healing and protection. The Great Mother provided protection and healing as she guided souls through the process of death into new life.

The brush/comb symbol has been found on figurines and pottery from southeastern Europe to Cyprus to Turkey. In Denmark, it was found carved into an amber pendant. The brush/comb was also depicted as a pendant itself on some figurines. In Central Europe this type of pendant was actually worn by rural people into the twentieth century as a talisman for protection and healing. Although the origin of this symbol is unknown, the shrine at Çatalhüyük provides a clue, with the brush/comb used to depict the wings of the vultures.

The triangle and hourglass shapes are also symbols of the Goddess as a bird of prey. The triangle symbolizes the Goddess's regenerative forces and powers of transformation. On figurines, it most often represented the pubic triangle. Triangular stones, either natural or chipped into shape, had markings to indicate their association with the Goddess and date back to the Paleolithic. Large, triangular stones were used in megalithic tombs and passage graves throughout the British Isles. In addition, triangular-shaped amulets of stone, clay, and bone have been found in numerous graves.

Figure 1.3: Symbols of death and regeneration: owl eyes, owl face, and radiant divine eyes, (top row); brush/comb, triangle, hourglass, and bird's claw (bottom row)

The hourglass shape is basically a set of converging triangles emphasizing not just original birth but rebirth. Hourglass figures were depicted with bird claws as hands and/or feet, and occasionally with wings. These have been found from Ireland to Spain and Italy. The hourglass shape has also been found with chevrons and owl eyes. An hourglass figurine from Spain also sported small, raised wings. Representing the rites of regeneration, hourglass figures portraying a row of dancers were used throughout Old Europe for about three thousand years.[34]

Depictions of bird's feet were used to represent this aspect of the Goddess, too. Accompanying triangles and hourglasses, bird's feet were painted red on cave walls and on vases. Marked with bird's feet, a ceramic cup found in Poland also had a handle topped by a bird's head. Often on vases, bird's feet were placed in rows or in alternating panels with triangles and hourglass figures.

The death/regeneration aspect of the Bird Goddess survived for thousands of years. An Etruscan urn dating to 500 BCE depicted a winged goddess of death with a pregnant belly.[35] In the Basque area of northern Spain, the goddess of death and regeneration was depicted as a vulture, a crow, or a woman with bird's feet. Although in later Greek myth the Harpies were portrayed as half bird/half woman monsters that carried people to the underworld, originally they bore away the bodies of the slain for healing and rebirth.

The main themes of this aspect of the Goddess and these symbols are that death and rebirth are a transition through which the Goddess leads and protects us. In the next chapter, we will see how we can incorporate these symbols and concepts into our practices and everyday lives.

---

34. Gimbutas, *The Language of the Goddess*, 242.

35. Johnson, *Lady of the Beasts*, 89.

Chapter 6:

Connecting with the Death-Wielder/Regeneratrix

As we have seen, the ancient people of Old Europe viewed death as part of a cycle. Symbols of death were accompanied by symbols of life and renewal; thus endings are followed by beginnings. We can use the endings and beginnings in our lives to recognize this aspect of the Goddess. In addition, we can use her symbols at Samhain or when a death occurs and ask for her blessings for those who have departed this world.

Endings and Beginnings Ritual

For this ritual you will need a white candle, dried herbs, and a cauldron or safe container in which to burn the herbs. Use a large sewing needle or a fine-point marker to draw several of the death/regeneration symbols, such as the triangle, owl face, or bird's claws, on the candle. Other objects to use on your altar include decorated eggs or egg-shaped objects and bird pictures or figurines, especially birds of prey. The ritual is written as a solo practice that can easily be adapted for a group.

Once your altar is set up, light the candle. Raise your hands in the epiphany gesture with arms out to the sides at shoulder height, elbows bent, and hands raised with palms facing forward. As you do this say: *"To the people of the past, white was the color of death, of bare bone. It signified the completion of death so rebirth could begin. I call on the Bird Goddess to be with me so I may understand her eternal cycles and find balance in life and death, and the endings and beginnings in my life."*

Create sacred spacing through breath and toning. Slowly inhale and exhale three times, and then chant the sound *OOOO* (as in *who*) for as long as you can with a single breath. Stand in silence for a moment or two and then say: *"Now in sacred space, I bring that sacredness within me as I enter the realm of the Bird Goddess."*

To the people of Old Europe, death was seen as part of the cycle of renewal. Death and regeneration also symbolize the endings and beginnings that occur throughout our lives. Stand in front of your altar, take a piece of herb, and hold it for a moment. Let it symbolize an emotion, a thought, a situation, or an aspect of your life that has ended or is ending, or that you wish to release in order to bring renewal. Touch the herb to the candle flame and as it burns, drop it into the cauldron and say: *"I accept this ending. Now I begin a rebirth."*

When the herb is finished burning, stand in silence for a few moments. In the days and weeks ahead, think of the cycle that you have acknowledged in this ritual and know that the Goddess will support you.

Honor the Goddess with chant and send your energy out to the universe. Say: *"May the birds of the Goddess be messengers to carry my intention and energy forth."*

And then chant:

> *From the Goddess I am born.*
> *And to her I shall return.*
> *She is the bright spark of life,*
> *That forever and always burns.*

When it feels appropriate, end the chant. Stand in the epiphany gesture in silence as you ground and center your energy. Extinguish the candle and then say: *"May I learn to recognize and honor the transitions in my life and realize that the beauty of endings is that they are also beginnings. Blessed be."*

A Symbol for Samhain

A feather ladder, also known as a witches' ladder, can symbolize the descent of Inanna into the otherworld and her return to the light and life. Hang a feather ladder above your altar on Samhain and contemplate Inanna's journey as well as the Goddess's power of death and regeneration.

Figure 1.4: A single-strand style of feather ladder

To make a garland-style feather ladder, you will need three strands of yarn or light cord—one black, one white, and one red. Cut them into three-foot lengths, which will make the ladder about one foot long. You will also need nine feathers. Read the information in chapter 10 about consecrating the feather ladder as well as information about collecting feathers.

Knot the strands of yarn together at one end. Place something heavy on the knot to anchor it while you braid the strands. When you get near the end of the yarn, knot it, and then lay the braid out on a table. Arrange the feathers in a row along the braid. Place the largest feather at the center of the row and arrange the others by descending size at even intervals out to both ends. When finished, the largest feather will be at the bottom of the ladder.

At each point where you placed a feather, tie a knot in the braid, and then push the shaft of the feather through it. Form a circle by knotting the ends of the braid together. Raise the ladder in one hand, and then gently pull the center feather down so it hangs straight toward the floor. The other feathers will jut out to the sides, creating the steps of the ladder.

A feather ladder can also be used to honor a loved one when he or she passes. After making it, place the ladder in the center of your altar. Write or carve the name of the person into a white candle, light it, and place it alongside the feather ladder. Spend time recalling your relationship and how he or she touched your life. When it feels appropriate, blow out the candle and place a piece of candy in the middle of the feather ladder to symbolize your wish that your loved one's journey be sweet. Allow these things to remain on your altar for three days. After that, wrap the feather ladder in a scarf or a soft cloth and store it with your ritual items for use in Samhain sabbats.

Eggs and Bones

As we have seen, eggs represent birth and rebirth. Decorate a couple of eggs with symbols of regeneration such as an hourglass, triangle, or brush/comb for your Samhain, Imbolc, and Ostara altars. Instructions for creating and hanging decorated eggs can be found in chapter 4. Also consider making a special egg when someone you know passes. Write the person's name on the egg along with symbols of regeneration. Keep it on your altar for nine months, and then bury it in the ground. In Ukrainian folk tradition, a decorated egg was often placed in a coffin to accompany the deceased.

Bones, of course, represent death. Instead of discarding chicken bones after dinner or bones from your Thanksgiving turkey, wash them off and let them dry. Using paint or markers, draw owl eyes or an owl face on them. Place the bones on your altar at Samhain and Imbolc to acknowledge the death and regeneration aspect of the Goddess. At Samhain, let the bones remind you of the fragility of life, and what a blessing it is to be alive. Also let the bones serve to strengthen your faith in the Goddess. Know that she is there to receive you when this life ends and to prepare you for the next.

Instead of bones, use a white bird figurine on your altar to represent a stiff white lady figurine. Use red paint or markers to simulate red ochre and draw several symbols of regeneration. Place it on your altar for Samhain or Imbolc as well as for dark moon rituals.

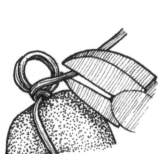
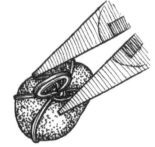

Figure 1.5: Making a stone amulet

Triangular Stone Pendant

The triangle symbolizes the Goddess's regenerative forces and powers of transformation. This is a simple yet powerful symbol that can be worn as an amulet, as people of ancient times did. Go for a walk and look for stones with a natural triangular shape. If you prefer a crystal, use white or clear quartz.

Make the crystal or stone into an amulet that you can wear as a pendant. This can be created by wire-wrapping the stone. There are many techniques for wire-wrapping stones; some are fancy and others simple. The following is an easy method that does not require a lot of skill (only a little patience). You will need: 18-gauge craft wire, a small pair of needle-nose pliers, a small pair of round-nose pliers or a pencil, and wire cutters.

Begin by cutting an eight-inch length of wire. Make a circle in the middle of the wire by winding it around a pencil or round pliers once or twice. Twist both lengths of wire around each other to keep the circle in place. Orient the stone so the finished pendant will be a downward-pointing triangle. Hold the circle of wire in place at the top of the stone opposite the downward point. Carefully bend both lengths of wire around the stone beginning at the bottom. Work the wire around to the top of the stone. Basically, you are making a little cage to hold the stone. Loop both ends of the wire around the circle at the top of the stone. Cut off excess wire, and tuck the ends into the loop by gently squeezing them with the pliers.

Flight Visualization

Visualization is another way to connect with the Goddess and her birds. Place a white candle and an image of an owl or other night bird on your altar. If you are so inclined, use eyeliner or a face-paint pencil to draw a triangle, an hourglass, or a bird's foot under each of your eyes. Alternatively, draw them on your eyelids so they are only visible when you close your eyes. Sit in front of your altar, light the candle, and gaze at the bird image or figurine. Slowly close your eyes and visualize that you are the bird. Imagine that you are sitting in a tree like an owl or on the ground like a nighthawk or nightjar. Feel the darkness like a cloak around you, providing protection.

Despite the dark, you can clearly see your surroundings. Although it is quiet, there are many faint sounds that allow you to identify the subtle nocturnal activity around you. Stretch your body tall, spread your wings, and lift into flight. The dark world slides away beneath you as air rushes past your face. It is such a simple thing, yet flight carries us closer to the Goddess who guides us on a never-ending cycle in, out, and back into the miracle of life.

Enjoy your flight, and then slowly return to your perch in the tree or on the ground. Feel the solidity beneath you. Take a couple of slow, deep breaths, and then return your attention to the room in which you sit. Slowly open your eyes and gaze at the bird image or figurine on your altar for a few moments. Take time to journal your experience, and then blow out the candle as you thank the Bird Goddess for her blessings.

Additional Activity

Just as the people of Old Europe used stones, so can we. Go for a walk to look for oblong stones that will serve as little owls. When you get home, wash them and let them dry. Paint owl eyes and a V or single line for the beak, or the radiant divine eyes. These can be placed on your altar for rituals or in your garden in the spring as symbols of regeneration. Because the Goddess is also a protector, use your little owl stones when casting spells of protection and call on the Bird Goddess for support.

Chapter 7

Are Her:
Transformer and Eternal Spirit

As mentioned in the introduction, Marija Gimbutas referred to this third aspect of the Goddess as transformation, timeless energy, and unfolding. To me, this represents the eternal spirit that links life and death, the manifest and unmanifest. Timeless energy and unfolding is the perpetual source of ongoing transformation and unfailing rhythm. Although eternal, the soul is in a continual state of becoming that flows with the pulse of life. It is constant, yet changing. It is what animates the clay of our physical bodies and it is the ultimate mystery. The energy of birds and their long association with spirit makes all birds appropriate for this aspect of the Goddess.

The Goddess As Bird

With its ephemeral fragility, the bird came to represent the transcendent quality of the human soul and its ability to rise and soar. The epiphany gesture that represents the presence of the Goddess can equally represent the human spirit rising to reunite with the Great Mother.

There have been two nearly universal and mystical functions of birds relating to spirit and soul. One is that the soul took the form of a bird at death. A bird's ability to fly symbolized freedom and the unfettered human spirit as it passed from this world into the next. The other function is that a bird served as a guide for the soul. Eagles depicted on Syrian tombs represented soul guides. Likewise Isis and her sister Nephthys were frequently depicted on sarcophagi as protectors and guides for the deceased.

As mentioned, the Egyptian ba represented a person's immortal soul that was released at death. The ba was originally depicted as a stork and later as a human-headed hawk. In both Greek and Celtic cultures it was believed that the dead could reappear as birds in the realm of the living. The Romans believed that the soul left the mouth as a raven; however, the souls of their emperors were said to take the form of eagles. In addition, there is a Turkish saying that a person's soul bird has flown away, which means that he or she has died.[36]

The metaphor of the soul departing as a bird at death or serving as a soul guide persisted in Europe and was carried to the New World. Funeral symbols on old gravestones include an angel releasing a bird from a wicker cage, a dove in the tree of life, or spring birds singing to awaken the soul to new life.

In addition to the spirit, birds have been associated with inspiration and widely used as metaphors in literature. This seems no coincidence as the words *spirit* and *inspire* come from the same Latin root *spir*, meaning "to breathe."[37] When we are inspired, our thoughts soar, and when we are in-spirit, our souls soar. Inspiration also relates to the breath and brings us full circle to the belief that the soul took the form of a bird and left the body on the last breath.

Eggs: The Circle of Life

The egg relates to all aspects of the Bird Goddess. As life-giver, it represents birth as well as the Goddess's power as cosmic creatrix. In her aspect as death-wielder and regeneratrix, it represents double birth or rebirth. In this transformer and eternal spirit aspect, the egg represents the power of transformation and the promise of new life.

---

36. Constance Victoria Briggs, *Encyclopedia of the Unseen World* (San Francisco: Red Wheel/Weiser, 2010), 60.

37. E. Bernard Jordan, *The Laws of Thinking: 20 Secrets to Using the Divine Power of Your Mind to Manifest Prosperity* (Carlsbad, CA: Hay House, 2006), 136.

Being of circular shape, the egg is a symbol that encompasses and represents the eternal cycle of life into death and death into life. Images of eggs and splitting eggs were widely used by Neolithic people as symbols of becoming and the energy of change. These depictions were used along with spirals, whirls, and Xs to represent becoming and life in transition.

On Minoan vases, eggs were depicted as the source from which trees (possibly the tree of life) sprang and grew. Much later, in medieval literature, the egg symbolized the four elements, which all together represented cycles and completeness. The egg also represented life and its various manifestations as well as an incubator of enlightenment and source of divine light.

Symbols of Transformation and Energy of Spirit

Symbols associated with this aspect of the Goddess are dynamic, representing the pulse of life. Defying stagnation, the energy of these symbols portrays the movement or transition from one place, stage, or phase to another. The essence of this energy is easily seen in the movement of a flock of birds as it flies in unison and creates vigorous, flowing patterns.

The spiral is an ancient symbol of energy that is still widely used although it is not often regarded as sacred today. Dating to about 16,000 to 13,000 BCE, the oldest-known use of the spiral was found in the area of present-day Siberia.[38] Carved into a piece of mammoth ivory, a spiral was created with a series of dots that wind around seven times from a hole drilled into the center of the ivory. This center spiral is flanked by six smaller ones.

To the people of Old Europe, the spiral embodied energy and cyclic time. Like the meander, it symbolized a path between the worlds of the seen and unseen. The spiral has been found on pottery dating to 6500 BCE, and it was in common use throughout Old Europe by 3500 BCE.[39]

On vases, the spiral was used singly, in running bands, or as an S-shaped double spiral. Bands of spirals represented the energy that awakens dormant life forces. Echoing the mammoth ivory, a spiral was sometimes drawn in the center of a dish with circles around it. On figurines, spirals occasionally took the place of the Goddess's eyes, or were located on her breasts. The intention has been interpreted as amplifying her life-force en-

---

38. Baring and Cashford, *The Myth of the Goddess*, 23.
39. Gimbutas, *The Language of the Goddess*, 279.

ergy. I wonder what the people of Old Europe would think if they knew that our galaxy was just one of many vast spirals formed by stars.

Not surprisingly, another important symbol was the circle. Like the spiral, it implies continual motion and cycles. As keen observers of nature, the people of Old Europe were in tune with the ongoing transformation of the earth through its seasons. Punctuating spring and autumn, the arrival and departure of migrating birds would have seemed like harbingers of change. In addition to emerging from circular-shaped eggs, when birds molt their feathers they themselves embody transformation.

Figure 1.6: Symbols of energy and transformation: spiral, double spiral, and triple spiral (top row); the cross/quartered circle, whirl, and tri-line (bottom row)

From the Paleolithic onward, ring or circle dances have been depicted—first on cave walls and later on pottery. In addition, the imprints of human feet in a circle have been found in the caves of France, suggesting that these were places for sacred dance. Through dance, people could attain ritual or shamanic ecstasy as well as communicate with the Goddess. Besides circle dances, stone circles represented the power of Goddess energy. Standing stone circles are mostly found in the British Isles. While over nine hundred still exist, the best known, of course, is Stonehenge.[40]

---

40. Gimbutas, *The Language of the Goddess*, 313.

The circle symbol was often quartered with two lines, a cross, in the middle. Pagans and Wiccans should not shy away from the cross just because it is a symbol of Christianity. In older times, crossed lines represented the four directions and the four phases of the moon. It also served as a symbol of life and elemental energy. Together, the circle and cross is a fourfold motif representing the unifying power of nature that encompasses the four seasons. Found in Central Europe and Italy, some fourfold designs contain a center circle surrounded by four circles within which are Ms, zigzags, or crosses. Taken altogether these represent the completeness and predictable rhythm of the natural world and the wheel of life.

Round like a circle, the earliest loaves of bread were often marked with a cross before being baked. In Egypt, a cross was incised on loaves that were dedicated to Isis in the springtime. Thousands of years later, the people of Elizabethan England believed that eating a loaf decorated with a cross would provide protection for a year

The whirl is a symbol that is best described as a cross in motion. An example of one that is still commonly used is Brigid's cross. The whirl was a symbol of becoming that was used throughout Old Europe and found on a range of sacred and secular objects. As a sign of becoming, Brigid's cross is the perfect symbol for Imbolc. Whirls stir energy, and their presence seemed to be critical for healing or when used in tombs for aiding the process of regeneration. According to Gimbutas, "whirling signs seem to ensure a smooth transition from one phase to the next." [41]

The power of three is an ancient concept that had special meaning to the people of Old Europe, perhaps because of the Bird Goddess's association with water. She was regarded as the source of water that fell from the heavens, that flowed on the surface of the earth, and that welled up from under the ground. The Goddess's power encompassed the sky, the earth, and the underworld. The power of three was also prevalent in the trinity of woman, bird, and egg. The symbol that represented the power of three was the simple tri-line, or three parallel lines. It was commonly included on beaked Bird Goddess figurines beneath the eyes or down the neck. Tri-lines were sometimes accompanied by chevrons on figurines, and sometimes it was the only marking on vases.

Associated with energy and symbols of becoming, tri-lines have been found inside circles, in the center of whirling patterns, and with spirals. Tri-lines were used on spindle whorls, altars, vases, pebbles, and pendants. Depicted in the center of an egg, it echoed a cosmic connection among the domains of the Bird Goddess. In temples, flat triangular

41. Gimbutas, *The Language of the Goddess*, 295.

stones or clay altarpieces were marked with meanders and tri-lines. In addition, symbols and objects appear to have been used in threes, including triple columns and shrines with three rooms.

The power of three was also an important concept in the megalithic culture outside of Old Europe. This is most famously represented by the triple spiral in the passage tomb of Newgrange in Ireland. As the winter solstice sunlight penetrates the dark passageway, it dramatically illuminates this spiral on the back wall of the structure. In addition, the large horizontal curbstone in front of the entrance to Newgrange was carved with triple spirals and other flowing symbols. Although not as ancient as the spirals in Ireland, the motif of a triple spiral or whorl of bird's heads has been found in both Wales and Germany.

The power of three echoes down the ages as we continue to draw on its significance for incantations, spells, and rituals. The power of three brings us full circle to the three important aspects to the Goddess, which also embody the three great mysteries of life, death, and spirit. In the next chapter, we will see how we can incorporate these symbols into our practices and everyday lives as we connect with this aspect of the Goddess and her birds.

Chapter 8

Connecting with the
Transformer and Eternal Spirit

As the transformer of energy and the keeper of our eternal souls, the Goddess embodies the perpetual rhythm of all that is. Spirit drives our personal journey like a dynamic spiral that links the manifest and unmanifest through the immanent presence of the Goddess. Existing everywhere on Earth, birds are the touchstone through which we can maintain our contact with her as well as with our own souls. Birds can also be instrumental to enriching our everyday experiences and to helping us through the changes in our lives.

Transformer and Spirit Ritual

For this ritual you will need a black candle, pictures and/or figurines of birds, and a feather (or a feather for each participant if you are doing a group ritual). Be sure to read the information in chapter 10 before collecting feathers. Using a large sewing needle or a fine point marker that will show up on black, draw or carve several energy symbols onto the candle. The ritual is written as a solo practice that can easily be adapted for a group.

Once your altar is set up, light the candle. Raise your hands in the epiphany gesture with arms out to the sides at shoulder height, elbows bent, and hands raised with palms facing forward. As you do this say: *"Black is the color of transformation. It represents the soul incubating in the darkness of the Goddess's womb. Bird Goddess, transformer and keeper of eternal souls, I call on you to be with me."*

Create sacred space with breath and a feather. Inhale and then hold the feather lengthwise in front of your mouth as you gently blow across it. Do this three times, and then say: *"Now in sacred space, I bring that sacredness within me as I enter the realm of the Bird Goddess."*

You may want to record the following visualization and play it back: *Try to imagine the time when nature was revered; when the seasons were important; when the circle of the moon was a marker of time. The Goddess was everywhere; she is still everywhere. When we open our hearts, we can feel her presence.*

Imagine that you are standing in the filtered shade of trees as you gaze across a wide meadow. It is morning and the sun slants golden ribbons of light across soft, green grass. Birds flutter and sing nearby. Take a deep breath and enjoy the sweet, earthy aromas.

Now, step from the shade of the trees into the meadow. Feel the long grass tickle your legs. As you move across the meadow, you can see a rolling green quilt of cultivated fields and meadows. Above you, the sky is a deep turquoise canopy that reaches from horizon to horizon. You can feel its limitlessness and serenity. You feel at peace with yourself in the stillness of the morning and the quiet meadow.

You have been in this meadow before and you have seen this view many times, but today is different because you can feel the presence of the Goddess. Her love and beauty are all around you and within you. You are relaxed and at ease with her gentle energy.

A bird circles around you, and then as you hold out your hand it alights on your wrist. You gaze into its eyes and it gazes back, reflecting the energy of life that is all around you. You feel a gentle sensation through your arm that moves up through your body to the heart center. Feel its vibrant flow.

The bird slowly flaps its wings and gently lifts from your wrist. Watch it as it circles and climbs into the sky. Experience the heady exhilaration of feeling totally alive. Your body feels warm and exquisitely invigorated by the luminous flow of energy. You feel in a state of grace, surrounded by a deep sense of compassion and spirit. You are profoundly moved because you know that you are touching the web of life and you have a sense of your place in it. Dwell in this knowledge for a few minutes. When you are ready to return your attention to the room in which you sit, take a few long, slow breaths and then open your eyes.

Stand up slowly, and begin to move. Listen for your inner music and feel it flow through you. Pick up your feather, and hold it as you move with the energy.

As you move, you may want to chant:

> *Circle round, spiral down;*
> *Rise up singing from the ground.*
> *Goddess, keeper of my soul;*
> *Transformation make me whole.*

When it feels appropriate, end the chant. Stand in the epiphany gesture in silence as you ground and center your energy. Extinguish the candle and then say: *"May the energy and spirit of the Bird Goddess remain in my heart. Blessed be."*

Walking a Spiral

A spiral can be used like a labyrinth. Because it is one of the Goddess's ancient symbols, it helps us connect with her and to work with bird energy. Like a labyrinth, the spiral has one path into the center that takes us back out again. Because of this, the movement of energy is both clockwise and counterclockwise (deosil and widdershins). I have found that walking a spiral can provide just as profound an experience as walking a labyrinth.

When we walk a spiral, going toward the center is symbolic of moving inward toward the self as well as moving toward the primal source. Walking a spiral is both a descent and ascent that provides an opportunity to find balance and wisdom. Each journey on a spiral provides a unique opportunity for us to gain personal insight and connect with the energy of the Goddess and her birds.

To make a spiral, clear as much floor space as you can, or, if you have privacy, create one in your backyard. The easiest thing to use for a spiral is a long piece of rope. Begin laying it out at the center of the spiral and leave enough space to sit. If you are not comfortable sitting on the floor, place a chair in the center. Make the space between each wind of the spiral wide enough to form a path for walking.

It is helpful to take something with you when you walk the spiral, such as a feather, a bird figurine, or an egg decorated with Goddess symbols. When you are ready, stand at the entrance for a moment or two with your eyes closed and focus your mind before stepping onto the path. Move slowly and with intention. If you feel the need to pause during the walk, do so.

The walk into the center provides time to release the flurry of thoughts that usually occupies our minds. As we walk, we are symbolically spiraling inward, releasing the ego's control as well as any thoughts or emotions that tend to hold us back. This walk toward inner self also prepares us to reach outward to connect with the Goddess and her birds.

When you reach the center of the spiral, sit down. You may want to close your eyes or focus your gaze on whatever object you brought with you. Let your body relax; listen with your heart. Take your time in the center of the spiral, and then let your intuition guide you for the appropriate time to begin your walk out. Stand up, and then pause for a moment before initiating your return walk.

The power of the inward and outward movement can make us feel extremely grounded or a little wobbly from the energy that has been generated. Take your time and pause when necessary as you walk out. Upon emerging from the spiral, it is helpful to take a few minutes to stand or sit in silence. You may want to journal your experience.

Insights may occur right away or they may take several days or even longer. Be mindful of any birds that begin to show themselves, as they may hold meaning for you. Refer to chapter 9 and the profiles to help you interpret their meaning.

Genius Loci and Spirit of Place

Birds provide a strong connection with the natural world and keep us in sync with the rhythms of nature. This is why it is helpful to work with the energy of our local birds. They bring an intangible atmosphere to the landscape around us, giving it an identity that fosters our sense of belonging.

Find out what birds are native to your area, which ones are year-round residents, and which ones may only stop by while on migration. Go to a place where you can easily observe them. Reach out with your energy and explore the sensations they create in the environment around you. Also do this in your backyard to connect with the birds closest to your home.

As you open yourself to their energy, you may find that you are seeing more birds or more types of birds. However, if one type of bird consistently presents itself, look up its profile in this book and spend time connecting with its energy. You may want to consider keeping a journal of bird sightings because it is easy to forget details. Comparing your observations over time often reveals patterns and aids in identifying and understanding messages.

Flight Patterns

The spiral and flowing symbols associated with this aspect of the Goddess are forms found in nature and in the flight patterns of birds. Find a place outside where you can sit comfortably and watch the movement of birds that fly in flocks. Early evening just before dusk is the best time, especially in the autumn and winter. This is because many types of birds form large roosting flocks after the breeding season.

Unlike the linear flight of geese, pelicans, and other waterfowl, some birds fly in dense groups. While starlings are well known for their aerobatic group displays, blackbirds also form large flocks that perform amazing maneuvers. Other birds to look for include pigeons, larks, meadowlarks, and robins.

When you go to a place to observe birds in flight, take a handful of birdseed along with you. As the birds synchronize their movements, watch for spirals, whorls, and circular patterns. Follow the fluid motion with your eyes and energy. Allow the birds' flight patterns to pull you into their unity. Let it inspire a sense of connection with them and with all the people who have gone before and witnessed the Bird Goddess speaking through these symbols created by her creatures. When the birds begin to settle down or move off from where you are, make one of her energy symbols by sprinkling the birdseed on the ground. Stand in silence for a moment and then say: *"Bird Goddess, Mother of all, thank you for touching my life with your blessings."*

Additional Activities

Another way to observe flowing patterns and symbols is with incense. Light it in a slightly darkened room where you will be able to observe the smoke. Hold a feather over it and gently blow across the length of the feather. Observe the flowing movement of the incense and watch for whorls and other symbols related to the Goddess. After watching the smoke, close your eyes for a moment and experience the energy of her blessings.

Last but not least, Ostara is the perfect sabbat to incorporate the life-stimulating energy symbols of the Goddess. While hot cross buns are a Christian tradition, the cross or quartered circle is an important symbol of the Bird Goddess. Incorporate this food into your Ostara ritual or meal.

Chapter 9
Bird Guides and Messages

Even if you have not felt an affinity with birds before, as you begin to work with their energy you may develop a special connection with a particular type of bird. A bird guide may stay with you forever or a new one may come into your life as you change and grow. In addition to a special bird guide, others may become important to us at different times. You may even find that these avian contacts change through the seasons as some birds migrate. Another level of relationship with birds are the messengers that make temporary contact to bring or help us interpret information or deal with a situation.

Finding Your Bird Guide

Visualization and meditation are useful methods for finding your bird guide. Sit quietly and close your eyes in a room where you will not be disturbed. Rest your hands in your lap with palms upward and open. Take three long, deep breaths, each one slower than the one before. Become aware of the energy in your heart center. Visualize your heart energy opening like a flower. Now, image that it is late afternoon and you are sitting in a beautiful field or outdoor place that you enjoy. Keep your senses open to the smells and sounds around you. Perhaps there is a gentle breeze. Stay present and keep your mind focused on this scene. Simply breathe and wait.

If a bird appears, just observe it. The bird may approach you or keep its distance. Because you have only just met, it needs to get to know you. Allow events to unfold. It may fly off to end its first meeting with you or simply fade away. Slowly return your attention to the room in which you are sitting and journal the details of any encounter that may have occurred. Over the next few days or weeks, you may notice images of the bird everywhere you go, or you may actually see the type of bird more frequently. This is confirmation that you met your bird guide. Alternatively, do this exercise outdoors and see if a flesh-and-blood bird approaches you. However, your bird guide may or may not be one that is local to you.

Once you know the type of bird that is your guide, find out all you can about it. Begin with the information in part 2 of this book, which provides basic details, historical information, and the bird's associations and powers relevant to Pagans and Wiccans. Your bird guide may have connections with you that stem from events in your life, your family background, or various other aspects that have shaped who you are. Take time to examine these things as well as the bird itself. Study its physical and behavioral characteristics, which may reveal things about yourself as well as your path. Also, keep in mind that your bird guide may not be local to your area.

If a bird does not come to you, don't try to force the visualization. Or, if you get fidgety or lose focus during the visualization, this may not be the best time for your bird guide to find you. Alternatively, your bird guide may choose to make itself known to you in a dream or by continually appearing. Appearances can include actual bird sightings, the same type of bird showing up in the media, or bird figurines and pictures in shops. Whether a bird came to you in the visualization or not, you will know when your bird guide chooses to make itself known. Don't be in a rush; it will happen when the time is right.

An important point to keep in mind is that your bird guide may not be a fabulous eagle, owl, or peacock. Don't be disappointed; even the smallest or humblest of birds holds a great deal of power and, of course, a connection with the Goddess.

When you find your bird guide, honor it. Keep an image or figurine of it on your altar or any other place in your house or on your property that serves as a meaningful touch point. Decorate a special egg and mark it with the common or species name of your guide bird. Glue a small image of your bird onto it, or paint it to resemble the coloring and markings of your bird guide's eggs. Keep this on your altar or in a special place where you will see it often.

Messages and Guidance

As mentioned, sometimes certain birds come to us as messengers, and sometimes we may seek an outside force for guidance. The ancient Romans called this a "bird-telling."[42] If a particular type of bird keeps appearing and has not made itself known as your guide, then it may be bringing information for you. Alternatively, its appearance may help you understand something in your life or alert you to pay more attention to a certain situation. These appearances may also occur in dreams.

Ask the bird outright, vocally or in your mind, what the message is. You may receive a forthright response; however, the message is most often revealed by the action or location of the bird. For example, if the bird is always perched on a house, examine your home life and situation. If it is always flying, perhaps there is something you want to escape from, remove from your life, or change. If it is on a fence, there may be barriers that you need to remove in some aspect of your current situation. Because each of us and each bird is unique, there are no hard and fast guidelines. However, they are not difficult to figure out.

For example, a fence can be a barrier, a hurdle, or a challenge, but it can also symbolize something that unites and defines. It can mean that you need to make a decision about something. Interpretations depend on our personal circumstances and how we view them. If the messenger bird appears on different objects, it can indicate a connection or a progression. Keep track of the bird's activities in a journal, and then take time to review them. Think it through and keep notes because, like dreams, our interpretations can come and then be gone like a gossamer mist.

If you are uncertain of your interpretation, take your time but don't overanalyze it. Quite often the first or simplest interpretation is the correct one. It is also normal to question our conclusions and perhaps feel a bit skeptical. If this is the case, the messenger bird may provide confirmation for you. It may appear with food or a flower in its beak for you. The confirmation you receive will make sense to you.

Sometimes a message can be very simple and may come in the form of a feather. The first time I stepped out on the back porch of my house in Maine, I heard seagulls

---

42. Diane Skafte, *Listening to the Oracle: The Ancient Art of Finding Guidance in the Signs and Symbols All Around Us* (San Francisco: HarperSanFrancisco, 1997), 11.

overhead. Having spent childhood summers by the shore, it was a sound I loved. When I returned my gaze to the porch, I found a white feather right beside me. I felt that I had been welcomed to my true home.

Another way to ask for guidance or to work with a bird is to randomly open this book to a page in the profiles section. This method can also be used to aid in interpreting dreams if they included an unidentifiable bird. Read the information about the bird. Do any of the characteristics relate to you in some capacity? Some of the ways that a bird can offer guidance may be included in the magical workings section of its profile. Take time with the information as you analyze the significance of the bird and how it relates to you or your situation.

The Bird Ogham

The Celtic ogham, also known as the tree alphabet, provides a unique way to connect with avian energy because birds are associated with the characters. The bird ogham was one of many types of ogham included in *The Book of Ballymote*. Like many of the old "books" of Ireland, *The Book of Ballymote* is a collection of manuscripts. There are several ways that we can use this ogham when working with bird energy. One is to use the ogham character in place of a bird's name when inscribing it on candles or other objects used for rituals or spells. If you have a set of ogham staves or cards, randomly choose one and then use the profiles in this book for information on a potential message.

Table 1.1 lists the ogham names, letters, and their associated birds. Because a few of the birds are not included in this book, I have offered their cousins as alternatives. You may want to explore some of the birds from the original list if they pique your interest.

Since the number of birds represented by the ogham is so limited, another way to use it is by letter. For example, if you want to work with the energy of a falcon, you could use the ogham character Fearn, which represents the letter *F*. For letters not represented by the ogham, there are common substitutions that can be used. For example, when working with the energy of a kingfisher use the ogham Coll, which represents the letter *C* and is the substitute for *K*. The *forfeda* are five characters that were not part of the original ogham. While each character is not linked with an individual bird, the crane is associated with the *forfeda* as a group, so any of these ogham characters may be used for crane.

Table 1.1 The Bird Ogham			
Character	*Name*	*Letters*	*Original Birds/ Alternates*
	Beith	B/P	Pheasant
	Luis	L	Duck
	Fearn	F/V	Gull
	Saille	S	Hawk
	Nion	N	Snipe / Sandpiper, Plover
	Huath	H	Night Raven / Raven
	Duir	D	Wren
	Tinne	T	Starling
	Coll	C/K	None / Owl
	Quert	Q	Hen / Chicken, Peahen
	Muin	M	Titmouse / Chickadee
	Gort	G/J	Swan
	nGetal	NG	Goose
	Straif	Z	Thrush / Bluebird, Robin
	Ruis	R	Rook / Crow

Character	Name	Letters	Original Birds/ Alternates
			Table 1.1 The Bird Ogham (cont.)
⊥	Ailm	A	Lapwing / Sandpiper, Plover
⊥⊥	Onn	O	Cormorant
⊥⊥⊥	Ur	U/W	Lark
⊥⊥⊥⊥	Eadha	E/Y	Swan
The Forfeda			
⚹	Eabhadh	EA	Crane
◇	Oir	Oi	
⊐	Uilleann	Ui	
⋈	Elfin	Ia	
▦	Eamhancholl	Ae	

When working with birds, especially when randomly selecting one from the profiles section or choosing an ogham, information may not be understood immediately. In fact, it may take a few days, a week, or more. Be patient. Information often comes softly like the flutter of wings.

Chapter 10

Feathers

Throughout time and around the world, feathers have been a powerful symbol because they allow birds to defy gravity. Like the egg, feathers have been regarded as special and magical. Carrying the transformative power of birds, feathers have been used for cloaks and headdresses or as tools to invoke the presence of bird spirits and helpers. Feathers are also associated with divination, second sight, and the otherworld, and they have been used as talismans.

Before Collecting Feathers

Picking up a feather from the ground seems innocent; however, unless you are exceptionally good at identifying the species of bird from which it came, you could be breaking the law. According to the Migratory Bird Treaty Act, it is "illegal for anyone to take, possess, import, export, transport, sell, purchase, barter, or offer for sale, purchase, or barter, any migratory bird, or the parts, nests, or eggs of such a bird except under the terms of a valid permit issued pursuant to Federal regulations." [43]

You may be wondering what this means for those of us who do not deliberately hunt protected birds, destroy nests, or catch birds to sell as pets. Unfortunately, collecting feathers (even those found on the ground), nests, or eggs is illegal. Simply possessing one these things is illegal because the law does not distinguish between picking up a discarded feather or eggshell and poaching them.

Many birds are protected by the Migratory Bird Treaty Act, the name of which is somewhat misleading. This is because the act covers some birds that simply "migrate" for food within their year-round habitat. At any rate, this law originated in 1918 to protect bird populations that were being decimated by the fashion industry's use of feathers. While the law has been updated from time to time, it may be a surprise to find certain birds on the list, such as the American crow and the herring gull. Nevertheless, they are included and protected. The entire text of the Migratory Bird Treaty Act and a complete list of birds included in this law can be found online.

So where does that leave us if we want to work with feathers? There are native species that are not included in the migratory list, such as pheasants, ruffed grouse, wild turkey, starlings, and others. Feathers sold in craft stores come from birds not protected by the act and are legal to own. In addition to turkey and pheasant feathers, stores sell feathers from chickens, certain species of geese, and the mute swan, as well as peacock feathers and ostrich plumes. Often these are dyed to look like other types of feathers, such as eagle or hawk, as well as colors or patterns not found in the wild.

These feathers can be used as symbols for birds in general and surrogates for the specific species we may want to work with that are protected under the law. After all, intention is intertwined with magic, and so with intention and willpower we can symbolically work with a particular bird using the feather of another.

The Wonder of Feathers

Feathers make birds colorful creatures, and they make it possible for birds to fly. Feathers are light, flexible, and tough. There are six basic types, each with a different role. The contour feathers cover a bird's body and provide a sleek, aerodynamic contour. They also make up most of the wing feathers. Semiplumes are shaped like contour feathers but are not as stiff and can be fluffed. Down feathers are short and can be fluffed like the

---

43. http://www.fws.gov/migratorybirds/RegulationsPolicies/mbta/mbtintro.html.

semiplumes. Both of these are underneath the contour feathers and provide insulation to keep a bird warm or cool.

Filoplume feathers are tiny and are believed to help a bird sense their contour feathers and make adjustments when necessary. Bristles are very stiff, short feathers, and not all birds have them. On some birds they help protect the eyes and on others they help keep dust out of the nostrils. Swallows, nightjars, and woodpeckers have bristles. The other type of feather is called powder down and only a few birds have them. These constantly growing feathers are very delicate and break off to create a water-resistant powder. Herons have powder down feathers.

Molting is a process of losing and re-growing feathers to replace broken or worn ones. Most birds have one complete molt or one complete and one partial molt each year. Some birds have two complete molts. A partial or one complete molt occurs before the breeding season to acquire special plumage for attracting a mate. A full molt occurs after the breeding season, which is when birds with only one molt will lose their feathers. The molt is a gradual process that proceeds in a particular order, which varies from one type of bird to another.

Feathers give wings the shape necessary for getting a bird off the ground. The flight feathers are specialized contour feathers that have very rigid shafts to withstand the forces of flight. Other small contour feathers on the leading edge of the wing cover the bases of the larger feathers, creating a smooth, aerodynamic surface. Owls and nightjars can fly almost silently because the leading edges of their primary flight feathers are fluffy, which muffles sound. In addition to moving their wings up and down, birds can also move them forward or back, which helps them maneuver.

Tail feathers are often used as brakes for landing and can flare out like a fan. In addition, woodpeckers and nuthatches use the stiff feathers of their tails to brace against trees when climbing. Now, let's see how we can incorporate feathers into our magic, rituals, and everyday lives.

Feather/Witches' Ladder

In chapter 6, I recommended using a witches' ladder at Samhain to symbolize Inanna's underworld descent and return. Instructions on how to make the ladder are also included there. Historically, witches' ladders have been used in spells for both white and black magic. More recently, they have been used as talismans and hung in homes for protection. According to folklore, a witches' ladder was hung outside a house to prevent a specific person from entering.

Also called a witches' garland, they are most often fashioned as braided, knotted cord with the ends tied together, forming a circle. However, a witches' ladder can also be just a single length of rope with a small loop at the top from which to hang it. The shafts of feathers are then pushed through the rope at intervals so they are perpendicular to the rope.

Because a feather ladder is a magical tool, you may want to consecrate it before using it. I like to use mugwort for cleansing and setting intentions but if you have a different herb or incense that you like, use that instead. Place an incense burner or cauldron on your altar along with other objects that relate to your purpose for the ladder. Because the ladder is made with feathers, consider including pictures or figurines of birds or the Bird Goddess. Light the incense or burn the herb, and then pass the ladder through the smoke three times as you state your purpose for making it. Leave the ladder on your altar for three days before using it.

As an alternative to rope for making the single-strand style of feather ladder, try drapery cord, which is available in a wide range of colors and styles. When working with this type of ladder, swing it back and forth while chanting or reciting a spell. In addition to spells and ritual use, experiment holding a feather ladder of either style when working with bird energy.

A Quill Pen for Magic

Until the early nineteenth century, a quill pen was the best instrument for writing. Nowadays there are many options for those of us who enjoy writing in longhand. For magical purposes, a quill pen is a delightful throwback to the past. It may take a little practice the first time you make or use one, but it is worth the effort. Of course, when working with birds for magical purposes, it provides a unique way to connect with their energy.

To make a pen, you will need a stiff feather that is large enough to feel comfortable when writing. A turkey feather that is about twelve inches long works well. You will also need a small, sharp knife, a pair of tweezers, a cutting board or block of wood, and a soup can filled with sand. Of course, you will also need a bottle of ink.

First, hold the feather as though you are going to write to see if you may need to trim back some fluff to provide a large enough bare area on the shaft to grip the pen. Make the first cut to shape the pen nib by holding the feather sideways on the cutting board. Make a slanted cut at about a 45-degree angle to remove a small part of the point. Use the tweezers to remove any material inside the feather shaft.

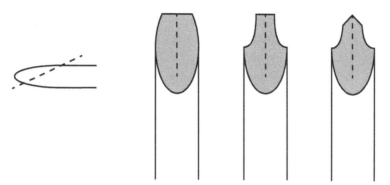

Figure 1.5: The steps for cutting a feather to make a quill pen.
The first view is shown from the side; the others show the pen nib from below.

Next, temper the shaft to strengthen it. Put the can of sand in a 350-degree oven for about 15 to 20 minutes. Carefully remove it from the oven and stand the bare part of the feather shaft in the sand. Leave it there until the sand cools.

Now you are ready to shape the nib. Hold the feather flat so the longer side of the slanted cut is against the cutting board. Cut across the end so it is squared off, and then gently make a small slit up the middle of the shaft. Next, shape the end by cutting both sides to make the squared-off nib narrower, and then slightly pointed. Now, it is ready to use. Dip the nib in the ink and practice writing until you get a feel for it. Avoid using heavy pressure as this can bend or break the nib.

Additional Feather Uses

As an alternative to a feather ladder, simply hold a feather as you meditate to work with bird energy or when connecting with your bird guide. Also, stand a few feathers in a jar to keep on your altar or anywhere in your home to serve as a reminder of your connection with birds and the Bird Goddess. I also keep one in my car as a travel amulet.

Feathers attached to a walking stick aid in connecting with the rhythms of the natural world as you explore it. In addition to feathers, carve or paint an image of a bird on your walking stick, or attach a small figurine. You may also want to carve a few of the Bird Goddess symbols into the stick.

In place of wind chimes, hang a feather charm. This can be as simple or elaborate as you like. Start with a fairly straight branch that is about a foot long. The bark can remain on the branch, or strip it off and let the wood dry. The branch can be stained or left natural. Also consider carving or painting some of the Goddess symbols on it. Cut a two-foot length of thin twine or decorative thread, and tie it to the ends of the branch. This will be used to hang the feather charm. Using a fine thread, attach one end to the shaft of a feather and tie the other end to the branch. Cut different lengths of thread to attach other feathers so they will hang at various lengths. When it is finished, consecrate it by passing it through the smoke of incense or burning herb, and then hang it up. The feather charm can be consecrated for a specific purpose, or it can be used to move and activate energy wherever you hang it. Of course, it can also be dedicated to the Bird Goddess or your bird guide and hung in a special place.

Part Two

THE PROFILES

Most of the birds included in this book are common, some are legendary, a few are pets, several are domesticated farmyard birds, and some may only be seen in zoos. The birds profiled here are North American because that is where I live. While a few of the birds do not call North America home, to be totally inclusive would have made this a monumental task and would require more than one volume. However, although most species covered in this book are native to the Americas, a great deal of European folklore has been ascribed to them because settlers brought their worldview with them. As a result, birds such as American blackbirds, which are not related to the blackbirds of Europe, have had Old World folklore ascribed to them.

While a number of the birds profiled here may have a wide range over most of North America, many do not. To compensate, more than one species is presented in many of the profiles to cover as much territory as possible.

Because we have a good idea of how big (or small) some birds are but not others, comparative sizes are noted to aid in identification. Familiar birds such as the sparrow, robin, and crow are used as categories of comparative sizes. For example, if you are not familiar with magpies and mockingbirds, it is helpful to know that a magpie is about the size of a crow and a mockingbird the size of a robin. Having a good idea of the size and description of a bird also aids in visualization when working with its energy.

These categories relate to an average bird size, which is a measurement of its length from the tip of the bill to the tip of the tail. So while we may think that egrets, ibis, and storks should be classified as very large, their long legs are not included in this standard form of measurement. Also keep in mind that sizes are approximations and some birds with which we are familiar may seem bigger or smaller than these sizes.

Table 2.1 Comparative Bird Sizes	
Category	*Approximate Body Size*
Very small	Smaller than a sparrow
Sparrow	3 to 7 inches
Robin	8 to 11 inches

Table 2.1 Comparative Bird Sizes (cont.)	
Category	*Approximate Body Size*
Pigeon	11 to 14 inches
Crow	15 to 20 inches
Red-tailed hawk	19 to 25 inches
Goose	25 to 45 inches
Very large	Larger than a goose

Also included in the profiles are a couple of terms to understand when describing birds. The "upperparts" refer to the crown of the head, nape of the neck, back, wings, and rump. The "underparts" refer to the chest, abdomen, and flanks. A physical description is provided to help in visualizations and to identify birds when observing them.

While we can work with a bird's energy regardless of where we live, knowing its habitat and range also aids in our visualizations and experiences. The ranges provided in this book encompass a bird's breeding, wintering, and migration areas. Because Alaska is not contiguous with the lower forty-eight states, I have noted these separately as Alaska and the United States. For specific details on these ranges, the Cornell Lab of Ornithology has an excellent website at www.allaboutbirds.org. The Lab also has a bird identification app called Merlin that can be downloaded from merlin.allaboutbirds .org/. The National Audubon Society also has an online bird guide at www.audubon.org /field-guide. Audubon offers a mobile app called Audubon Birds Pro, which is available at www.audubon.org/apps.

Both the Cornell Lab and Audubon websites and apps include samples of bird calls and songs. Sound is a great way to identify birds, especially since we often hear them without seeing them.

Also included in each profile is a description of the bird's eggs. As previously suggested, in addition to decorating eggs with Goddess symbols you may want to paint them in the style of a particular bird. This can be used to honor the bird as well as aid you in connecting with its energy. I have included suggestions for ways to connect with each bird. However, because we are all unique, and so are birds, the way we contact them and how they make their presence known will vary. Follow your intuition and let the Bird Goddess guide you.

Birds provide us with a simple yet powerful way to stay in touch with the natural world and its seasonal markers. By working with birds we can attune ourselves to the subtle energies around us to enhance rituals, boost magic work, and expand a range of practices. Each bird has its own particular wisdom that can enrich our lives.

Albatross:
Black-Footed Albatross, Snowy Albatross

Black-Footed Albatross (**Phoebastria nigripes**)

This legendary storm rider and wanderer is the largest creature of the air. It is also a true seabird, as it does not hug the coastline but ventures across the widest expanses of water. The albatross was unknown to Westerners until European explorers encountered it while looking for a shortcut to the Spice Islands and the riches of the East. Originally regarded as a type of pelican, it was named accordingly.

The name *albatross* evolved from the Arabic name for pelican, *al-qadous,* which went through several Spanish and Moorish translations and emerged as *alcatraz.*[44] This, in turn, was anglicized to *albatross* because of the Latin *alba,* meaning "white." The genus name of the legendary snowy albatross comes from Diomedes, a mythical Greek hero in the story of the Trojan War. Returning from the battle, his companions were turned into birds for grumbling about their conditions. The species name *exulans* means "homeless" or "exile" and was chosen because this bird wanders so far from shore.[45]

Soaring on air currents high above the waves, the albatross was regarded by early mariners as the bringer of winds. Stories from sailors filtered back to England, where this bird was given spiritual associations. Because of their habit of following ships as well as their lonesome cries, albatrosses were believed to be the restless souls of drowned sailors.

44. John A. Burton, *Birds of the Tropics* (London: Orbis Publishing, 1973), 111.
45. Terence Lindsey, *Albatrosses* (Collingwood, Australia: CSIRO Publishing, 2008), 6.

English poet Samuel Taylor Coleridge's famous work "The Rime of the Ancient Mariner" linked the albatross with penance and redemption.

In Japan, the albatross was considered auspicious and was regarded as a servant to the sea gods. For the Maori people of New Zealand, the albatross is a common motif for ship prows and a talisman for smooth sailing.

Magical Workings

This amazing oceanic wanderer can show us the ethereal realms beyond our world and within our hearts. With a wingspan greater than other seabirds, albatross can shepherd our journey and steer us in the direction we are meant to travel. Albatross can help fine-tune intuition, receive messages, and interpret omens. In addition, it can be instrumental for weather divination.

The freedom this bird symbolizes requires adaptability, patience, and creativity, which are important capabilities for meeting challenges and dealing with problems. Call on the power of albatross for support and guidance in journeying on the astral plane and for spiritual quests. Use a picture of albatross as a talisman for protection during physical travel.

Known for strength and endurance, the energy of this bird can be instrumental when seeking transformation. In ritual, call on albatross to bring spiritual purification through the elements of air and water.

Make Connection

Windy days are good opportunities to connect with the energy of albatross. Go to a place where you will not be disturbed. Take along a picture of an albatross, a crystal, or anything to serve as a talisman. Face into the wind and close your eyes. Stretch out your arms and imagine that you are gliding across the ocean. The water passes smoothly under you as you soar effortlessly. You are a mighty albatross: bird of legend, strength, and spirit. Draw this power into you so you can remember how it feels deep within your body, and then release it into the crystal or other object you hold. When you return home, place the crystal or picture on your altar and use it whenever you want to connect with albatross.

Associations

Zodiac: Aquarius

Element(s): Air, water

Bird Identification

BLACK-FOOTED ALBATROSS (*PHOEBASTRIA NIGRIPES*)

Size: 25 to 30 inches

Wingspan: 76 to 85 inches

Comparative size: Goose—large for a seabird but small for an albatross

Description: Mostly brown with white at the base of the bill and under the eyes; black tail; long, narrow wings; grayish-black bill

Range: West Coast of North America and the northern Pacific Ocean

Habitat: Open ocean, but also seen just off the coast

Eggs: White with brown speckling

SNOWY ALBATROSS (*DIOMEDEA EXULANS*)

Also known as: Wandering albatross, white-winged albatross

Size: 42 to 53 inches

Wingspan: 8 to 11 feet

Comparative size: Goose to very large—largest wingspan in the world

Description: White body with black and white wings; pinkish bill and feet

Male: Wings more white than female's wings; tips and edges black

Range: Circumpolar in the southern oceans

Habitat: Open ocean and coastal areas

Eggs: White with a few spots

Collective noun(s): A flight, a rookery, or a weight of albatross

Blackbird:
Brewer's Blackbird, Rusty Blackbird, Red-Winged Blackbird

Red-Winged Blackbird (Agelaius phoeniceus)

The legendary "four-and-twenty blackbirds baked in a pie" were European members of the Thrush family, not the blackbirds that we are familiar with in North America. Even though the genus name *Euphagus* of the American birds means "good to eat," New World blackbirds were not menu items as they had been in parts of Europe.[46]

In addition to naming birds according to the familiar ones in Europe, immigrants to North America attached their folklore to these birds, too. As in Italy, the last two days of January and the first of February were known as the blackbird days. According to Italian folklore, the blackbird was originally white, but after taking shelter in a chimney during a very cold winter it turned black.

Other lore that became associated with the North American blackbird came from Celtic legends where blackbirds served as gatekeepers to the otherworld and the fairy realm. If a blackbird sang before Christmas (prior to its normal time in mid-February), the month of February would start with a cold spell.

---

46. Diana Wells, *100 Birds and How They Got Their Names* (Chapel Hill, NC: Algonquin Books of Chapel Hill, 2002), 12.

Magical Workings

Black creatures blend into the night and convey a sense of mystery. Blackbird can be called upon to draw on the energy of the Goddess in new moon rituals. This bird reminds us to embrace the dark, to go deep, and to incubate ideas or explore mysteries. Blackbird's energy stokes creativity and heightens awareness for psychic work. It is also instrumental for defense.

Blackbird provides support and guidance for shamanic work, retrieving ancient wisdom, and interpreting omens. Blackbirds themselves are omens, and seeing two means good things are on the horizon. It is particularly helpful at Samhain, bringing access to the otherworld and contact with loved ones who have passed.

Red-winged blackbird has a strong connection with life-giving Goddess energy. It is especially associated with the Fates and other goddesses associated with spinning and weaving.

Make Connection

Connect with blackbird energy by sitting in a dark room or outside at night if weather permits. Reach out into the darkness with all of your senses. Imagine the darkness as a blanket that enfolds you like a cloak of black feathers. You may feel guided to other realms or carried inward to new levels of discovery and wisdom. This is blackbird accepting you and acting as guardian and teacher.

Associations

Zodiac: Cancer

Element(s): Air, water

Time of day: Dusk

Sabbat(s): Samhain

Goddesses: Athena, Bertha, the Fates (red-winged), Freya (red-winged), Frigg, Holda/
   Holle, Isis, Minerva, Neith, the Norns (red-winged), Rhiannon

Bird Identification

BREWER'S BLACKBIRD (*EUPHAGUS CYANOCEPHALUS*)

Size: 8 to 10 inches

Wingspan: 14 to 15 inches

Comparative size: Robin

Description: Slim body; fairly long tail and legs; long beak with thick base

Male: Glossy black with a purplish-blue sheen on the head and greenish iridescence on the body; yellow eyes

Female: Dull brownish-gray with darker wings and tail; dark eyes

Habitat: Damp woods, wooded swamps, marshes, and meadows

Range: From British Columbia to Ontario in Canada, down through the western United States to the Midwest, into the southeastern states and northern Florida, and into Mexico

Eggs: Pale gray to greenish white, spotted with brown, pink, yellow, violet, and gray

Rusty Blackbird (*Euphagus carolinus*)

Size: 8 to 10 inches

Wingspan: 14 to 15 inches

Comparative size: Robin

Description: Medium body; medium-length tail; slightly down-curved bill

Male: Overall mostly rusty color; pale yellow eyes with buff-colored eyebrows; during breeding season, dark with bluish-green iridescence

Female: Gray-brown with rusty feather edges; pale eyes and light eyebrows

Habitat: Wet woodlands, fens, bogs, and swamps

Range: From Alaska across Canada to New England, down through the eastern states, Midwest, and eastern plains states to the Gulf Coast

Eggs: Blue-green to pale gray with brown markings

Red-Winged Blackbird (*Agelaius phoeniceus*)

Size: 7 to 9 inches

Wingspan: 12 to 15 inches

Comparative size: Sparrow to robin

Description: Stocky, broad-shouldered; medium-length tail; slender, conical bill

Male: Glossy black with red and yellow shoulder patches; no yellow on birds in California

Female: Brown upper body; streaked brown underparts; orange and white shoulder patches

Habitat: Fresh and saltwater marshes, meadows, fields, and pastures

Range: From southeastern Alaska across Canada to Newfoundland and south throughout the United States and central Mexico

Eggs: Pale blue-green to gray with black or brown zigzag markings

Collective noun(s): A cloud, a cluster, a flock, or a merl of blackbirds, and a keg of Brewer's Blackbirds

Bluebird:
Eastern Bluebird, Mountain Bluebird

Eastern Bluebird (Sialia sialis)

Impressed with this little bird, American naturalist John Burroughs (1837–1921) wrote that the bluebird "carries the sky on its back and the earth on its breast." [47] With a robin-like song, the mountain bluebird begins its melody at first light and ends just after sunrise. The bluebird's genus name, *Sialia,* was derived from the Greek *sialis,* meaning a "kind of bird." [48]

The bluebird's cheery song and bright colors made it the symbol of happiness in France. Long romanticized and considered magical in Europe, the bluebird held a special place in the hearts of English settlers in North America. This bird was reminiscent of the robin redbreast back home and they called the American bird blue redbreast. The colonists were also fond of bluebirds because of their willingness to nest in human-made boxes as well as feed in open areas where they could be seen and enjoyed.

According to folklore, if the first bird you see in the spring is a bluebird, you will have good luck. However, if you eat a bluebird's eggs, you will be restless for as long as

---

47. Budd Titlow, *Bird Brains: Inside the Strange Minds of Our Fine Feathered Friends* (Guilford, CT: Lyons Press, 2013), 141.

48. James Sandrock and Jean C. Prior, *The Scientific Nomenclature of Birds in the Upper Midwest* (Iowa City, Iowa: University of Iowa Press, 2014), 132.

you live. Weather lore notes that when a bluebird is seen, it is an indication that the following day will be fair. Although this bird was long associated with happiness, Belgian playwright Maurice Maeterlinck's (1862–1949) fairy tale entitled *The Blue Bird* coined the phrase "the bluebird of happiness." Also, in current sales jargon a bluebird refers to an opportunity that lands in your lap from out of the blue.

Since early times, blue has been considered a spiritual color as well as the color of heaven. Known as the mother of gods, Phoenician goddess Tanit had a bird as her emblem and was depicted in a blue gown wrapped in such a way that its folds suggested wings. In the Minoan temple of Knossos on Crete, the bluebird fresco wall painting represented spring and renewal.

Magical Workings

The bluebird heralds change and foretells good things to come. This unassuming little bird can help us find confidence and motivation to accomplish our goals. Call on bluebird to provide a gentle boost to love spells.

Place a piece of blue lace agate, larimar, celestine, or lapis lazuli on your altar to work with this bird's energy for aid in spiritual growth or transformation. Bluebird can hold us in a time that is outside of time to connect with spirit. Call on bluebird to activate creative forces for artistic expression as well as for fertility. Use a bluebird figurine as a talisman to invite happiness into your life. As the wheel of the year turns, bluebird brings renewal as well as continuity to hearth and home.

Make Connection

With "the sky on its back and earth on its breast," bluebird is symbolic of above and below. Although it is the color of the sky, blue is also symbolic of rain, snow, and ice and connects us with the heavenly waters. Take a walk in the rain or snow to feel the sacredness of this water that comes from above to below. Bluebird instills a flowing yet grounded feeling, as though you can touch the sky while keeping your feet on the earth. When you feel this as you walk in the rain or snow, bluebird is with you.

Associations

Element(s): Air, earth, water

Goddesses: Aphrodite, Tanit

Trees: Elder, hackberry, holly, oak, pine

Bird Identification

EASTERN BLUEBIRD (*SIALIA SIALIS*)

Size: 6 to 8 inches

Wingspan: 9 to 12 inches

Comparative size: Sparrow to robin

Description: Large, rounded head; plump body; tail and legs fairly short; short, straight
   bill

Male: Vivid blue upper body; rusty reddish throat and breast

Female: Grayish upper body; bluish tinge on wings and tail; orange-brown breast

Range: East of the Rocky Mountains across southern Canada and down to the Gulf
   of Mexico

Habitat: Rural gardens, orchards, and suburbs near farmland

Eggs: Pale blue

MOUNTAIN BLUEBIRD (*SIALIA CURRUCOIDES*)

Size: 6 to 8 inches

Wingspan: 11 to 12 inches

Comparative size: Sparrow to robin

Description: Large, rounded head; chunky body; long wings; medium-length tail

Male: Sky-blue to turquoise colored head, upper body, wings, and tail; paler blue
   underparts; white belly; dull brownish blue in winter

Female: Head and back bluish-gray; pale sky-blue rump, wings, and tail; white eye rings

Range: From central Alaska through western Canada and throughout the mountains
   and western prairies and parts of California to Arizona, New Mexico, and western
   Texas into Mexico

Habitat: High mountain meadows, ranch land, fields, and prairie or forest edges

Eggs: Pale blue; sometimes white

Canary

Canary (Serinus canaria domestica)

Native to the Canary Islands, located in the Atlantic off the coast of northern Africa, this unassuming little bird has a long history of fascinating people. The ancient Greek writer Homer identified the Canary Islands as the fabled Elysium, an enchanted otherworld and isle of the blessed. "Poised at the edge of the world, whose inhabitants knew no sorrow," these little yellow birds symbolized cheerfulness.[49] Although the islands eventually became known as the Fortunate Islands, finding them overrun by wild dogs, the Romans dubbed them *Insula Canaria*, "Island of Dogs."[50] The Latin *canaria* is also the root for the English word "canine."

Centuries later, the Canary Islands were rediscovered by the Spanish, who named the yellow birds for the islands. Captivated by the canary's singing, the Spanish imported them to the Continent, where they became popular as pets throughout Europe. Four hundred years of selective breeding has resulted in over two hundred species of these charming domesticated songsters. At this point, not all breeds have the quintessential yellow color.

---

49. Robert G. Pasieczny, *DK Eyewitness Travel Guide: Canary Islands* (New York: Dorling Kindersley, 2013), 29.

50. Bill Sherk, *500 Years of New Words* (Tonawanda, NY: Dundurn Press, 2004), 57.

Folklore has portrayed this bird with double meanings. On the one hand, it was considered good luck to own a canary; however, if it sang after dark the owner would not have a long life. Also, if another person's escaped canary entered your house and fluttered in front of a mirror, you could expect a death in the family. According to other legends, it was good luck for a bride to wear a canary feather, and if she owned one that had just laid eggs she could expect to have as many children as eggs in the bird's nest. However, if she or her groom owned a canary and it died on their wedding day, it was advisable to postpone the event.

In North America, goldfinches and escaped domestic canaries are often mistakenly identified as the Atlantic canary (*Serinus canaria*), which can be found in the wild in parts of Europe. As pets, canaries are one of the most popular birds in the United States. My grandfather was a devoted canary owner. He kept its cage in the dining room and had an after-dinner custom of whistling a duet with it.

Magical Workings

Just as caged canaries were taken into coal mines to warn of dangerous gases, this bird may bring warnings to us and aid in developing intuition. Famous for singing, canary can help us find and activate our inner voices as well as other talents.

Originating on the fabled Fortunate Islands, this bird is instrumental in finding your soul path and exploring spirituality on a deeply meaningful level. Canary's association with Elysium can also help us weave together connections with past lives, which can bring healing, harmony, and well-being. Let this bird guide you when you want to consecrate sacred space through singing and chanting.

Carve this bird's name on a yellow candle and place it on your altar to invite happiness and beauty into your life. Symbolic of sensitivity, canary can guide you in matters of companionship as well as creativity. Call on canary's help by using a pinch of saffron in spells for love and luck.

Make Connection

Connect with canary energy by burning dragon's blood incense. The dragon's blood tree (*Dracaena draco*) is also a native of the Canary Islands. Place a yellow candle with the word *canary* carved into it on your altar and light it along with the incense. Close your eyes for a few moments and bring the image of a canary into your mind. When the image is clear, open your eyes and sit in silence as you observe the smoke of the incense. As it rises, visualize it forming a connection between you and canary. If the color of the smoke seems to change to somewhat yellowish, canary is making contact with you.

Associations
Solar system: Sun

Bird Identification
Canary (*Serinus canaria domestica*)

Size: 4 to 8 inches

Wingspan: 9 to 11 inches

Comparative size: Sparrow to robin

Description: While the quintessential canary is solid yellow or white, their colors include blue, green, and cinnamon as well as a mix of variegated shades

Range: Households worldwide

Habitat: A clean cage with enough space to flit around

Eggs: Almost white, to blue, to greenish-blue; may have light reddish-brown or dark brown speckles

Collective noun(s): An aria or an opera of canaries

Cardinal:
Northern Cardinal

Northern Cardinal (Cardinalis cardinalis)

At one time, the cardinal was thought to be a cousin of the red crossbill (*Loxia curvirostra*) because of the shape of its beak. Later, when it was determined that the two species were not closely related, the scientific name was changed to *Cardinalis virginianus* with the common name Virginia cardinal. After several other changes, it was finally named *Cardinalis cardinalis* with the common name northern cardinal because it is the only cardinal in the Northern Hemisphere. The species name *Cardinalis* was chosen because its plumage was reminiscent of the bright red color of Catholic cardinal robes. Considered precious because the dye was very expensive, red was a color of power and affluence.

Unique to North America, the cardinal was unfamiliar to early European settlers who simply called it the red bird. Also fascinated with their songs, people often caught them to keep as pets. In folklore, a cardinal seen flying upward meant good luck, while a downward-flying one meant the opposite.

The cardinal is one of only a few North American songbirds where the female also sings. While mated pairs usually share song phrases, the female tends to have a slightly more complex melody. Male cardinals often defend their territories through the use of song. Like many birds, the cardinal's singing ends at the conclusion of the breeding season, but in late December, this brilliant bird resumes its song. In addition to their melodies, cardinals have an unmistakable metallic "chip" note.

With its bright plumage, this bird stands out against the mostly dull winter landscape. It is no wonder that the cardinal is a popular symbol of winter and the Yuletide season. In addition, the color red associates it with holly berries and the Goddess's life-giving blood.

Magical Workings

Like red ochre, a cardinal's color associates it with the energy of renewal and regeneration. Symbolizing the blood of the Mother Goddess, this bird brings the promise of fertility and the continuance of life. Use a picture or a figurine of cardinal on your Yule altar to draw the energy of the Goddess into your ritual. This bird symbolizes the vitality of life and the importance of nurturing family and friends. Include cardinal in magic work relating to family and pregnancy.

Although its color seems a stark contrast to winter, cardinal aids us in finding balance and well-being during a time of year that is filled with joy, yet sometimes fraught with emotional challenges. Long nights and cold weather are conducive to turning inward and cardinal can aid us in seeking knowledge and clarity by listening for that inner voice. With this bird's aid we can fine-tune intuition and stoke creative juices while building confidence and self-worth.

Of course, we can't ignore the fact that cardinal's red plumage is associated with love and passion. Include an image of this bird when working spells of romance.

Make Connection

To connect with cardinal's energy, clear everything from your altar except one red candle. If you have a picture or a figurine of a cardinal, place it on your altar, too. Sit in a darkened room with only the candle lit. Gaze at the color and then imagine that you are red like the bird. Amidst the darkness, visualize yourself becoming a glowing red beacon. When you open your eyes, don't be surprised if the whole room seems to have a reddish glow. This is a sign that cardinal is present. Listen for a soft "chip" note to confirm this.

Associations

Element(s): Air, fire

Sabbat(s): Yule

Trees: Dogwood, hawthorn, maple, pine

Shrubs: Blackberry, rose

Bird Identification

NORTHERN CARDINAL (*CARDINALIS CARDINALIS*)

Also known as: Virginia cardinal, Virginia nightingale, cardinal grosbeak

Size: 8 to 9 inches

Wingspan: 9 to 12 inches

Comparative size: Robin

Description: Short, thick bill; long tail; prominent crest; black face around bill

Male: Brilliant red all over; reddish bill

Female: Pale brown; reddish tinge on wings, tail, and crest; red-orange bill

Range: From southern Canada and New England across the eastern United States to the Gulf Coast, through the plains states to Arizona and into Mexico

Habitat: Brushy areas, backyards, parks, woodlots, and shrubby forest edges

Eggs: Grayish white, buff white, or greenish white with pale gray to brown speckles

Collective noun(s): A college, a conclave, a deck, or a radiance of cardinals

Chickadee:
Black-Capped Chickadee, Carolina Chickadee, Mountain Chickadee

Black-Capped Chickadee (**Poecile atricapillus**)

Constantly active, chickadees are good birds to have around a garden because they like to feed on pests, including caterpillars and budworms. Sometimes chickadees flock with downy woodpeckers, titmice, and nuthatches. On very cold winter nights, these birds go into torpor with depressed body functions, which helps them survive in low temperatures. Black-capped and Carolina chickadees hybridize in areas where their ranges overlap. As a result, their offspring can sing the songs of both species.

This bird's common name comes from its song, which sounds like "chick-a-dee-dee-dee." In their complex communication, the more "dees" that are sung indicate a heightened level of threat. They also use a song similar to the eastern phoebe's (*Sayornis phoebe*), which is a drawn out "fee-bee" with a drop in pitch at the end. Two or more counter-singing together can sound like a game of Marco Polo.

In a star legend of the northeastern Micmac tribe, the chickadee is one of three birds (along with robin and moosebird) that hunt a big bear represented by the constellation Ursa Major. Of the seven stars in the Big Dipper, chickadee is represented by the middle star in the handle. Author and shamanic practitioner Ted Andrews associated this bird with the number seven because there are seven species of chickadees.

Magical Workings

Although usually associated with spring, the chickadee is a tough little character that can handle fierce winter weather. Perhaps it's an attitude of cheerfulness that keeps it in balance: something we can call on when we need a lift. Also, chickadee understands moods and can be called upon for help in dealing with attitudes, as it knows how to use them. It is also an asset in overcoming fear.

Whether we are learning a divination or psychic skill or determining our chosen paths, chickadee is a bird of the mind and can aid us when seeking knowledge. Because of torpor, it is familiar with altered states and supports practices such as shamanic journeying and astral travel. Chickadee is instrumental in awakening inner wisdom especially when we need to get to the core truth in a situation or with ourselves. This bird reminds us to speak the truth.

When you need to take action, count on chickadee to energize the situation and back you up. Because chickadee is a good communicator and able to speak the language of other birds, call on it when compassion, diplomacy, or eloquence are needed. Because of this, chickadee is also helpful when creating rituals.

Make Connection

Because chickadee is associated with the number seven and fairies, draw the seven-pointed fairy star (also called the witches' star) on a picture of the bird. Alternatively, carve the star into a candle along with the name *chickadee*. As you light the candle, say three times: *"Tiny bird, Chickadee; I call on you to befriend me."* When it is ready to contact you, you may hear a slight rustle of wings or a faint "chicka-dee-dee-dee."

In the Northern Hemisphere, the Ursa Major constellation is visible year round. Go outside on a starry night and locate the Big Dipper. Look for the middle star at the bend in the handle and visualize it as a little chickadee and ask for its blessing.

Figure 2.1: The seven-pointed fairy star can be used to represent chickadee.

Associations

Element(s): Air, earth

Magical beings: Fairies

Trees: Alder, birch, pine

Shrubs: Bayberry, winterberry

Bird Identification

Black-Capped Chickadee (*Poecile atricapillus*)

Size: 4½ to 6 inches

Wingspan: 6 to 8 inches

Comparative size: Sparrow

Description: Round body; short bill; long, narrow tail; black cap and bib; cap extends below the eyes; white cheeks; gray back; buff flanks and white underparts; gray wings edged with white

Range: From Alaska across Canada to Newfoundland; south through the Mid-Atlantic states, the Appalachians, and Smoky Mountains; across the plains states and up to Oregon and Washington

Habitat: Forests, thickets, swampy areas, wooded areas in cities, and backyards

Eggs: White with tiny reddish-brown speckles

Carolina Chickadee (*Poecile carolinensis*)

Size: 4 to 5 inches

Wingspan: 6 to 8 inches

Comparative size: Sparrow

Description: Resembles the black-capped chickadee; black cap and bib; gray wings and back; whitish underparts; short neck; large head

Range: Southeastern Kansas to New Jersey, south to central Florida, the Gulf Coast, and Texas

Habitat: Deciduous woodlands, riparian areas, suburban and urban areas

Eggs: White with light brown speckling

MOUNTAIN CHICKADEE (*POECILE GAMBELI*)

Size: 4 to 5½ inches

Wingspan: 6 to 8 inches

Comparative size: Sparrow

Description: Large head; small bill; long, narrow tail; rounded wings; black and white coloring on head; gray elsewhere; pale underparts; white stripe over eyes

Range: British Columbia and south through the Rocky and Cascade-Sierra Mountains to Arizona and New Mexico, and parts of California

Habitat: Evergreen, mountainous forests

Eggs: White, sometimes with reddish speckling

Collective noun(s): A banditry or a dissimulation of chickadees

Chicken:
Domestic Chicken

Domestic Chicken (Gallus gallus domesticus)

The red junglefowl (*Gallus gallus*) of southeast Asia is believed to be one of several ancestral sources for today's chickens. This bird is estimated to have been domesticated around 6000 BCE in China and the Indus Valley region of Pakistan. Chickens were depicted in Egyptian hieroglyphs dating to 1500 BCE.[51] By the fourth century BCE, raising chickens for eggs and meat, and the sport of cockfighting, had spread to Greece and then Rome. The Romans took chickens with them into northern Europe and Britain.

The domestication of chickens also spread east from Asia, and European explorers found them throughout the Pacific Islands. On Easter Island, chickens were used in magic and religious rituals, and their feathers were incorporated into headdresses. On Hawaii and a world away in Europe, white chickens were thought to possess magical properties and were used for divination. In Greece, chickens were associated with healing and were sacrificed to Asclepius. These birds also had the role of guiding souls to the otherworld and initiating rebirth. According to English folklore, a crowing hen could bring the devil from his den.

Carrying a sun emblem on its head, the cock was a universal solar symbol and believed to have the ability to manifest light. It was associated with sun and war gods in

---

51. Annie Potts, *Chicken* (London, England: Reaktion Books, 2012), 12–13.

Greece and Rome. In Norse myth, a cockerel sat atop Yggdrasil, the world tree, to warn the gods of approaching enemies. Centuries later, a cock on a weathervane represented a guardian and protector. Associated with fertility, the cockerel was used in rituals when crops were sown and harvested in Britain.

As the world's most common bird, it is not surprising that the chicken has various and specific names. A chick is a baby of either sex, a pullet is a young female, a hen is a female old enough to lay eggs, and a biddy is an older hen that no longer lays. A cockerel refers to a young male, and a cock is a mature male. Associated with sexual prowess, it is no surprise that in many cultures the name for the male chicken is usually the same as the penis. Modesty in the Victorian era ushered in a change with the name *rooster*.

While it is known that birds evolved from the dinosaurs, the humble chicken may be the living genetic descendant of *Tyrannosaurus Rex*.[52]

Magical Workings

The chicken is a bird of abundance, fertility, and healing. Call on this bird to aid in spells of prosperity and fertility. Place an image or figurine of a chicken on the altar of a healing circle. Call on the hen or cock at Samhain to help you connect with the spirits of those who have died, or ask this bird to guide a loved one at their passing.

For support, incorporate a chicken feather or a picture into your divination practices. Use an image or a figurine of a cockerel to boost sex magic and protection spells, especially for psychic protection.

Make Connection

To connect with chicken energy, get up before dawn and observe the sky as it gradually fades from black into soft blue. When the first rays of the sun can be seen, stand up and softly crow as you visualize your ability to manifest the light. As the sunlight grows stronger, see yourself as a rooster or a hen standing proudly as you welcome a new day. No matter where you live, listen for the sound of a cock crowing for a sign of contact.

Associations
COCK
Zodiac: Gemini
Element(s): Earth, fire

---

52. Jane S. Smith, *In Praise of Chickens: A Compendium of Wisdom Fair and Fowl* (Guilford, CT: Lyons Press, 2012), 3.

Time of day: Dawn

Sabbat(s): Lughnasadh, Samhain

Goddesses: Amaterasu, Artemis, Brigid

Gods: Apollo, Ares, Asclepius, Attis, Helios, Hermes, Jove, Lugh, Mars, Mercury, Mithras, Osiris, Skanda, Zeus

Tree: Ash

Solar system: Sun

Hen

Element(s): Earth

Sabbat(s): Samhain

Goddess: Cerridwen

Ogham: Quert

Bird Identification

Domestic Chicken (*Gallus gallus domesticus*)

Size: Varies widely according to breed; size of an average breed, the Rhode Island Red: 11 to 17 inches

Wingspan: 24 to 36 inches

Description: Small head; large body; bare, scaled legs; pointed beak; wide variety of colors and patterns; each breed has special types of feathers

Distinctive features: Comb and two wattles—the comb is a red appendage on the top of the head; wattles are two appendages under the chin

Male: More prominent comb and wattles; typically brighter, bolder plumage; large swooping tail; pointed feathers on the neck called hackles; may have spurs on legs

Female: Less colorful than the male

Range: Chickens are domesticated around the world

Habitat: From backyards and small organic farms to massive poultry-production facilities

Eggs: Depends on breed; white, brown, green, pink, or blue

Collective noun(s): A brood, a flock, or a peep of chickens and a chattering or a clutch of chicks

Cormorant:
Double-Crested Cormorant, Great Cormorant

Great Cormorant (**Phalacrocorax carbo**)

Unusual as it may seem for a seabird, the cormorant's feathers are not waterproof, which is why they are frequently seen sitting on rocks with their wings outstretched to dry. This practice gives them an eerie appearance and perhaps gave rise to their being regarded as the spirits of those who had perished at sea. While the lack of oil in their feathers may seem like a drawback for a bird that spends so much time in the water, cormorants actually use this to their advantage. They give their feathers a good soaking while hunting for fish, which helps them sink faster when diving after them.

From approximately 1600 to 770 BCE in China, jade carvings of cormorants holding fish were placed in graves, which is believed to have carried the intention of providing food for the deceased.[53] Both the Chinese and Japanese trained these birds to catch fish, and images of cormorants were used as talismans by fishermen. Native people of Kodiak Island, Alaska, also used an image of a cormorant for luck in hunting and fishing. Training cormorants for fishing became fashionable in England when King James I (1566–1625) kept a flock on the Thames River alongside Westminster. Later in the seventeenth

---

53. Hope B. Werness, *The Continuum Encyclopedia of Animal Symbolism in Art* (New York: Continuum International, 2006), 105.

century, this bird acquired a negative connotation when John Milton portrayed the devil as a cormorant in his epic poem *Paradise Lost*.

Two eighteen-foot copper cormorants grace the top of the Liver (rhymes with *diver*) building and serve as the symbol of the city of Liverpool, England. In South America, cormorants were frequently depicted on Mayan pottery, and they may be one of the morphing creatures portrayed in the ancient Nazca lines of Peru.

The common name *cormorant* comes from the Latin *corvus marinus*, which means "raven of the sea."[54] In Ireland and Wales, this bird was regarded as a magical sea raven that wove together the forces of air and water. I can understand this connotation when I kayak in the Gulf of Maine and see cormorants on rocky outcrops. Standing in groups with their wings outstretched as though in the epiphany gesture, they look like they are engaging in some kind of mystical ritual.

Magical Workings

At Samhain or anytime someone you love passes to the other side, place an image of cormorant on your altar. This will symbolize your wish that they find nourishment and plenty in their new state of being.

Cormorant can help us find where we belong in our communities, as well as bolster our courage for independence. As an expert diver, cormorant teaches us to go deep within ourselves for a profound sense of who we are, especially if we seek spiritual transformation.

Call on this bird for guidance in finding and developing your skills, especially those related to prophecy and divination. For ritual and magic, cormorant can aid in drawing on the forces of nature, particularly the elements of air and water.

Make Connection

To connect with cormorant energy, pour water into a bowl on your altar. Raise your hands in the epiphany gesture with arms out to the sides, elbows bent, and hands raised with palms facing forward as you say: *"Corvus marinus, raven of the sea; I call on you to visit me."* Visualize that you are standing on a rocky outcrop surrounded by water. Reach out with your energy and in your mind's eye watch for a cormorant to approach. If one joins you, sit down beside it and allow events to unfold.

---

54. Wells, *100 Birds and How They Got Their Names*, 34.

Associations

Element(s): Air, water

Sabbat(s): Ostara, Samhain

Ogham: Onn

Bird Identification

Double-Crested Cormorant (*Phalacrocorax auritus*)

Size: 27 to 35 inches

Wingspan: 45 to 48 inches

Comparative size: Goose

Description: Small head; long, hooked bill; long, kinked neck with orange throat pouch; black all over; short tuft of white feathers over the eyes during breeding season

Range: From the Alaskan coast, across southern Canada to Newfoundland, and throughout the United States

Habitat: Lakes, rivers, swamps, and coastal areas

Eggs: Pale blue-green

Great Cormorant (*Phalacrocorax carbo*)

Size: 33 to 36 inches

Wingspan: 51 to 63 inches

Comparative size: Goose

Description: Long, glossy black body; thick neck with yellow throat pouch; blunt, hooked bill; white patch at base of bill; shaggy head plume

Range: Along the Atlantic coast from Georgia to the Canadian Maritime Provinces

Habitat: Rocky coasts, sea cliffs, and inland waters

Eggs: Pale bluish-green with white, chalky covering

Collective noun(s): A flight, a gulp, a paddling, or a swim of cormorants

Crane:
Sandhill Crane, Whooping Crane

Whooping Crane (Grus americana)

The genus name *Grus* is actually the Latin name for this bird, and the common name *crane* is said to have been derived from their haunting calls.[55] The whooping crane is the tallest bird in North America and its trumpet-like call can be heard for several miles. Cranes are known for their flamboyant courtship dances that include wing flapping, head tossing, and dramatic leaps into the air. This elaborate performance is sometimes used to daze predators, but it also seems to take place for no apparent reason.

According to Greek and Roman mythology, flying groups of cranes inspired some of the letter shapes in their alphabets. In Egypt, the sun bird deity Benu was depicted as a crane, and images of cranes have been found in ancient temples and tombs. Folklore throughout the Mediterranean region mentions cranes ferrying smaller birds on their backs to cross wide expanses of water. Native Americans in Montana have similar stories.

In Japan, cranes were referred to as marsh gods and have been considered auspicious creatures. Wishing someone "one thousand cranes" means to wish them good luck, happiness, and longevity times one thousand.[56] Throughout Asia an origami crane symbolizes good fortune, and chains of paper cranes are hung in temples as offerings. According to Vietnamese legend, cranes lift the souls of the dead to heaven.

---

55. William Young, *The Fascination of Birds: From the Albatross to the Yellowthroat* (Mineola, NY: Dover Publications, 2014), 63.

56. Ibid., 42.

Celtic myth abounds with stories and references to cranes. Many legends tell of women shape-shifting into cranes. The famous crane bag of Manannan mac Lir was made from such a bird when the woman died. The bag was said to hold magical objects and things of power. According to legend, Manannan added the fifth group of characters, called the *forfeda*, to the ogham. The *forfeda* is sometimes referred to as the crane bag.

Magical Workings

Found throughout Celtic myth, the crane is associated with death, rebirth, understanding deep mysteries, and truth. Through Manannan's crane bag, this bird is associated with the ogham and divination in general. Buy or make a drawstring bag for your divination tools and decorate it with the *forfeda* characters and the name *Grus*. Refer to table 1.1 in chapter 9 for the bird ogham.

Crane provides support for astral travel and shamanic work and becomes a guardian when connecting with the otherworld. Call on this bird for magic involving justice, honor, and the protection of children. As a symbol of grace and endurance, crane can help us find peace and patience.

When seeking self-knowledge or wisdom of the ancients, crane brings focus for introspection. It teaches us how to be independent and to keep secrets. Call on crane for spells of abundance or reversal and to stoke creativity. This bird also brings healing, longevity, and well-being. Cranes are beautiful symbols of balance that go well on an Ostara or Mabon altar.

Make Connection

In Celtic myth, a ritual crane posture of standing on one leg with one eye closed was said to have been employed by Lugh and the Dagda. While this was used for general spellwork, it was also instrumental in performing a form of magic known as *corrguinecht*, "crane-wounding."[57] I mention this not to advocate the use of retributive magic but to illustrate the power associated with this bird. Use this posture as you visualize yourself being graced with the stately presence of a crane. You will know it is with you when you feel firmly grounded yet lifted by an energy from outside of you.

Associations

Element(s): Air, earth, fire, water

Sabbat(s): Ostara, Mabon

---

57. Sharon Paice MacLeod, *Celtic Myth and Religion: A Study of Traditional Belief, with Newly Translated Prayers, Poems, and Songs* (Jefferson, NC: McFarland & Company, 2012), 120.

Goddesses: Artemis, Athena, Badb, Cailleach, Hera, the Morrigan

Gods: Apollo, Benu, the Dagda, Hephaestus, Hermes, Lugh, Manannan, Midir

Solar system: Moon, Sun

Tree: Willow

Magical beings: Fairies

Ogham: *Forfeda*

Bird Identification

SANDHILL CRANE (*GRUS CANADENSIS*)

Size: 34 to 48 inches

Wingspan: 72 to 78 inches

Comparative size: Goose to very large

Description: Long neck and legs; gray or somewhat reddish body; red forehead; white cheeks; tufted rump feathers

Range: From Alaska east through most of Canada to Quebec, south through the plains states into Texas and Mexico, and west to the coast; also parts of the Midwest to Florida

Habitat: Open grasslands, meadows, and freshwater marshes

Eggs: Pale brownish, irregularly marked with darker brown

WHOOPING CRANE (*GRUS AMERICANA*)

Size: 45 to 50 inches

Wingspan: 84 to 90 inches

Comparative size: Very large

Description: Long neck and legs; white all over with black wingtips; tufted rump feathers; red forehead and cheeks

Range: A narrow band from Alberta, Canada, through the Dakotas to the Texas Gulf Coast

Habitat: Freshwater bogs and coastal areas

Eggs: Light brown with variable brown blotches

Collective noun(s): A dance, a family, a flock, a herd, a sedge, or a siege of cranes, and a kettle of Sandhill Cranes

Crow:
American Crow

American Crow (Corvus brachyrhynchos)

Crows are mentioned in the mythology of many cultures throughout the world and are often portrayed as guides for traveling between the worlds. In European folklore, crows were believed to convene courts, pass judgments, and execute guilty members. Associated with the Goddess's death aspect, crows came to be regarded as evil or fearsome. In medieval times, finding the foot of a crow, commonly called a witches' foot, was regarded as a sign of death.

The Greeks regarded crows as messengers of the gods bearing wisdom and secrets. These birds were also prevalent in Roman and Norse mythology. In India, a crow landing on a nearby tree was a sign of good luck. In addition, Hindu legends tell of crows delivering messages and offerings to people's ancestors.

Crows are prominent in Celtic lore and considered to be on the edge between light and dark, life and death. In Ireland, crows and ravens represented the goddess known as the Morrigan in her trinity with Badb and Macha. The name *Badb* means "crow," and this goddess was said to carry souls to the otherworld after battle.[58] According to legend, Macha flew over battlefields in crow form to warn of approaching enemies. In Gaul, the goddess Nantosuelta was depicted with a crow or raven and a dovecote. The dove

---

58. Eason, *Fabulous Creatures, Mythical Monsters and Animal Power Symbols*, 54.

and crow (or raven) together represented the intertwined life/death aspects of the Great Goddess.

Considered among the most intelligent of creatures, crows learn quickly, solve problems (often in cooperation with each other), use tools, and even play. In addition, they are extremely inquisitive. I'm not sure what my neighborhood crows are up to, but they seem to enjoy messing with the seashells and other small things I place on my outdoor altar. Sometimes they knock these items to the ground, and other times they pick them up and place them in the birdbath or even fly off with them.

The common name *crow* comes from the Anglo-Saxon *crawe*, which describes the classic sound they make.[59] These birds actually have a wide range of vocalizations, which includes imitating human speech. Crows can be extremely aggressive, especially when mobbing a predator, such as an owl or hawk, for defense.

Magical Workings

Crow is a harbinger of change, bringing messages from other realms and at times warning of danger. Associated with war and death, it leads the way into the afterlife. While the destructiveness it seems to bring may cause fear, crow provides wisdom to see beyond into the fertile womb of darkness where rebirth and manifestation begin.

Fostering growth, crow's darkness is a cradle for creativity and intuition where it can help incubate talents. Crow is also instrumental in opening awareness for divination and all forms of communication. Whenever you find yourself at a crossroads, crow can reveal which direction offers the best opportunity. In addition, call on crow for support in past-life exploration and shamanic work.

This bird holds a great deal of power that can be called upon to boost spells, especially spells for defense and protection, and even love. Crow shows us that adaptability and honor are essential when working within one's community. It also tells us that intelligence and spirituality are keys to longevity.

Make Connection

Connect with crow energy by visualizing that you are completely black, even your eyes. At night you are practically invisible and during the day you are but a shadow and can be seen only when you want. Visualize yourself as a crow moving unseen through the world. Feel yourself as the holder of secrets and collector of wisdom as you carry mes-

---

59. Wells, *100 Birds and How They Got Their Names*, 43.

sages from one realm to another. As you do this, be attentive for signs that crow is moving with you.

Associations

Element(s): Air, earth, water

Goddesses: Amaterasu, Athena, Badb, Cailleach, Macha, Maeve, the Morrigan, Rhiannon

Gods: Apollo, Asclepius, Buddha, Loki, Lugh, Mercury, Mithras, Saturn

Solar system: Moon, Saturn, Sun

Trees: Evergreens

Bird Identification

AMERICAN CROW (*CORVUS BRACHYRHYNCHOS*)

Size: 15 to 20 inches

Wingspan: 33 to 39 inches

Description: Thick neck; heavy, straight bill; short and rounded or squared tail; completely black including legs and bill; old feathers appear brownish or scaly during molt

Range: From British Columbia across Canada to Newfoundland and south throughout most of the United States

Habitat: Woodlands, orchards, farmland, suburbs, and cities

Eggs: Dull bluish-green to olive green with brown blotches

Collective noun(s): A caldron, a clan, a company, a mob, a murder, or a rookery of crows

Cuckoo:
Black-Billed Cuckoo, Yellow-Billed Cuckoo

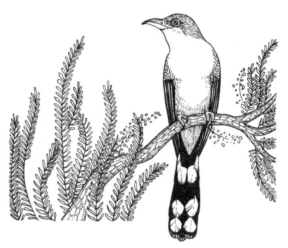

Yellow-Billed Cuckoo (Coccyzus americanus)

American cuckoos occasionally lay eggs in nests of other birds; however, they do this far less than their European cousins. This practice was the basis for the term *cuckold*, meaning "the husband of an unfaithful wife." However, this term originally had a broader meaning of "adulterer" or "deceiver."[60] The Greeks associated the cuckoo and this habit with lust. Gods, especially Zeus, used the guise of this bird for amorous pursuits. The cuckoo was also regarded as a messenger of Thor, and it was believed to become a sparrow hawk during the winter.

A common but shy bird, the cuckoo is heard more often than it is seen. In Europe, this bird has been considered uncanny because it is hard to distinguish from which direction its sound is coming. This gave rise to a wide range of folklore. In addition, if a cuckoo was heard in the wee hours of the morning, the interpretation of its calls depended on the current moon phase.

April was considered the month of the cuckoo, when it returned to many parts of Europe and England. Numerous legends were centered around the first time a cuckoo was heard in the spring. For example, if a person had money in their pocket when this occurred, they would have a prosperous year.

---

60. Peter Tate, *Flights of Fancy: Birds in Myth, Legend, and Superstition* (New York: Bantam Dell, 2007), 29.

Greek writer, farmer, and astronomer Hesiod (c. 700 BCE) considered the cuckoo a weather forecaster. The timing of this bird's arrival in the spring was said to foretell summer weather, which was important for the year's planting and harvesting. In America, the cuckoo's tendency to make more noise as storms approached was the basis for its nickname rain crow.

In Celtic lore, the cuckoo was a bird of the otherworld that could call forth the souls of the dead. It was also a herald for Lugh on the summer solstice.

Magical Workings

As folklore through the ages has pointed out, the cuckoo is a bird of prophecy. Place a picture or figurine of it on your altar or wherever you practice divination. Also, call on cuckoo to aid you in developing and strengthening intuition. This bird's connection with the otherworld makes it an ally for shamanic work as long as your intentions are clear.

As a harbinger of spring and the herald of Lugh, place an image or figurine of cuckoo on your altar for Ostara and Litha, as well as for an April esbat ritual. Invite this bird into your life when entering a new stage, situation, or relationship. It can help you ease through changes, find balance, and foster growth.

Employ cuckoo to boost love spells, especially when marriage is involved or to banish jealousy. Call on it for luck when seeking justice and to eliminate negative energy.

Make Connection

Connect with the energy of cuckoo by sitting quietly in front of your altar. Hold your divination tools or any object that represents prophecy. Very slowly, in a whisper, begin to chant *"coo-koo"* over and over like a mantra until you begin to feel slightly mesmerized. Stop chanting and tune in to the silence for a minute or two with your mind and soul open for messages. You may find this exercise especially useful at the beginning of your divination sessions.

Associations

Zodiac: Aquarius

Element(s): Air, earth, fire

Sabbat(s): Ostara, Litha

Goddesses: Athena, Hera, Juno

Gods: Agni, Lemminkäinen, Lugh, Pan, Thor, Zeus

Trees: Aspen, birch, hawthorn, poplar, willow

Solar system: Moon, Sun

Magical beings: Fairies

Bird Identification

BLACK-BILLED CUCKOO (*COCCYZUS ERYTHROPTHALMUS*)

Size: 11 to 12 inches

Wingspan: 13 to 15 inches

Comparative size: Robin to pigeon

Description: Slender body; long tail; brown and gray back and head; whitish underparts; red eye ring; black bill

Range: Maine to eastern Montana and just north of the Canadian border, and south to eastern Colorado and South Carolina, through the Gulf Coast states into Mexico and Central America

Habitat: Woodlands, thickets, overgrown pastures, and orchards

Eggs: Greenish-blue

YELLOW-BILLED CUCKOO (*COCCYZUS AMERICANUS*)

Size: 10 to 12 inches

Wingspan: 15 to 7 inches

Comparative size: Robin to pigeon

Description: Slender body; long tail; brown upper body and whitish underparts; mostly yellow, down-curved bill; dark mask across face; yellow eye ring

Range: From the East Coast to the Dakotas, south through Texas to Florida; also in Cuba and parts of Mexico

Habitat: Woodlands with dense cover, thickets along streams, old orchards, and scrublands

Eggs: Pale bluish-green that lightens to greenish yellow

Collective noun(s): An asylum, a cooch, or a family of cuckoos

Dove:
Mourning Dove

Mourning Dove (Zenaida macroura)

One of the most widespread and adaptable birds in North America, the mourning dove makes its familiar cooing sounds when nesting and claiming territory. Its common name stems from its drawn-out, lament-like call. Its species name, *macroura*, is Greek and means "long-tailed." [61] When taking flight, their wings make a distinctive whirring sound.

Associated with all three aspects of the Goddess, this bird became the ultimate symbol of peace, spirit, and divinity. Domesticated by the Egyptians around 2600 BCE, these birds are mentioned throughout history and mythology.[62]

Because doves were regarded as suitable sacrificial offerings to deities, many temples throughout the Mediterranean region included onsite dovecotes to furnish a convenient supply. Instead of actual birds, figurines of doves were used as votive offerings in the temples of Hera in Greece. Likewise in France, dove images served as offerings to Sequana, the Gallo-Roman goddess of the River Seine.

---

61. Sharon Sorenson, *Birds in the Yard Month by Month* (Mechanicsburg, PA: Stackpole Books, 2013), 343.

62. Edward A. Armstrong, *The Life and Lore of the Bird: In Nature, Art, Myth and Literature* (New York: Crown Publishers, 1975), 131.

Greek writer Homer noted that doves carried messages for Zeus. However, the oracle speakers at the sacred oak grove in Dodona, Greece, were called *doves* long before the god was associated with the site. While depictions of the Phoenician goddess Atargatis almost always included doves, this bird was also the emblem of Astarte.

Although in earlier times the dove was believed to possess the power of regeneration, as the Goddess's aspects were separated and diminished, so too were this bird's functions. Perhaps because of their courtship displays, doves became associated with love and fertility goddesses. In medieval Europe there were conflicting beliefs about the devil and doves. Some people believed that the devil could take the form of this bird; however, others believed the dove was so pure that the devil could not do so.

While it may seem odd that this present-day symbol of peace was also associated with death, the dove came to symbolize the soul's journey after physical death. This is also true in India, where a dark-colored dove is associated with spirit and death.

Magical Workings

The dove is a bird of duality and balance: life/death and grief/happiness. Call on dove for support when mourning the death of a loved one. Its gentleness is especially helpful for healing at a time when we can feel so terribly fragile. Use a figurine or image of dove on your altar to honor the deceased and help to carry him or her toward rebirth.

Dove represents hope, forgiveness, and compassion. Associated with Aphrodite, Venus, and other goddesses of love, it can be instrumental for magic relating to love and sex. Call on dove to stoke passion and sensuality as well as to restore fidelity and harmony in a relationship. As an ancient symbol of springtime and the future, this bird is an aid for fertility, pregnancy, and childbirth. It can also boost prosperity spells.

Dove's long association with prophecy makes it an ideal talisman to use for receiving messages from other realms as well as general divination practices. More than anything, this bird is a powerful symbol of peace, wisdom, and spirit. In addition, dove can help ground and center energy after ritual and magic work.

Make Connection

To connect with dove energy, spend some quiet time alone. Focus on your breath and wrap your arms around your body as though you are giving yourself a hug. Imagine your arms as great wings enfolding you with the breath of life and spirit. Very quietly, coo like a dove. Know that you are loved and that you can always find healing and harmony in the wings of doves.

Associations

Zodiac: Libra, Taurus

Element(s): Air, earth, water

Times of day: Dawn, dusk

Goddesses: Aphrodite, Astarte, Atargatis/Derceto, Athena, Demeter, Freya, Hera, Holda/Holle, Inanna, Ishtar, Isis, Maia, Nantosuelta, Rhea, Sequana, Venus

Gods: Apollo, Zeus

Solar system: Venus

Trees: Olive, willow

Bird Identification

Mourning Dove (*Zenaida macroura*)

Size: 9 to 13 inches

Wingspan: 16 to 17 inches

Comparative size: Robin to pigeon

Description: Plump body; small head; long, slender, pointed tail; short legs; soft brown to buff-tan all over; black spots on back and wings; white edge on tail feathers

Range: Across southern Canada to New Brunswick and throughout the United States into Mexico and Central America

Habitat: Open fields, parks, and lawns with trees and shrubs

Eggs: White

Collective noun(s): An arc, a cote, a cove, or a flight of doves, as well as a funeral of mourning doves

Duck:
American Pekin Duck, Mallard, Wood Duck

Mallard (Anas platyrhynchos)

With legs set back on their bodies, ducks are ungainly on land but powerful swimmers. They are also strong fliers. The common name *duck* comes from the Anglo-Saxon *duce*, which means "diver."[63] However, not all ducks are divers. The species included here are called dabbling ducks, which means they feed in the water by tipping forward to get at underwater plants rather than diving.

The mallard is the ancestor of nearly all domestic breeds and the most familiar of all ducks. The name comes from Latin *masculus*, which means "male."[64] However, what we consider as the standard duck quack is the sound of the female mallard. Unlike most waterfowl, wood ducks perch and nest in trees and are comfortable flying through woods. Like the cuckoo, they often lay their eggs in other birds' nests.

The Egyptians raised ducks for food and commonly used them for sacrifice. While ducks sometimes represented the evil spirits of the marshes, they also symbolized fertility. The Romans kept ducks and even hatched their eggs in incubators. The goddess Sequana of Gaul was often depicted in a duck-shaped boat. Throughout European folklore, hearing

---

63. Jonathan Alderfer, ed. *National Geographic Complete Birds of North America* (Washington, DC: National Geographic Society, 2006), 147.

64. Ibid., 19.

a duck quack was an omen of prosperity and ducks fluttering their wings was a sign that it would soon rain.

I couldn't resist adding the domestic duck to this book because I had a pet duck when I was a child. The first white Pekin ducks (also called Peking ducks) were imported into North America in 1873.[65] The following year they were bred in New York and were called Long Island ducks.

Magical Workings

Since ancient times, ducks represented abundance and comfort. Use a picture of a duck in spells to draw on this age-old symbolism and to bring prosperity into your life. Being birds of the water, ducks are associated with emotions and can help bring clarity and foster affection. Call on the female duck for nurturing energy and the male for relieving stress.

As a symbol of fertility, the duck engenders fidelity and communication in marriage. Duck is a bird of support, providing protection as well as attracting opportunities. It is also a helper in shamanic work when seeking connection with past lives, guidance, and transformation. Through its familiarity, duck provides comfort and support.

Make Connection

Connect with duck energy by keeping a little rubber ducky in your bathroom. This slightly comical figure will serve as a reminder that while we are all ungainly at times, each of us has particular strengths and special beauty. Hold the duck in the water with you after bathing, close your eyes, and visualize the type of duck that resonates with you. Its power may surprise you.

Associations

Element(s): Air, earth, water

Goddess: Sequana

Ogham: Luis

---

65. Susanna Hoffman and Victoria Wise, *Bold: A Cookbook of Big Flavors* (New York: Workman Publishing, 2013), 174.

Bird Identification

AMERICAN PEKIN DUCK (*ANAS PLATYRHYNCHOS DOMESTICA*)

Size: 25 to 35 inches

Wingspan: 54 to 60 inches

Comparative size: Goose

Description: Broad, round head; broad, orange bill; body elevated in front sloping downward in back; long, thick neck; stout legs; legs and feet yellow/orange; tapered wings; fan-shaped tail; cream or creamy-white color all over

Male: Develops a curled tail feather

Range: Ducks are domesticated around the world

Habitat: From small organic farms to massive poultry-production facilities

Eggs: White

MALLARD (*ANAS PLATYRHYNCHOS*)

Size: 20 to 26 inches

Wingspan: 32 to 37 inches

Comparative size: Red-tailed hawk

Description: Large with hefty bodies; rounded heads; wide, flat bill; white-bordered, blue patch on wing

Male: Dark, iridescent-green head; white neck ring; bright yellow bill; gray body with brown breast and black rear

Female: Mottled brown all over; white tail; orange-brown bill

Range: From Alaska across Canada to Newfoundland and south throughout the United States and Mexico

Habitat: Lakes, ponds, marshes, rivers, and coastal habitats, as well as city and suburban parks and residential backyards

Eggs: Creamy to grayish or greenish buff

WOOD DUCK (*AIX SPONSA*)

Size: 18 to 21 inches

Wingspan: 26 to 28 inches

Comparative size: Crow

Description: Boxy, crested head; thin neck; broad tail; short, broad wings

Male: Glossy green head with crest; white throat, partial neck ring and chin strap; pink
bill; red eyes; chestnut breast; buff-colored sides

Female: Brownish-gray; darker crown; broad white eye ring tapering back to a point;
gray-brown body; white-speckled breast

Range: Throughout the eastern United States to the Great Plains; parts of the Southwest
and Mexico, the northwestern United States and California

Habitat: Wooded swamps, marshes, streams, and ponds

Eggs: Glossy creamy white to tan

Collective noun(s): A brace, a daggle, a flush, a paddling, or a raft of ducks. There is also
a fleet or a sword of mallards and a discomfiture of wood ducks.

Eagle:
Bald Eagle, Golden Eagle

Bald Eagle (Haliaeetus leucocephalus)

Long considered the king of birds, the eagle is a solar symbol that has represented leadership and power throughout the ages. The bald eagle was revered by Native Americans and became the national symbol of the United States. Its scientific name comes from the Greek *halos*, meaning "sea"; *aetos*, meaning "eagle"; and *leucocephalus*, "white-headed." [66]

While these large birds may seem fierce, they have a playful side. Bald eagles have been observed playing an aerial game of catch with sticks, plastic bottles, and other objects. Known for their maneuverability in flight, golden eagles have been clocked in aerial dives at nearly two hundred miles an hour.

The eagle appears frequently in Greek and Roman myth. As symbols of power, eagle emblems were displayed on Roman shields and banners of war. As we have seen, the eagle was a common symbol of sky gods. The fact that they are one of the longest-living birds may have fostered the myth that they were immortal. Coupled with this, the legend that eagles flew into the sun and then plummeted into the ocean and emerged renewed may have given rise to the mythical phoenix.

In Norse myth, the eagle was one of the three birds of Odin; the other two were ravens. Odin could also shape-shift into an eagle. In Celtic lore, the eagle is one of the oldest and

---

66. Wells, *100 Birds and How They Got Their Names*, 59.

wisest creatures, and it is associated with prophecy and power. In the myths of India, an eagle messenger from the god Indra brought *soma*, a ritual drink of deities, to earth for humans. According to a legend of the Chumash people of California, the shadow of an eagle's wings causes the phases of the moon. In addition, the constellation Aquila (Latin for "eagle") has been regarded as an eagle for over four thousand years. Aquila is visible in the Northern and Southern Hemispheres from July to October.

Magical Workings

Above all, when we think of eagles we think of power, strength, courage, and authority; however, these birds offer so much more. We can call on the energy of eagle for these qualities as well as guidance, motivation, and success.

Eagle is instrumental in shamanic work, traveling between the worlds, and receiving visions. It can aid in developing psychic abilities, interpreting messages, and contacting spirits. Employ the power of eagle in purification rituals and for healing. In regards to spirituality, this is a bird of awakening that can bring knowledge and clarity.

Eagle can help us adapt to changes and seize opportunities with confidence. It can provide the spark of inspiration to get creative juices flowing and ignite passions. When judicious communication is necessary, eagle can tweak intuition and lead us to hidden truths. As a symbol of the sun and renewal, this bird can help us discover new levels of freedom.

Call on eagle to build energy for summer and winter solstice celebrations. Although this high-flying bird is less nimble when walking, it is an aid for grounding energy after ritual or psychic work and helps us find balance.

Make Connection

Connect with eagle energy by climbing a hill where you can see out over the land. Hold your arms straight out to the sides at shoulder height and visualize that you are flying. Imagine seeing the ground slip beneath you as you gain altitude, circling higher and higher. The sun warms your back, but the air rushing past your face is cool. If you feel that strong wings are holding you aloft, eagle has connected with you and is helping you soar above the world.

Associations

Zodiac: Aquarius, Gemini, Leo, Scorpio

Element(s): Air, fire

Sabbat(s): Litha, Yule

Goddesses: Isis, Justitia/Iustitia

Gods: Agni, Ares, Belenus, Indra, Jupiter, Lugh, Odin, Pan, Vishnu, Zeus (golden eagle)

Solar system: Jupiter, Sun

Trees: Conifers

Ogham: Iodho (young eagles)

Bird Identification

BALD EAGLE (*HALIAEETUS LEUCOCEPHALUS*)

Size: 28 to 38 inches

Wingspan: 70 to 80 inches

Comparative size: Goose

Description: Heavy, dark brown body; brown wings; large, white head and tail; heavy, bright yellow, hooked bill; yellow legs

Range: From Alaska across Canada to Newfoundland, south to Florida, and throughout most of the United States

Habitat: Lakes, rivers, ponds, reservoirs, marshes, and coastal areas

Eggs: Dull white

GOLDEN EAGLE (*AQUILA CHRYSAETOS*)

Size: 27 to 33 inches

Wingspan: 72 to 86 inches

Comparative size: Goose

Description: Dark brown all over; golden sheen on the back of the head and neck; head relatively small; long, broad wings; long tail

Range: From Alaska throughout most of Canada and the United States except for the southeastern and Gulf Coast states

Habitat: Mountain forests and open grassland; may winter on salt marshes in the east

Eggs: White to cream or pale pink, usually with small brown blotches

Collective noun(s): An aerie, a convocation, an eyrie, a jubilee, or a soar of eagles

Egret:
Great Egret, Snowy Egret

Great Egret (Ardea alba)

Even though the egret is a type of heron, I have included it as a separate entry because of the ethereal and otherworldly energy of this bird, which differs from other herons. The name *egret* comes from the French *aigrette*, meaning "little heron."[67] To the Maori people of New Zealand, seeing an egret was considered a great blessing. This is understandable to me, as I have felt fortunate whenever I have encountered these elegant birds while kayaking through our local marshes.

Throughout most of the year, the egret has a svelte appearance. However, during the breeding season, it develops long, wispy plumes that make it look shaggy. These temporary feathers are called nuptial plumes, and they were so much of a fashion rage in the late nineteenth and early twentieth centuries that the egret was hunted nearly to extinction. Founded to protect birds from being killed for their feathers or other frivolous uses, the National Audubon Society uses the great egret as its symbol.

According to wildlife biologist and nature writer Les Beletsky, the Egyptian hieroglyph that is interpreted as a phoenix actually depicts a bird that looks more like an egret

---

67. Ian Fraser and Jeannie Gray, *Australian Bird Names: A Complete Guide* (Collingwood, Australia: CSIRO Publishing, 2013), 64.

or heron. Along with the crane, egrets were believed by the Celts to have a close affinity with the supernatural world. Although he was usually depicted as a woodsman, Esus, considered a fertility god by Continental Celts, was associated with egrets.

Magical Workings

Before embarking on astral travel, spirit communication, or any exploration of the otherworld call on egret to help bring you into stillness with its calm, grounding energy. This bird also provides guidance and protection between the worlds. Visualize holding one of its feathers as a talisman as you journey.

Draw on egret's wisdom at Samhain to connect with ancestors as well as those who have more recently passed beyond the veil. This bird can help answer questions and carry messages between you and your loved one.

Egret's beauty is symbolic of peace and stability. Meditating on its image conveys a deeply-rooted confidence that can serve as an aid for all of your endeavors.

Make Connection

Connect with the energy of egret by standing as still as you can while you imagine a thin, white, veil-like mist surrounding you. Feel the shimmering, ethereal quality of the mist enfolding you into a separate and magical realm. As the mist slightly parts, a brilliant white egret stands before you. It looks at you but does not move, only watches you with interest.

Reach forward toward one of its wings as you bow your head. If it brushes your hand with its bill, you will be allowed to touch it. When you make contact with the feathers, you will be filled with a sense of peace. Don't be discouraged if it does not touch you the first time you seek connection. Egret may want to teach you patience and the art of coming into stillness.

Associations

Element(s): Air, earth, water
Sabbat(s): Samhain
God: Esus

Bird Identification

Great Egret (Ardea alba)

Size: 37 to 40 inches

Wingspan: 51 to 57 inches

Comparative size: Goose

Description: Tall and slender; all-white body; long, black legs; yellowish-orange, daggerlike bill; long, S-curved neck; long lacy plumes on back during breeding season

Range: Throughout most of the lower forty-eight except Rocky Mountain states and parts of California and the Pacific Northwest; throughout Mexico, Central America, and most of South America

Habitat: Fresh and saltwater marshes, marshy ponds, and marine wetlands

Eggs: Smooth, pale greenish blue

Snowy Egret (Egretta thula)

Size: 22 to 26 inches

Wingspan: 38 to 40 inches

Comparative size: Goose

Description: Small and delicate; all-white body; black bill with yellow patch of skin at the base; black legs; greenish-yellow feet that turn orange-yellow during breeding season; long lacy plumes on head, neck, and back during breeding season

Range: From northern California and east to New England; mainly on the coasts but also inland waters; south into Mexico and South America

Habitat: Fresh and saltwater marshes, ponds, swamps, and mudflats

Eggs: Pale greenish blue

Collective noun(s): A colony, a congregation, a heronry, a stand, or a wedge of egrets

Falcon:
American Kestrel, Merlin, Peregrine Falcon

American Kestrel (Falco sparverius)

The peregrine falcon is the largest falcon in North America and the American kestrel is the smallest. From medieval Latin, *peregrine* means "wanderer" or "foreigner." [68] The common name *merlin* comes from an Old French name for the species, *esmerillon*, and its scientific name means "falcon dove." [69] The family name of these birds, Falconidae, is Latin and means "a sickle," which describes the shape of their beaks and talons.[70]

Falcons have a signature aerial dive called a "stoop," where they seem to hang still in the air and then shoot downward like an arrow. They are powerful and fast, which has made them prized sporting and hunting birds. Falconry dates to approximately 1700 BCE in Iran and 650 BCE in China.[71] Because of its smaller size, the merlin was the preferred falcon for European noblewomen. Mary Queen of Scots (1542–1587) is said to have used this type of falcon for hunting.

---

68. Mary Beath, *Hiking Alone: Trails Out, Trails Home* (Albuquerque, NM: University of New Mexico Press, 2008), 11.

69. Wells, *100 Birds and How They Got Their Names*, 144.

70. Ibid., 66.

71. Armstrong, *The Life and Lore of the Bird in Nature, Art, Myth and Literature*, 110.

Falcon-headed Horus was one of the oldest Egyptian deities, and the falcon hieroglyph meant "that which is above."[72] Not surprisingly, falcon amulets have been found in both royal and common Egyptian burials. In addition, according to Norse mythology, Freya's falcon-feathered cloak was used for shape-shifting.

Magical Workings

Since ancient times, falcon has been a bird of power, strength, and magic. It can provide clarity when interpreting omens and messages and when engaging in any form of psychic work. This bird teaches us how to sharpen our perceptions for greater awareness of what may be going on around us.

Falcon can be instrumental in personal growth as well as healing the soul. Call on it to accompany you as a guide no matter what level (physical or spiritual) your journey may be on. While this bird can be a fierce adversary, it demonstrates the importance of loyalty and truth. Because of its association with the sun, summer, and fire, invite falcon to your summer solstice celebrations by placing a figurine or picture of it on your altar.

Make Connection

Connect with falcon energy by making a talisman. Using a felt-tip marker, draw the symbol of the Eye of Horus on a flat stone or crystal. Go outside at dusk when there are fast-moving clouds, hold the talisman between your hands as you gaze up at the sky and say: *"Falcon, falcon, moving so swift, I call to you and offer this gift. This talisman I hold as a tribute to you, guide my work and I will be true."* When you return home, place the talisman on your altar for three days. During this time be attentive for images, sightings, or dreams of falcons, which will indicate that your gift was accepted.

Figure 2.2: The Eye of Horus is a powerful talisman that helps us connect with falcon.

---

72. Arin Murphy-Hiscock, *Birds: A Spiritual Field Guide* (Avon, MA: Adams Media, 2012), 72.

Associations

Zodiac: Capricorn

Element(s): Air, fire

Sabbat(s): Litha

Goddesses: Freya, Frigg, Nephthys

Gods: Horus, Khonsu, Loki, Ra, Woden

Solar system: Sun

Bird Identification

AMERICAN KESTREL (*FALCO SPARVERIUS*)

Also known as: Sparrow hawk

Size: 8 to 12 inches

Wingspan: 20 to 24 inches

Comparative size: Robin

Description: Long, narrow wings; long, square-tipped tail; rusty brown upperparts spotted black; black band near tip of tail; pale face with pairs of vertical black stripes

Male: Slate-blue wings

Female: Reddish-brown wings

Range: From central Alaska across Canada to the Maritime Provinces, and throughout the United States, Mexico, Central America, and parts of South America

Habitat: Meadows, grasslands, farmland, cities, and suburbs

Eggs: White, yellowish, or light reddish brown with violet-magenta, gray, or brown mottling

MERLIN (*FALCO COLUMBARIUS*)

Also known as: Pigeon hawk

Size: 9 to 11 inches

Wingspan: 21 to 27 inches

Comparative size: Robin to pigeon

Description: Stocky body; dark, streaked coloration all over; broad, streaked chest; pointed wings dark underneath; medium-length tail with narrow, white bands

Male: Slate-gray to dark gray

Female: More brown than gray

Range: Throughout Alaska, Canada, the United States, Mexico, Central America, and parts of South America

Habitat: Open forests, grasslands, and coastal areas

Eggs: Rusty brown with brown or chestnut markings

PEREGRINE FALCON (*FALCO PEREGRINUS*)

Also known as: Duck hawk

Size: 14 to 21 inches

Wingspan: 39 to 43 inches

Comparative size: Pigeon to crow

Description: Dark head; thick sideburns; gray, hooked bill with yellow base; long, pointed wings; long tail; blue-gray upperparts; barred underparts; yellow lower legs and feet

Range: From Alaska and Arctic Canada, south through the western mountains to the West Coast and Southwest, along the East and Gulf Coasts into Mexico, Central, and South America

Habitat: Open country along rivers, lakes, and coasts as well as in cities

Eggs: Pale creamy to brownish, with brown, red, or purple blotches

Collective noun(s): A bazaar, an eyrie, or a flight of falcons. There is also a cage or a wandering of peregrines, a hover or a soar of kestrels, and a cast of merlins.

Finch and Goldfinch:
House Finch, Purple Finch, American Goldfinch

American Goldfinch (Spinus tristis syn. Carduelis tristis)

These cousins can be distinguished from other small birds by their bouncy flight patterns. This is especially useful in the winter when goldfinches have molted their breeding plumage and look more like sparrows. Unlike their yellow cousin, the male house finch and purple finch retain their rosy coloring throughout the year. Finches are master weavers, constructing nests that are so tight that some can actually hold water.

Finches have been kept as pets for their pretty coloring as well as for their singing. Originally the house finch's range covered just the western United States into Mexico. In 1940, after a plan to sell them as pets called Hollywood finches failed, the captive stock was turned loose on Long Island, New York.[73] House finches now range throughout most of the eastern United States and southern Canada.

In medieval Europe, a belief persisted that the goldfinch provided protection against the plague. These birds were also symbols of fertility. In other folklore, if the first bird a young woman saw on Valentine's Day was a goldfinch, she would marry into a wealthy family.

---

73. John Eastman, *The Eastman Guide to Birds: Natural History Accounts for 150 North American Species* (Mechanicsburg, PA: Stackpole Books, 2012), 239.

Magical Workings

These little high-energy creatures have the vitality to help us awaken and activate talents that we may not know we possess. Whenever introspection is needed, call on finch to aid you in heightening your awareness. As a songbird, finch helps us realize the power of the voice and communicate on all levels, including with spirits. Goldfinch, in particular, is an aid for contacting spirits.

Associated with enchantment, finch can open the gateway between the worlds for contacting the fairy folk. Call on this bird to enhance your summer solstice celebration by placing a figurine or picture on your altar during ritual. Invite finch to aid in spells dealing with fertility, for resolving family issues, and for attracting wealth.

Make Connection

To connect with finch, go to a place where you are comfortable singing out loud. Don't worry about having a good voice; birds don't concern themselves with that. Just express yourself. You don't have to sing a song with words, you can simply follow a melody by making vowels sounds such as "*ah*" or "*oo*." Lift your voice and let your spirit soar with the finches and you may feel yourself flying among them.

Associations

Element(s): Air

Sabbat(s): Litha

Tree: Cedar

Flower: Thistle

Magical beings: Elves, fairies

Bird Identification

AMERICAN GOLDFINCH (*Spinus tristis* syn. *Carduelis tristis*)

Also known as: Thistle bird, wild canary, yellow bird

Size: 4 to 5 inches

Wingspan: 7½ to 8½ inches

Comparative size: Sparrow

Description: Short, conical bill; small head; long wings; short, notched tail

Male: Bright yellow; black forehead; black wings with white markings; white patches above and beneath tail. In winter: drab brown; blackish wings with two pale wing bars

Female: Duller yellow underparts; olive above; black wings and tail

Range: Throughout southern Canada, most of the United States, and the Gulf Coast of Mexico

Habitat: Weedy grassland and farmland with shrubs and trees, thickets, and suburban areas

Eggs: Pale bluish white; may have small faint brown spots around large end

House Finch (*Haemorhous mexicanus* syn. *Carpodacus mexicanus*)

Size: 5 to 6 inches

Wingspan: 7½ to 9½ inches

Comparative size: Sparrow

Description: Short wings; large beak; long, flat head; shallow notch in tail

Male: Red head, upper breast, and flanks; streaked brown back, belly, and tail; red rump

Female: Grayish-brown; streaked head

Range: Throughout most of the United States except for eastern Texas and a strip up through the central plains states to Canada; also in parts of Mexico

Habitat: Rural areas, suburbs, and cities

Eggs: Pale blue to white, finely speckled with black and pale purple

Purple Finch (*Haemorhous purpureus* syn. *Carpodacus purpureus*)

Size: 4½ to 6 inches

Wingspan: 8½ to 10 inches

Comparative size: Sparrow

Description: Chunky body; big, conical beak; short, notched tail

Male: Pinkish-raspberry red head and breast; brown streaks on back; whitish belly

Female: Strong facial markings; brown eye line; broad white eyebrow; underbody brown streaking

Range: From the Eastern Seaboard into the plains states, across southern Canada, and along the West Coast

Habitat: Evergreen forests, mixed upland woods, orchards, parklands, and suburban
areas

Eggs: Pale greenish blue with brown and black markings

Collective noun(s): A charm, a company, or a trimming of finches, as well as a chirp or a
glister of goldfinches

Flamingo:
American Flamingo

American Flamingo (Phoenicopterus ruber)

More than a funky lawn ornament, flamingos belong to one of the oldest families of birds and have a lineage that dates back at least thirty million years.[74] This bird's genus name, *Phoenicopterus*, comes from the Greek *phoiniko-pteros*, which means "crimson winged."[75] In addition, its species name, *ruber*, means "red" in Latin.[76] These names are in reference to the distinctive coloring of these birds, which ranges from pale pink to reddish.

The flamingo's coloring is not exactly natural. It is caused by the carotenoids in the bird's diet, without which its feathers would be white. In captivity, they have to be fed a special diet to keep their classic coloring. Flamingo chicks are born white or gray and do not develop pink feathers until they are about two years old and have consumed enough beta carotene–rich food. Also related to food is this bird's unusual hooked beak, which is adapted for its unique method of feeding. Flamingos turn their heads upside down in

74. Tim Harris, ed., *National Geographic Complete Birds of the World* (Washington, DC: National Geographic Society, 2009), 54.

75. Fraser and Gray, *Australian Bird Names*, 64.

76. Wells, *100 Birds and How They Got Their Names*, 70.

the water and use their beaks as a filter, not unlike the baleen plates of certain whales, for collecting algae, small crustaceans, and fish.

The Creek and other Native American tribes of the southeastern United States used flamingo feathers as pendants on their smoking pipes. Flamingo feathers were also used for ornamentation on short cloaks. To the ancient Egyptians, the flamingo was a symbol of the sun and served as a hieroglyph for the color red. Because of their coloring and the fact that they often lived on volcanic lakes, these birds became associated with the phoenix and its power of transformation. According to the Upanishads, ancient Hindu texts, the flamingo was a symbol of the soul migrating from darkness to light. Along with storks, flamingos were depicted in cave paintings in southern Spain that date to between 6000 and 4000 BCE.[77]

Although the meat of this bird was not often eaten, the Romans considered its tongue a delicacy. Flamingo tongues, along with other avian morsels, were served as offerings to the goddess Minerva. Surrounding themselves with color, wealthy Romans adorned the walls of their gardens with paintings of flamingos. Two millennia later, the kitsch American lawn ornament, which got its start in the 1920s, came to symbolize bad taste.

Magical Workings

Associated with night magic, flamingo is linked with transformation from dark to light. Call on it for spellwork done just before dawn as well as when seeking illumination for events that may seem mysterious. It is also appropriate to grace an Imbolc altar with a flamingo as we move from the dark of the year toward spring. And, of course, at summer solstice it brings the essence of lighthearted summer fun.

As a bird of knowledge, flamingo can bring enlightening information that will lift your heart and soul. It can be instrumental when building community and stability in the home. Call on this bird to boost spells for attracting abundance. If you feel a strong affinity with flamingo, dare to put a plastic one in your garden. As an alternative, work images of this bird into your bathroom decor.

Make Connection

To connect with flamingo energy, dress your altar in all things pink and include a picture or figurine of this bird. Light a pink candle and use a blanket, piece of clothing, or anything pink that is large enough to wrap around your body. Gaze at the candle and then

---

77. Stephen Moss, *A Bird in the Bush: A Social History of Birdwatching* (London: Aurum Press, 2004), 27.

the image/figurine of flamingo. After a few minutes, close your eyes and meditate on the color, and then visualize a pink glow surrounding you. It is soft, warm, and comforting like the feathers of a flamingo. Enjoy the feeling of being nurtured by this unique and beautiful bird, and know that whenever you summon this sensation you can connect with flamingo.

Associations

Element(s): Air, water

Sabbat(s): Imbolc, Litha

Goddess: Minerva

Solar system: Sun

Bird Identification

AMERICAN FLAMINGO (*PHOENICOPTERUS RUBER*)

Also known as: Caribbean flamingo, greater flamingo

Size: 46 to 48 inches

Wingspan: 55 to 65 inches

Comparative size: Very large

Description: Long neck; long legs; webbed feet with three toes; mostly pink all over; pointed wings with black tips; heavy, hooked, down-curving bill with black tip; coloring ranges from pale pink to rosy pink to reddish

Range: Southern Florida, the Caribbean, and the Yucatan Peninsula

Habitat: Shallow coastal lagoons, inland waters, and mudflats

Eggs: White

Collective noun(s): A colony, a flamboyance, a flurry, or a stand of flamingos

Goose:
Canada Goose, Snow Goose

Canada Goose (Branta canadensis)

Although geese spend a lot of time on land, they are the quintessential waterbird in the life-giving aspect of the Goddess. As noted in chapter 3, the flying-V formation of waterbirds inspired symbols of abundance and fecundity. They are also harbingers of the changing seasons.

Kept domestically in ancient Egypt, the goose was sacred to Isis, Osiris, and Horus. It was associated with the solar god Amun as well as the earth god Geb. In Egyptian creation myth, a goose laid the cosmic egg that became the sun. In India, the goose was also a solar symbol and a creature worthy of drawing the chariot of Vishnu. Also according to Hindu legend, the god Brahma rode a goose. In China, geese were believed to be messengers between heaven and earth.

Votive offerings in the form of geese figurines were left in the temples of Hera. Geese guarded the temple of Juno in Rome, which is not surprising as geese can be very aggressive, and through the centuries they have served as barnyard defense. A white goose was associated with Aphrodite and was sacred to Bertha, a Germanic earth goddess. In Norse mythology, Freya was noted as goose-footed. Geese were used widely as a sacrificial animal and a frequent offering to Odin at Mabon.

The familiar post-Thanksgiving dinner tradition of wishing on the turkey's breastbone was a divination practice that centuries ago involved a goose bone. As today, two people would pull on a wishbone, and the one who ended up with the larger piece when it broke was in store for good luck. In medieval Germany, divination with the breastbone of a goose was used to foretell the severity of the coming winter. A male is called a gander, a young goose of either sex is a gosling, and a female is simply a goose.

Magical Workings

Domesticated for their eggs, meat, and feathers, geese symbolize comfort, abundance, and domesticity. Also on the home front, these birds represent love, marriage, fertility, and fidelity. Call on goose to aid you in any of these areas of life.

Goose also provides support for divination practices, especially interpreting messages and omens. In addition, this bird aids in working with spirits and can serve as a guide in otherworld journeys. Acting as a guardian, goose is instrumental for warning of danger. For travel in the physical world as well as other realms, call on it for protection and a safe return.

Although considered noisy by some, goose brings clear communication and fosters cooperation. Spiritually, it can be a guide for soul pathway working, deeply meaningful quests, and personal growth. Sparking inspiration and imagination, goose can help us find true freedom and happiness.

Make Connection

To connect with goose energy, go to a children's zoo, farm, or a place in the wild where you can observe geese. Listen to their calls long enough that you can keep the sound in your mind, and then go to a place where you can sit quietly. Replay the sound in your mind and imagine that you are calling out to goose. Listen for a callback to acknowledge contact.

Associations

Zodiac: Capricorn (snow goose), Libra
Element(s): Air, earth, water
Sabbat(s): Mabon, Yule (snow goose)
Goddesses: Aphrodite, Bertha, Freya, Hera, Isis, Juno
Gods: Amun, Brahma, Geb, Horus, Odin, Osiris, Ra, Vishnu

Solar system: Sun

Moon phase: Full (snow goose)

Ogham: nGetal

Bird Identification

CANADA GOOSE (*BRANTA CANADENSIS*)

Size: 30 to 43 inches

Wingspan: 50 to 70 inches

Description: Long neck; large webbed feet; wide, flat bill; black head, bill, and neck; white cheeks and chinstrap; cream to light tan breast and underparts; brown back

Range: Part of Alaska, throughout Canada and most of the United States, and part of the Mexican Gulf Coast

Habitat: Lakes, bays, rivers, marshes, grassy fields, and suburban or urban parks and lawns

Eggs: Creamy white

SNOW GOOSE (*CHEN CAERULESCENS*)

Size: 27 to 33 inches

Wingspan: 52 to 54 inches

Description: Stout body; hefty pink bill with a dark line called a "grinning patch"; long, thick neck; white body; black wingtips; dark-colored snow geese are called blue geese and have a white face, dark brown body; white under the tail

Range: Canadian Arctic, Mid-Atlantic coast of the United States, Gulf Coast, and southern California

Habitat: Near water on open grassy areas

Eggs: Creamy white, elongated oval

Collective noun(s): A drove, a flock, a gaggle, a skein, or a string of geese. There is also a wedge of Canada geese, a blizzard of snow geese, and a brood or a shoal of goslings.

Grouse:
Dusky Grouse, Ruffed Grouse

Ruffed Grouse (**Bonasa umbellus**)

A grouse is a forest game bird that relies on its camouflage to provide protection. The combination of its coloring and slow, careful walk allows this bird to remain unseen until it bursts out of cover. A grouse can be most startling in the winter when it seems to explode out of snow banks, where it dove into soft snow to spend the night.

In the winter, projections grow from their toes and act as built-in snowshoes that help them walk on top of deep snow. According to folklore, grouse were used for weather divination. If their toe feathers were especially thick, a harsh winter was on the way. Early American settlers called these birds grewes and grows.[78]

Living in a forest and sporting perfect camouflage limits the type of tactics grouse can use for attracting a mate. As a result, the male grouse has developed an elaborate courtship dance and drumming to attract females. The sound has been described as ghostly because it is difficult to pinpoint the direction of the noise. Although it looks and sounds like the bird is drumming on a fallen log, it is not actually striking the log. Instead, by rapidly flapping his wings, the grouse creates mini sonic booms.

At one time, the dusky grouse was considered a subspecies of the blue grouse, but DNA tests suggested otherwise. The ruffed grouse is so named because of the longer,

---

78. Wells, *100 Birds and How They Got Their Names*, 99.

dark neck feathers, which are more prominent on males and used for mate-attracting displays.

Magical Workings

The grouse's dancing and drumming activities make it a powerful ally for shamanic work and for reaching different levels of consciousness. If you have a drum, place an image of grouse next to your instrument when not in use. Also, slip an image or figurine of this bird in your pocket when you go to a drumming circle to really elevate the energy.

Grouse helps us learn how to flow with the rhythms of the natural world. As each new cycle brings challenges, it shows us how to meet them without fear. Call on grouse for support in divination, especially related to weather. The true wisdom of this bird is in finding what brings us satisfaction in life. Grouse can also teach us how to hold secrets.

Make Connection

Connect with grouse energy by dancing or drumming. Begin by walking slowly and carefully in silence or drumming very slowly, and then find a rhythm or a movement that you can sustain for a while. As you do this, visualize yourself in a forest surrounded and shielded by thick vegetation. Also imagine the smells and the texture of the forest beneath your feet. Carry on for as long as you can do so comfortably. When it feels appropriate, end your dancing or drumming and sit in silence. If you feel the energy enfolding you like the camouflage of a grouse, you have attracted its attention. A sign from grouse may come immediately or in a few days.

Associations

Element(s): Air, earth

Trees: Aspen, birch, oak, pine, spruce

Bird Identification

DUSKY GROUSE (*DENDRAGAPUS OBSCURUS*)

Size: 15 to 21 inches

Wingspan: 26 to 46 inches

Comparative size: Crow

Description: Plump, pear-shaped body; fan-shaped tail with gray band along the tip

Male: Gray to bluish-gray body; orange-yellow or red comb over eyes; reddish or purplish patch of skin on neck surrounded by a rosette of white feathers; wings slightly mottled; black tail

Female: Mottled brown; darker tail

Range: From the southern Yukon and Northwest Territories of Canada south to California, Colorado, Arizona, and New Mexico

Habitat: Grass and scrublands, mountainous forests, and subalpine areas

Eggs: Cream with light brown spots

RUFFED GROUSE (*BONASA UMBELLUS*)

Size: 16 to 20 inches

Wingspan: 20 to 25 inches

Comparative size: Crow

Description: Plump body; short crest on head; gray or reddish-brown with dappled patterns of bars and spots; dark bars from neck onto belly; barred tail with one wide, black band near tip

Male: Large neck ruff and crest; two or more whitish dots on rump feathers

Female: Smaller ruff; shorter crest; dark blotchy tail; one dot on rump feathers

Range: From Alaska through most of Canada, the northern United States, and down through the Appalachians and the northern Rockies

Habitat: Mixed forests with clearings and dense undergrowth

Eggs: Milky to cinnamon-buff; plain or with reddish spots

Collective noun(s): A brace, a covey, or a pack of grouse

Hawk:
Cooper's Hawk, Red-Tailed Hawk

Cooper's Hawk (Accipiter cooperii)

The hawk family name, Accipitridae, means "to seize," which describes how these birds take their prey.[79] The hawks included in this book, red-tailed and Cooper's, come from different genera. The accipiters (Cooper's) are speedy with shorter wings that enable them to maneuver through forests as they pursue their prey. The buteos (red-tailed) are less fast, relying on eyesight and stealth. The red-tailed hawk is considered the most common in North America. It has a shrill, raspy call that is most often used by filmmakers to portray the sound of a hawk, regardless of species.

Using birds for hunting was a widespread practice before the advent of guns. Later, hawks were included in the sport more widely known as falconry; however, it was also called hawking. Today, hawks fly a fine edge with farmers who value them for rodent control but also shoot them for killing chickens.

The name of the Greek goddess Circe is the feminine form of *kirkos*, meaning "hawk" or "falcon."[80] *Kirkos* also means "circle," which describes the hunting flight pattern of these birds. In Celtic myth, one of the oldest animals was the hawk of Achill, which was said to hold memories from the deep past. In addition, the ancient Welsh legends called the *Mabinogi* mention Arawn, the king of the otherworld, hunting with hawks.

---

79. Eastman, *The Eastman Guide to Birds,* 149.

80. Judith Yarnall, *Transformations of Circe: The History of an Enchantress* (Champaign, IL: University of Illinois Press, 1994), 28.

Elsewhere in Celtic legend and fact, hawks were important in gift exchanges along with horses and hounds.

Even though the goddess Artemis came to be associated with the moon, amulets of solar hawks have been found in her early shrines. Also, figurines of her priestesses were depicted with these birds. Hawks were regarded as messengers that could travel between this world and the otherworld. Shape-shifting heroes and gods such as the Norse Loki often took the form of a hawk. The Egyptian soul bird, called the ba, was frequently depicted as a hawk with a human head.

Magical Workings

As in Celtic and Egyptian traditions, hawk links us with the otherworld and the afterlife, bringing messages and representing omens. It is a creature of memory that helps us tap into our past-life experiences. Call on hawk for aid in developing psychic abilities, especially clairvoyance. It will also help you learn to trust your intuition, especially when interpreting visions. This bird can bring clarity to communications on all levels and help to strengthen awareness. Hawk can bestow illumination when seeking truth about a situation or oneself.

As a bird of power and wisdom, it can serve as a guide to help traverse the astral realm. Use a picture or figurine of hawk on your altar during spring or autumn equinox rituals to boost and hold the energy. Call on hawk to bolster courage when confronting problems or any situation that requires confidence. This bird aids in fostering leadership skills and the ability to seize opportunities. It also stimulates creativity.

Make Connection

To connect with hawk energy, sit in front of your altar or other quiet place and close your eyes. Become aware of your body, your contact with the floor, and ultimately with the earth until you feel grounded. Bring your awareness up to the top of your head and then visualize a hawk hovering above you like depictions of the Egyptian ba. Reach out with your energy until you can feel hawk's presence and perhaps a slight whisper of a breeze from its wings as it continues to hold its position. Once you make contact, you will be able to call on hawk whenever you need guidance and protection.

Associations

Zodiac: Aries (red-tailed), Scorpio
Element(s): Air, fire

Sabbat(s): Mabon, Ostara

Goddesses: Artemis, Cerridwen, Circe, Danu, Hera, Isis, Nephthys

Gods: Apollo, the Dagda, Hermes, Loki, Mercury, Ra

Solar system: Sun

Moon phase: New

Ogham: Saille

Bird Identification

COOPER'S HAWK (*ACCIPITER COOPERII*)

Size: 14 to 15 inches

Wingspan: 24 to 35 inches

Comparative size: Pigeon to crow

Description: Broad, rounded wings; dark cap; steely blue-gray upper body; warm reddish bars on the underparts; thick, dark bands on the tail, which has a rounded tip

Range: Throughout the United States, parts of southern Canada, Mexico, and parts of Central America

Habitat: Woods with clearings or nearby meadows and leafy suburban backyards

Eggs: Pale blue to bluish white

RED-TAILED HAWK (*BUTEO JAMAICENSIS*)

Size: 19 to 25 inches

Wingspan: 45 to 52 inches

Description: Large, stocky body; broad, rounded wings; short, wide tail; dark brown upper body; white breast; brown band across belly; brick red underneath tail; coloration varies by region

Female: Larger than male

Range: From Alaska to Nova Scotia and south throughout the United States, Mexico, and Central America

Habitat: Broken woodland, grasslands, fields, scrub land, suburbs, and urban areas

Eggs: White or buff with brown or purple blotches or speckles

Collective noun(s): An aerie, a cast, an eyrie, or a kettle of hawks

Heron:
Great Blue Heron, Green Heron

Great Blue Heron (Ardea herodias)

The great blue heron is the largest of the North American species. Specially shaped vertebrae allow herons to curl their necks into an *S* shape for aerodynamic flight. The heron also has a high percentage of photoreceptors in its eyes, allowing it to hunt at night. The little green heron is one of a few birds that uses tools to catch prey. It floats light objects such as feathers, insects, or pieces of bread on water to lure fish to the surface, where they are easier to snatch.

The name *heron* is believed to come from the Old English *hragra*, the pronunciation of which was said to imitate the sound of these birds.[81] Up until the seventeenth century, herons were known as henshaws and heronshaws.[82]

Heron hawking was a popular sport in England and parts of Europe that involved the release of hawks or falcons to capture a heron. In the early days of the sport, an outing ended with the heron as dinner (they were considered a delicacy). By the mid-nineteenth century, the sport had become a competition that drew crowds to watch a pair of falcons spiral down to the ground with a captured heron. The bird was then banded with a brass ring bearing the name of the falcon club and released unharmed.

---

81. Fraser and Gray, *Australian Bird Names*, 64.
82. Wells, *100 Birds and How They Got Their Names*, 106.

In Egypt, the heron was a symbol of abundance and blessings. In India, a heron landing on the roof of a house was considered good luck.

Magical Workings

Believed to possess the power of the otherworld, heron is an ally for shamanic work and traversing the astral realm. Call on this bird for guidance when seeking your life path and for developing psychic skills. Heron teaches the importance of focus for introspection or any type of self-work that fosters transformation.

As a symbol of abundance, heron can bring opportunities and security. In addition, it is an aid for cultivating assertiveness. This bird teaches the power of keeping secrets and the wise use of authority. Turn to heron for help in unlocking your magical abilities. Call on its power and connection with the moon by placing an image or figurine of it on your altar during esbat rituals.

Make Connection

To connect with heron energy, go to a place where you can wade in shallow water. It only needs to be ankle-deep. If you choose a swimming pool, go at a time when it is quiet and few people are around. As an alternative, especially in winter, the bathtub in your home works just as well. If possible, do this at twilight, an in-between time of day when heron likes to hunt. Slowly step into the water and then stand as still as you can. Visualize an image of this bird. It will make itself known through a majestic presence at the core of your body, and you will feel the liminality of the in-between time and space of heron.

Associations

Zodiac: Capricorn

Element(s): Air, fire, water

God: Amun

Solar system: Moon

Magical beings: Fairies

Bird Identification

GREAT BLUE HERON (*ARDEA HERODIAS*)

Size: 38 to 54 inches

Wingspan: 65 to 79 inches

Comparative size: Goose to very large

Description: Long neck and legs; thick, daggerlike bill; overall slate-blue with lighter to grayish areas on the shoulders and breast; white forehead and top of head; black crown, crest, and legs; during breeding season, both males and females develop long plumes on the head, neck, and back, giving them a shaggy appearance

Range: From coastal Alaska throughout most of the United States, through Mexico and Central America

Habitat: Fresh and saltwater marshes, swamps, rivers, and lakes

Eggs: Pale blue

GREEN HERON (*BUTORIDES VIRESCENS*)

Also known as: Green-backed heron

Size: 16 to 19 inches

Wingspan: 25 to 27 inches

Comparative size: Crow

Description: Short, yellow legs; thick neck; broad, rounded, dark gray wings; long, daggerlike bill; deep green back; chestnut neck and breast; dark cap often raised into a short crest

Range: Throughout the eastern United States through the plains states; Pacific Northwest coast through California, parts of the Southwest, Texas, the Gulf Coast, Mexico, Central America, and part of South America

Habitat: Wooded ponds, marshes, rivers, reservoirs, and estuaries

Eggs: Pale green to bluish

Collective noun(s): A colony, a hedge, a heronry, a sedge, or a siege of herons

Hummingbird:
Ruby-Throated Hummingbird, Rufous Hummingbird

Ruby-Throated Hummingbird (Archilochus colubris)

If I had to choose just one word to describe these tiny birds, it would be "amazing." On its migration to winter roosts in Central America, a ruby-throated hummingbird has to fly five hundred miles in a single go to cross the Gulf of Mexico. Rather than flying a direct migration route back and forth, the rufous hummingbird makes a clockwise circuit of western North America each year. In addition, the rufous is known as one of the feistiest hummingbirds, standing its ground against bigger birds and even chasing chipmunks away from its nest.

Hummingbirds are well known for their aerobatics of flying straight and fast, stopping instantly, hovering, and even flying backward. John James Audubon (1785–1851) noted that they look like "glittering fragments of rainbows."[83]

Explorers who accompanied Columbus on his voyages took note of these birds in the Caribbean. Unsure of what they were, they described hummingbirds as some kind of mix between bird and insect or butterfly. The Taino people of the Caribbean called hummingbirds *colibri*, meaning "god bird."[84] To the Taino, this bird symbolized rebirth.

---

83. Murphy-Hiscock, *Birds: A Spiritual Field Guide*, 99.
84. Esther Quesada Tyrrell, "Jewels of the Sky", *Islands* Vol. 14, No. 6. (Nov–Dec 1994): 52–56.

Hummingbirds represented vitality to the Aztecs, who associated them with the sun and war. Warriors kept dead hummingbirds as talismans for success in battle. It was also believed that these warriors were eventually transformed into hummingbirds. While the purpose of the Nazca Lines remain a mystery, the hummingbird was considered important enough to the ancient people of Peru to be included as one of the giant geoglyphs. In the American Southwest, these birds were associated with rain by the Hopi and Zuni people, who depicted them on water jars.

Magical Workings

The strength and vitality of this tiny bird can be called upon to stoke courage and to call on the spirit of the warrior for spells of defense. Hummingbird also boosts spells for travel protection.

This bird aids in holding secrets and knowing when to be discreet. It is an honor to receive wisdom from it. Hummingbird's association with the sun makes it an appropriate symbol for a Yule altar as we welcome the return of the sun. Also use an image or figurine of hummingbird to invoke the enchantment of Midsummer's Eve, especially if you want to connect with fairies.

The energy of this bird can be instrumental to fostering motivation, independence, and optimism. Also call on hummingbird to aid with healing and issues of forgiveness.

Make Connection

To connect with hummingbird energy, gather a green agate and a red garnet or other green and red crystals to represent this little jewel of a bird. On a sunny day, stand outside with a crystal in each hand. As you feel the sun warm your body, close your eyes and hum just one note. As it reverberates through you, feel your energy rising as you visualize a tiny hummingbird hovering in front of you. When the image becomes clear, nod to the bird to acknowledge and honor it, and then let the experience run its course. Following this you may have dreams about hummingbirds.

Associations

Element(s): Air, fire

Sabbat(s): Litha

Trees: Birch, hackberry, hornbeam, maple, oak, pine, poplar

Flower: Sunflower

Solar system: Sun

Magical beings: Fairies

Bird Identification

RUBY-THROATED HUMMINGBIRD (ARCHILOCHUS COLUBRIS)

Size: 2½ to 3½ inches

Wingspan: 3 to 4 inches

Comparative size: Very small

Description: Slender, slightly down-curved bill; short wings; very short, black legs; metallic-green head, back, wings, and tail; whitish breast and belly

Male: Brilliant iridescent red throat

Female: White throat

Range: From Alberta, across southern Canada, south along the eastern half of the plains states to the East Coast, and into Mexico and Central America

Habitat: Open woodlands, forest edges, meadows, grasslands, parks, gardens, and backyards

Eggs: White

RUFOUS HUMMINGBIRD (SELASPHORUS RUFUS)

Size: 2½ to 3½ inches

Wingspan: 3 to 4 inches

Comparative size: Very small

Description: Slender, nearly straight bill; fairly short wings; tail tapers to a point when folded

Male: Bright orange back and belly; vivid iridescent-red throat

Female: Green upperparts; brownish-red flanks and patches on green tail; spot of orange on throat

Range: From southeastern Alaska and British Columbia through the western United States to parts of Mexico and Central America

Habitat: Open areas, yards, parks, and forest edges up to tree line

Eggs: White

Collective noun(s): A bouquet, a glittering, a shimmer, or a charm of hummingbirds

Ibis:
Glossy Ibis, White Ibis, White-Faced Ibis

White Ibis (Eudocimus albus)

The ibis is a tall wading bird that has been hunted for food as well as for its feathers. Once called the black curlew, the glossy ibis is fairly new to North America and expanded its range north along the Atlantic Coast in the early nineteenth century.[85] The ibis is easily confused with herons and storks, and it does not help that the only stork native to the Americas was originally called the wood ibis. Ibis belong to the family called Threskiornithidae, which is Greek and means "sacred bird."[86]

In Egypt, this bird was sacred to Thoth, the god of wisdom, who was usually portrayed with the head of an ibis. In addition to ibis statuettes as votive objects, the birds themselves were often sacrificed to serve as offerings to him. The Egyptians believed that the ibis possessed the gift of foreknowledge because its migration seemed to herald the flooding of the Nile, which brought renewal and abundance. Mummified ibises have been found in tombs, perhaps as a symbol of rebirth. The Greeks associated the ibis with Hermes, one of the Olympian gods and messenger to other deities.

85. Caroline Hill and Ina Stradins, eds. *American Museum of Natural History Birds of North America Eastern Region* (New York: Dorling Kindersley, Limited, 2011), 12.

86. Murphy-Hiscock, *Birds: A Spiritual Field Guide*, 102.

The crescent shape of this bird's beak is the source of its association with the moon. The length of its stride was said to be the basis for the ancient measurement called a cubit. The ibis was also said to have the power to kill a crocodile with one of its feathers.

Magical Workings

Known as the sacred bird of the Nile, ibis can help us connect with ancient wisdom. Call on its lunar association to boost the energy of moon magic and esbat rituals. Invite this bird to strengthen spells for drawing abundance into your life as well as for protection. It is also an aid for healing and supports well-being.

As a bird of Thoth, inventor of writing and patron of scribes, ibis is an aid for all forms of communication including human, animal, and spirit. Ibis is also a bird of prophecy and its power can be invoked to help develop sensitivity and divination skills. Place an image or figurine of ibis on your altar when seeking enlightenment.

Make Connection

To connect with ibis energy, go outside on the night of a crescent moon. Gaze at the moon for a few minutes and then close your eyes. Hold the image of the moon in your mind and then visualize ibis in the sky with the moon tucked into the curve of its bill. Feel the power of this great bird. Carried by moonlight, the energy of its blessings gently surrounds you. Remember how this feels and you will be able to contact ibis whenever you need it.

Associations

Zodiac: Cancer

Element(s): Air, water

Goddesses: Isis, Maat

Gods: Hermes, Thoth

Solar system: Moon

Bird Identification

GLOSSY IBIS (*PLEGADIS FALCINELLUS*)

Size: 18 to 25 inches

Wingspan: 34 to 36 inches

Comparative size: Crow to red-tailed hawk

Description: Long, down-curved, dark gray-brown bill; long, black legs; shiny, dark-green wings and tail; dark purple to black upper body, head, and neck, but rusty-red during breeding season

Range: Along the East Coast from Maine to the Gulf Coast of Texas

Habitat: Marshes, estuaries, coastal bays, flooded fields, and swamps

Eggs: Greenish-blue to dark blue

White Ibis (*Eudocimus albus*)

Size: 22 to 27 inches

Wingspan: 33 to 36 inches

Comparative size: Red-tailed hawk to goose

Description: All-white body; tips of wings black; long, down-curved, reddish-orange bill; reddish-orange face; long, gray legs that are reddish during breeding season

Range: East Coast from North Carolina south throughout Florida and along the Gulf Coast west to Texas, Mexico, and Central America

Habitat: Coastal freshwater, saltwater, and brackish marshes, mudflats, mangrove swamps, and lagoons; away from the coast in ponds or flooded fields

Eggs: Greenish-white with dark blotches

White-Faced Ibis (*Plegadis chihi*)

Size: 22 to 25 inches

Wingspan: 34 to 35 inches

Comparative size: Red-tailed hawk

Description: Long, down-curved, dark gray-brown bill; white band of feathers around face; red eyes and legs; chestnut-bronze all over; streaks on head and neck in winter

Range: From Oregon and sometimes as far east as Minnesota, south through California to Texas, Louisiana, and Mexico

Habitat: Salt and freshwater marshes and brushy coastal islands

Eggs: Pale blue-green

Collective noun(s): A colony, a congregation, or a stand of ibis

Jay:
Blue Jay, Steller's Jay

Blue Jay (Cyanocitta cristata)

It is a well-known fact that these birds love acorns and have a habit of caching them, which has aided in the reforestation of oak trees. Because of this, jays were believed to be the souls of Druids in British folklore. In Native American legend, jays carried messages between the realms and were associated with underworld journeys. French folklore says that the jay's piercing call is an omen of good things to come.

According to some sources, the name *jay* comes from the Old French *jai*, meaning "chatterer," a word often used in reference to a talkative person.[87] Other sources note that the name comes from the Latin *gaius* or *gaia*, which was a name used for both the jay and magpie.[88] In the past, the English word *jay* meant a silly person, and a *jaywalker* was a rustic bumpkin who did not understand the ways of the city. While these birds may be noisy chatterers, they understand the world around them and use this knowledge to their advantage.

Named for German naturalist Georg Wilhelm Steller, the Steller's jay is actually louder than other jays and often mimics hawks. Blue jays also imitate hawks, and in captivity they mimic humans and cats, as well. Jays are known for their intelligence and complex social

---

87. Wells, *100 Birds and How They Got Their Names*, 116.
88. Geoffrey W. Arnott, *Birds in the Ancient World from A to Z* (New York: Routledge, 2007), 78.

systems. These birds are protective of their families and have been observed taking care of older members unable to fend for themselves. Like their cousin the crow, jays mob predators or other potentially dangerous intruders to their territory.

Magical Workings

Jay's association with the underworld makes it an appropriate bird to grace a Samhain altar. Also call on it for guidance in otherworld journeys or for travel in the astral realm. Jay provides a connection between the worlds and aids in interpreting prophecies. As a bird of the forest, it can be instrumental in connecting with woodland energy and spirits.

This bird supports skill development, especially psychic abilities with an emphasis on learning to use talents for the common good rather than private gain. Call on jay for help with assertiveness or when you need to face personal fears. Ask for its help to boost magic spells, especially those relating to luck. Jay is also an aid when seeking higher knowledge and understanding how to use power wisely.

Make Connection

To connect with the energy of jay, hold an acorn between your palms, close your eyes, and visualize this bird. If you don't have an acorn, use a picture of one. When the image in your mind is clear and strong, recall the sound of this bird's piercing noise. After you hear the call say: *"Jay, Jay, bird of gray and blue; I bury this acorn in honor of you."*

Dig a small hole, plant the acorn, and repeat the incantation twice more. Ideally, plant the acorn outside, but if necessary, it can be buried in a pot with a houseplant. If you are working with a picture of an acorn, burn it and bury the ashes. After this, whenever you want to connect with jay, hold an acorn or a picture or figurine of the bird and bring the sound of his call into your mind.

Associations

Element(s): Air, earth

Sabbat(s): Samhain

Goddess: Gaia

God: Mars

Tree: Oak

Solar system: Mercury

Magical beings: Fairies, woodland spirits

Bird Identification

BLUE JAY (*CYANOCITTA CRISTATA*)

Size: 10 to 12 inches

Wingspan: 13 to 17 inches

Comparative size: Robin to pigeon

Description: Gray-blue crown and crest; various shades of blue, black, and white upperparts; bright blue wings and tail with white and black bands; black across throat and around head; off-white or gray lower breast and belly; black bill, legs, feet, and eyes

Range: Mainly east of the Rocky Mountains in southern Canada and throughout the eastern United States

Habitat: All types of forests especially oak, near edge of woods rather than deep forest; also common in suburban and urban areas

Eggs: Bluish or light brown with brownish spots

STELLER'S JAY (*CYANOCITTA STELLERI*)

Size: 12 to 13 inches

Wingspan: 16 to 17 inches

Comparative size: Pigeon

Description: Large, charcoal-black head with prominent triangular crest; blackish back and breast; deep blue belly, rounded wings, and long, full tail; long bill with slight hook; coloration varies throughout its range

Range: From coastal Pacific Northwest south through northern California and the Rocky Mountains into Central America

Habitat: High mountain slopes and coniferous forests of pine and oak; also common around campgrounds, parklands, and backyards

Eggs: Bluish-green spotted dark brown, purplish, or olive

Collective noun(s): A band, a party, or a scolding of jays

Kingfisher:
Belted Kingfisher

Belted Kingfisher (Megaceryle alcyon syn. Ceryle alcyon)

In Greek myth, this bird was called the halcyon and was said to lay its eggs at sea just before the winter solstice. The kingfisher was believed to have the power to calm storms, and the days of peaceful weather came to be known as halcyon days. In reality, kingfishers are not seabirds, despite the ancient belief that they floated nests like rafts on the ocean. Kingfishers actually nest in burrows that they excavate three to seven feet deep into soft riverbanks.

The kingfisher's legend is intertwined with the story of Alcyone, the daughter of Aeolus, god of the winds. Alcyone and her husband Ceyx affectionately called themselves Zeus and Hera, which was considered an affront by the supreme Greek god. When Ceyx was on an ocean voyage, Zeus sunk his ship with one well-placed thunderbolt. After Ceyx's apparition appeared to her bearing the news, Alcyone threw herself into the sea in grief over her beloved's demise. Instead of journeying to the underworld, they were both transformed into halcyons/kingfishers. As a bird, Alcyone laid her eggs on the beach around the time of the solstice. Her father subdued the winds and calmed the waves to allow her peace. Alcyone has been honored as the brightest star in the Pleiades, which are most prominent in winter.

In the past in Britain, this bird was known simply as a Fisher. According to folklore, sighting a kingfisher was an omen of good things to come and its appearance was believed to calm life's turmoil. The direction in which a kingfisher was sighted was important for weather divination.

In medieval Europe, the kingfisher was a symbol of protection and good luck, and keeping one of its feathers in your pocket was believed to hold misfortune at bay. The kingfisher's feathers were powerful in other ways, too. A woman who wore them was said to have more beauty than others around her. According to the Tartars of southern Russia, kingfisher feathers were powerful love talismans.

Magical Workings

Place an image of kingfisher on your altar on December 15 to mark Alcyone's feast day and the beginning of the halcyon days. More than anything, this legendary bird is a symbol of the winter solstice and the peace, hope, and harmony of this season. Also place an image or figurine of kingfisher on your Yule altar to engender these qualities and invite warmth to your ritual.

Call on this bird when you engage in any form of divination and prophecy to aid your concentration and bring clarity of purpose. Kingfisher is also an aid for spells dealing with love and marriage, especially when seeking fidelity and happiness. For centuries, this bird was portrayed in literature as a symbol of harmony among the elements. Kingfisher is also instrumental when inviting abundance and prosperity to the home. Call on it for protection from storms as well as stormy times in life.

Make Connection

To connect with kingfisher energy, sit on your knees in bed and pull the covers up over your head as you crouch forward, creating a tunnel to represent the kingfisher's burrow. Leave the opposite end open so you can easily breathe. Enjoy the darkness and warmth of this tunnel/nest. Kingfisher makes its presence felt with a gentle and calm sense of security. Let the experience run its course, and then thank kingfisher for its blessings.

Also connect with kingfisher by locating the Pleiades in the sky. They are visible from late autumn to early spring. To find them, locate the big hourglass figure of Orion. Orient yourself so the alignment of the three stars in Orion's belt looks higher on the right than the left. Follow the direction that the stars point to the right, and look for a cluster of six stars in a semicircle. It has the soft glow of a nebulous haze that can usually be seen with the naked eye.

Associations

Element(s): Earth, water

Sabbat(s): Litha, Yule

Bird Identification

Belted Kingfisher (*Megaceryle alcyon* syn. *Ceryle alcyon*)

Size: 11 to 14 inches

Wingspan: 19 to 23 inches

Comparative size: Pigeon

Description: Stocky body; large head with shaggy crest; straight, thick bill; short legs; medium-length, square-tipped tail; upperparts powder blue with white spotting on wings and tail; white underparts with a broad, blue breast band

Male: One blue band across the breast

Female: Two breast bands, one blue, one chestnut or rusty; more brightly colored than the male

Range: From Alaska across Canada and south throughout the United States, Mexico, and Central America

Habitat: Along the edges of streams, rivers, ponds, lakes, and calm marine waters

Eggs: White, smooth, and glossy

Collective noun(s): A concentration of kingfishers

Lark and Meadowlark:
Horned Lark, Eastern Meadowlark, Western Meadowlark

Horned Lark (Eremophila alpestris)

Although the lark and meadowlark are not related, they have remarkably similar plumage coloration and patterns as well as behavior and nesting habits, which has prompted their close association. Because of this, and the fact that their energy is so much alike, they are presented together in this book.

The horned lark is the only true lark in North America. While meadowlarks are actually in the blackbird family, these birds reminded early English settlers of the sky lark (*Alauda arvensis*) back home. The sky lark, and larks in general, were regarded as the bird of poets. Rising up from the ground singing, they were considered intermediaries between heaven and earth. Meadowlarks also angle their bodies upward on takeoff and sing in flight, enhancing their association with larks.

Sacred to the Gauls, the lark lingered in French folklore as a good omen. Its feathers were used in charms to provide protection from natural disasters as well as from negative people. While most birds in the blackbird family were indicators of rain in folklore, meadowlarks were just the opposite and foretold fine weather. Larks were an indication of good weather, as well.

The name *lark* comes from the Anglo-Saxon *lawerce*, meaning "traitor." [89] The only association with traitors is believed to come from the lark's enthusiastic early morning singing, which would rouse lovers who must part by dawn. This bird has been called the herald of the dawn, and rising early is called "getting up with the lark."

Magical Workings

Since early times, lark and meadowlark have been considered symbols of the future and springtime, making them appropriate birds to include on your Ostara altar. The cheerfulness and joy associated with these birds are not superficial qualities, but arrived at through introspection and awakening to the song that is in your heart. Call on lark and meadowlark for help with inner quests, finding clarity, and learning to trust intuition.

Because they help stoke the imagination, place an image of either bird on your desk, work table, or anywhere that you engage in creative activities. These birds can give your good luck charms or spells a boost, too. Although they soar to the heavens, lark and meadowlark aid in keeping us grounded. Call on them when centering and grounding after ritual.

Make Connection

To connect with lark and meadowlark energy, spend some solitary time in an open place. Sit on the ground if it is comfortable for you. Close your eyes and imagine yourself soaring up into the sky, rapidly descending, and then once more lifting high into the clouds. Again, you come back toward the earth, swooping low above the open ground, and then gently settling down in the short grass, feeling exalted and alive. If a sudden feeling of joy sweeps over you, lark or meadowlark is present.

Associations

Element(s): Air
Sabbat(s): Litha, Ostara
Solar system: Moon
Ogham: Ur (lark)
Magical beings: Fairies

---

89. Wells, *100 Birds and How They Got Their Names*, 133.

Bird Identification

Horned Lark (*Eremophila alpestris*)

Size: 6 to 8 inches

Wingspan: 11½ to 13½ inches

Comparative size: Sparrow to robin

Description: White or yellowish face and throat; black bib; broad, black stripe under eyes; black forehead with slanting feathers that give the appearance of horns; short, stout bill; heavily streaked brown upperparts; black tail with gray outer feathers

Male: Horn feathers usually erect

Female: Smaller bib; duller head and face; smaller horn feathers, rarely held erect

Range: From northern Canada, throughout most of the United States except southern Florida; into parts of Mexico

Habitat: Barren open fields, plains, beaches, and airports; prefers bare ground to short grass

Eggs: Pale gray with brown spots

Eastern Meadowlark (*Sturnella magna*)

Also known as: Common lark, field lark, meadow bird

Size: 9 to 11 inches

Wingspan: 14 to 16 inches

Comparative size: Robin

Description: Long, spear-shaped bill; short tail; rounded wings; brown-streaked upperparts; white-edged tail; bright yellow throat, breast, and underparts; black V on breast

Range: From southeastern Canada through eastern United States to Nebraska, Texas, and parts of the Southwest, into parts of Mexico and Central America

Habitat: Open country, meadows, and pastures

Eggs: White with brown and dull lavender spots

Western Meadowlark (*Sturnella neglecta*)

Also known as: Common meadowlark, field lark of the West, prairie lark

Size: 8 to 10 inches

Wingspan: 14 to 16 inches

Comparative size: Robin

Description: Long, slender bill; flat head; short, rounded wings; short, stiff tail; streaked brown upperparts; bright yellow underparts; black V on breast; yellow from throat onto cheeks

Range: From southern Canada, throughout the western United States into the Midwest, to the Gulf Coast into Mexico

Habitat: Meadows, plains, and prairies

Eggs: White spotted with brown, rust, or lavender

Collective noun(s): An ascension, a bevy, or an exaltation of larks

Loon:
Common Loon

Common Loon (Gavia immer)

The sound of the loon has been described as eerie, haunting, and otherworldly. According to author John McPhee, if the sound were human it would be "the laugh of the deeply insane."[90] Despite the phrase "crazy as a loon," the word *loon* is not related to *lunatic* but comes from the Old Norwegian *lom*, meaning "lame" or "clumsy."[91] While it is somewhat clumsy on land, in the water it's a whole different story, as this bird's scientific name reveals. *Gavia* is Latin for "aquatic bird" or "seabird," and *immer* comes from the Latin *immergere*, "to dive."[92]

Sometimes called a rain goose, loons are truly waterbirds and only go ashore to nest. The reason for their ungainliness on land is that their legs are placed far back on their bodies. This makes them great swimmers and powerful divers able to catch fish in underwater chases. The loon's only swimming equal in the bird world is the penguin.

While loons can fly, they need a long runway for takeoff because, unlike most birds, loons have solid bones. This makes them less buoyant in the water and enhances their diving abilities. Loons can dive about a hundred feet deep, earning them the name great

---

90. John McPhee, *The Survival of the Bark Canoe* (New York: Farrar, Straus and Giroux, 1982), 30.

91. Mark Nuttall, *Encyclopedia of the Arctic* (New York: Routledge, 2005), 497.

92. Sandrock and Prior, *The Scientific Nomenclature of Birds in the Upper Midwest*, 63.

northern diver in Britain.[93] Most loons ferry their hatchlings around on their backs until the young ones develop swimming skills.

In a Siberian creation myth, a loon and golden-eyed duck continually dove under water to collect mud and create land. Loons have also been featured in the legends of the Lakota Sioux and the Tsimshian of Alaska. The sound of the Ojibwa flute is said to have been inspired by the loon's call.

Being heard most often around sunset and calling to each other after dark has earned the loon an association with the night. In addition, this bird symbolizes the wildness and solitude of the north and has come to represent spiritual awakening.

Magical Workings

Loon is the bird to call on when you find yourself in a state of longing. Its hauntingly beautiful call expresses that deep, soul-felt tug at the heart from a source that is often unknown to us. Because of this, loon can help us reach new levels of consciousness and spirituality and help us find what we long for. Call on it for guidance with introspection and in finding solace.

As a bird that dives beneath the surface, loon can aid with dream work, help reveal and interpret past-life memories, and provide support when exploring the astral realm. It is a conduit to the imagination, inspiring satisfying expressions of creative energy. In addition, this bird helps us establish a deep connection with the natural world. Loon helps us find and kindle the spark of wisdom that flickers in the solitude of nature.

Make Connection

To connect with loon energy, place a tealight candle in a scallop shell or clamshell and float it on peaceful, calm water. This can be in a pond, a backyard pool, or even your bathtub. Sit in the dark and gaze at the candlelight as though you are gazing into the flame of your soul. Listen for the call of loon if you are within its range or hear it in your mind. Feel its call penetrate your soul with an ancient longing to understand the great mysteries. Hear loon call your spirit to follow and experience the natural world more deeply than you ever thought possible. When it feels appropriate, end the session, blow out the candle, and sit in silence to experience the solitude and solace of loon.

---

93. Laura Erickson, *For the Birds: An Uncommon Guide* (Duluth, MN: Pfeifer-Hamilton, 1994), 22.

Association

Element(s): Water

Bird Identification

COMMON LOON (*GAVIA IMMER*)

Also known as: Diver, great northern diver

Size: 26 to 36 inches

Wingspan: 41 to 52 inches

Comparative size: Goose

Description: Rounded head; red eyes; daggerlike bill; long, heavy body; short tail usually not visible; white throat and breast; black head and bill in summer, gray in winter; black-and-white spotting or striping on the back in summer, plain gray in winter

Range: From Alaska throughout most of Canada and the United States

Habitat: Seacoasts, inland reservoirs, and lakes

Eggs: Brown with dark splotches

Collective noun(s): A cry or a raft of loons

Magpie:
Black-Billed Magpie

Black-Billed Magpie (Pica hudsonia)

In thirteenth-century England, this bird was known by its French name, *pie*, which came from its Latin name, *pica*.[94] From the early fifteenth century, Mag, a diminutive form of the woman's name Margaret, became associated with idle chatter, and by the seventeenth century the two words were put together as *magpie* for the bird's name. As a relative of jays and crows, magpies know how to keep a flow of raucous calls going. Although magpies spend more time on the ground than many other birds, they band together in flight to mob a raptor or other predator that threatens their neighborhood.

Folklore attributed this bird with magical powers, and encountering magpies could indicate good or bad luck depending on how many were seen. This was the source of many magpie rhymes. To counteract any negative influence, it was customary to cross your fingers and say: *"I cross the magpie, the magpie crosses me; bad luck to the magpie; and good luck to me."* [95] Raising your hat or bowing to the bird could also counteract any bad influence. Seeing one fly away from the direction of the sun was a bad omen that

---

94. Mark Morton, *Cupboard Love 2: A Dictionary of Culinary Curiosities, Second Revised Edition* (Toronto, Canada: Insomniac Press, 2004), 225.

95. Armstrong, *The Life and Lore of the Bird in Nature, Art, Myth and Literature*, 62.

could be countered by saying: *"Bad luck to the bird that goes widdershins."* 96 In England, a magpie seen on the roof was a good omen, and in America it meant that the house would not be destroyed by a storm.

In China and Korea, magpies represent good luck and happiness. The Chinese celebrate Magpie Festival on the seventh day of the seventh lunar month of the Chinese calendar and is Valentine's Day for young women. It is based on a legend in which the Queen of Heaven forbade a weaver woman from marrying a cowherd and separated them by a river. Once a year, all the magpies in the world would gather to form a bridge over the river so the couple could be together.

Magpies, as well as crows and ravens, have been observed holding what can only be described as funerals. When one of their own is discovered dead, others gather around it. Some birds may leave and return with pieces of grass or pine needles that they place alongside their fallen friend. They usually stand by the corpse for several minutes and then fly off in silence.

Magical Workings

With starkly contrasting black and white feathers, magpie is a bird of balance that treads the realms between danger and death, and love and happiness. As an agent of prophecy it can aid in all forms of divination and the interpretation of messages and omens. Keep an image of magpie with your divination tools to draw its power into them.

Call on magpie to boost good luck spells and bring forth what you want to manifest. Listen carefully and you will learn to develop your skills, know when to seize the right opportunities, and discover how to use your willpower wisely. Magpie is also an aid for contacting spirits and can be called upon for support at Samhain.

Make Connection

To connect with magpie energy, sew or pin together two large pieces of cloth, one white and the other black. Hold an end in each hand and drape the cloth over your shoulders. Open your arms to spread your "wings" as you slowly circle the room reciting the magpie rhyme: *"One for sorrow, two for joy; Three for a girl, four for a boy. Five for silver, six for gold; Seven for a secret, never to be told."* 97 And then add: *"Magpie of wisdom, bird of prophecy; Use your skill, to guide me."* After this, sit in front of your altar for a few minutes

---

96. Tate, *Flights of Fancy*, 77.
97. Harry Oliver, *Black Cats & Four-Leaf Clovers: The Origins of Old Wives' Tales and Superstitions in Our Everyday Lives* (New York: Perigee Books, 2010), 47.

holding the image of a magpie in your mind, and then let it fade. Use the cloth draped over your shoulders whenever you want to call on magpie's energy and wisdom.

Visible from June to October, the Cygnus constellation can also be used to connect with magpie. The constellation, which represents a swan in the West, represents the magpie bridge in China. To find it, go outside about an hour after sunset and look straight up. The bright star directly overhead marks the tail of the swan and the top of the constellation's cross shape of stars. Recite the magpie rhyme when you see it to honor this bird and call on its wisdom.

Associations

Zodiac: Aries
Element(s): Air, earth
Sabbat(s): Samhain
Goddess: Aphrodite
God: Bacchus
Magical beings: Fairies

Bird Identification

BLACK-BILLED MAGPIE (*PICA HUDSONIA*)
Size: 18 to 24 inches
Wingspan: 22 to 24 inches
Comparative size: Crow to red-tailed hawk
Description: Long, diamond-shaped tail; black back, bill, head, breast, and flanks; blue-green iridescence on wings and tail; white belly and shoulder patches
Range: From southern Alaska across western Canada and south through the Rocky Mountains and western plains states
Habitat: Open woodlands, meadows, grasslands, and sagebrush plains
Eggs: Greenish tan with dark brown speckles

Collective noun(s): A charm, a mischief, a tiding, or a tribe of magpies

Mockingbird:
Northern Mockingbird

Northern Mockingbird (Mimus polyglottos)

A great deal of folklore is associated with this bird. In legends of the Pueblo people of the Southwest, a mockingbird granted humans the gift of speech. According to black folklore in the antebellum South, the mockingbird was a keeper of supernatural wisdom. In legends from Tennessee and North Carolina, a mockingbird sitting on your chimney and singing at night meant that someone in the house was going to die. If you heard it singing nearby all night, it meant that trouble was on the way. However, hearing it on a moonlit night meant that you would discover something that would make you happy. If an unmarried woman saw one fly over her, it was a sign that she would marry within the year.

Mockingbirds are rarely intimidated by animals or larger birds. In fact, they have been known to attack eagles. If they feel threatened by a cat, dog, or other terrestrial animal, they will harass it with dive-bombing maneuvers. Despite their wily reputations, these birds have been kept as pets, and they have captured people's imaginations. Mockingbirds have cropped up in songs such as the traditional lullaby "Hush Little Baby" and the mid-nineteenth-century popular song "Listen to the Mockingbird." A century later, the latter song was the theme for the cartoon birds Heckle and Jeckle, even though they were supposed to be magpies.

The mockingbird's scientific name, *Mimus polyglottos*, is Latin for "mimic" and "many-tongued," respectively.[98] These names are due to the bird's ability to mimic sounds—not only other birds but crickets, frogs, and even machinery and car alarms. Mockingbirds continually add new sounds to their repertoires throughout their lives. Erroneously believed to master the song of other birds, only about ten percent of the mockingbird's song is imitation of other bird's melodies; the rest is improvisation. They tend to sing loudest during twilight hours and sometimes during the full moon.

Magical Workings

Mockingbird is a creature of communication and imagination that can help stoke your creativity and help you find your unique method of expression. It can help you find the power of your voice and use it to foster understanding in those around you. Call on this bird to guide you through challenging experiences and to help you gain the most knowledge from them.

Mockingbird can boost spells for courage or aid you anytime you need to overcome fear. It can also be called upon for protection, especially for the home. Include this bird in personal rituals when seeking harmony in an intimate relationship. Honor this bird, which likes to sing during the full moon, at your esbat rituals.

Make Connection

To connect with mockingbird energy, sing like one, or more appropriately, improvise like one. During morning or evening twilight or a full moon, place a picture of a mockingbird on your altar and sit quietly while gazing at it. When you are ready, begin singing one of the mockingbird songs if you know them. If you are not familiar with them, choose a song that you feel relates to the mockingbird. Even if you don't know the complete tune or all the words, let your imagination take the lead and let the song evolve. You may begin to feel that your creativity is being guided. This is a sign that mockingbird has joined you.

Associations

Element(s): Air, fire

---

98. Murphy-Hiscock, *Birds: A Spiritual Field Guide*, 120.

Bird Identification
Northern Mockingbird (*Mimus polyglottos*)

Size: 8 to 10 inches

Wingspan: 12 to 14 inches

Comparative size: Robin

Description: Slender body; gray-brown upperparts; pale to whitish breast, belly, and underparts; small head; long, thin bill with a very slight downward curve; short, broad wings with two white wing bars; white patch under each wing can be seen in flight; long tail with white outer feathers

Range: Throughout the lower forty-eight states and into Mexico

Habitat: Open grassy areas in fields, parks, or suburbs with shrubby vegetation and fruiting bushes

Eggs: Pale blue or greenish-white with red or brown splotches

Collective noun(s): An echo, an exactness, or an impression of mockingbirds

Nighthawk and Nightjar:
Common Nighthawk, Eastern Whip-Poor-Will, Common Poorwill

Common Nighthawk (Chordeiles minor syn. Caprimulgus minor)

Creatures of the night are generally viewed with suspicion, and, like the owl, nightjars and nighthawks have been considered birds of ill omen. The nightjar's silent flight gives it a ghostlike quality, and its sound has been described as spooky or otherworldly. Loudest at dusk, the nightjar has been so named because of its jarringly loud sound.

Not to be outdone when it comes to strange noises, the nighthawk's flight pattern of swoops and sudden changes in direction creates a weird, some say UFO-like, buzzing sound. The bird uses this sound to get attention during mating season and at other times to startle predators. Its folk names include spinner bird and wheel bird because the buzzing sound has been likened to a spinning wheel. Despite its name, the nighthawk is not a hawk.

An earlier genus name for the nighthawk and nightjar comes from the Latin *capra*, meaning "nanny goat," and *mulgus*, "to milk."[99] To explain their unusually wide mouths, Aristotle wrote that these birds took milk from goats. In reality, their mouths allow them to catch large insects.

---

99. Adele Nozedar, *The Secret Language of Birds: A Treasury of Myths, Folklore and Inspirational True Stories* (London: Harper Element, 2006), 252.

Another unusual characteristic of nighthawks and nightjars is their large eyes, which have a reflective layer. This allows them to see extremely well at night. It also gives their eyes an eerie glow, which adds to their otherworldly reputation. In addition, nightjars lay their eggs according to the cycle of the moon so they hatch about ten days before a full moon.

Magical Workings

These birds of the night help us see into the inner and outer darkness. Call on either of these birds for support in divination practices and understanding messages of prophecy. The liminal nighthawk can help us develop heightened awareness and guide us through the in-between times of the day or year.

By their natures, nightjar and nighthawk provide a boost to night magic and any form of nocturnal practice. Also call on them for spells to bring success. Both of these birds aid in accessing the fairy realm and can teach us the fine points of adaptability and camouflage.

Make Connection

To connect with nighthawk and nightjar energy, sit in a completely dark room. Pull your energy in close to you and visualize yourself blending in with your surroundings. In a soft whisper say: *"Nighthawk, Nightjar, how I wonder where you are. Guide me through your world so dark, on this journey I now embark."* Listen carefully for any sounds and use your senses to feel what is around you. Although these birds are normally loud, contact in this manner is whisper-soft.

Associations

NIGHTHAWK

Element(s): Air, earth

Goddesses: Athena, the Fates, Freya, Frigg, Minerva, the Norns

Magical beings: Elves, fairies

NIGHTJAR

Element(s): Air, earth

Goddess: Lilith

God: Hypnos

Solar system: Moon

Moon phases: Full, waxing

Magical beings: Elves, fairies

Bird Identification

NIGHTHAWK

COMMON NIGHTHAWK (*CHORDEILES MINOR SYN. CAPRIMULGUS MINOR*)

Size: 8 to 9 inches

Wingspan: 21 to 22 inches

Comparative size: Robin

Description: A short neck gives the appearance of a large head; long, pointed wings with broad white wing bar; long, notched, or square-tipped tail; mottled brownish-black over all

Male: White throat patch; white tail bar

Female: Buffy throat patch; no tail bar

Range: From central Canada to Nova Scotia and throughout most of the United States into Mexico and South America

Habitat: Open woodlands, clearings, fields, suburbs, and urban areas

Eggs: Creamy white to pale olive-gray with gray, brown, and black speckles

NIGHTJARS

EASTERN WHIP-POOR-WILL (*ANTROSTOMUS VOCIFERUS SYN. CAPRIMULGUS VOCIFERUS*)

Size: 8 to 10 inches

Wingspan: 17½ to 19 inches

Comparative size: Robin

Description: Large, round head; large eyes; wide mouth with short bill and forward-facing whiskers (bristle feathers); stout chest; body tapers to long tail and wings; small feet and short legs; gray and brown mottling all over; black throat

Male: White tips on outer tail feathers; white patch below throat

Female: All brown tail with buff tips on outer tail feathers; light brown patch below throat

Range: From southern Saskatchewan to the Maritime Provinces in Canada and south through the Midwest to the East Coast, Florida, and around the Gulf Coast into Central America

Habitat: Dry, open woodlands near fields

Eggs: Cream or grayish-white, with lavender-gray, yellowish-brown, or pale brown marbling

COMMON POORWILL (*PHALAENOPTILUS NUTTALLII*)

Size: 7 to 8 inches

Wingspan: 12 to 13 inches

Comparative size: Sparrow to robin

Description: Large head and eyes; wide mouth with tiny bill and forward-facing whiskers (bristle feathers); short, rounded tail; rounded wings; tiny feet; mottled gray-brown all over; black throat with white patch beneath; outer tail feathers tipped with white

Range: From southern British Columbia and Alberta in Canada and throughout most of the western United States

Habitat: Dry, open grassy or sagebrush areas

Eggs: White or pinkish

Collective noun(s) for nightjars: A seek or an invisibility of whip-poor-wills. There is also a kettle of nighthawks.

Nuthatch:
Red-Breasted Nuthatch, White-Breasted Nuthatch

White-Breasted Nuthatch (Sitta carolinensis)

At first glance you may think that a nuthatch is a little woodpecker circling its way down a tree trunk. However, the giveaway is that this bird goes headfirst down the tree, which is something a woodpecker does not do. Nuthatches even hang upside down on branches to get insects and often roost upside down like bats. They can do these daring acrobatics because they have an unusually long back toe.

The name *nuthatch* is derived from the Anglo-Saxon *hakken* or *hacken*, meaning "to break."[100] This describes how they feed, by wedging nuts and hard seeds into crevices and then hacking them open with their sharp bills. The noise they make when doing this can be heard up to two hundred yards away.[101] This activity has earned the nuthatch the nicknames of woodcracker and jar bird. The nuthatch has also been called topsy-turvy bird and tree mouse. However, in Texas, these birds had the nickname devil-down-head because they were thought to hang upside down so they could face the devil.

According to Norse myth, the nuthatch was regarded as a bird of wisdom. One of the poems in the Poetic Edda tells how nuthatches directed the hero Sigurd to Gudrun, the

---

100. Wells, *100 Birds and How They Got Their Names*, 154.

101. W. Swaysland, *Familiar Wild Birds, Volume 4* (New York: Cassell and Company, 1901), 29–30.

woman who would become his wife. They also warned Sigurd about the betrayal by his foster father.

Magical Workings

This little climbing bird shows us the importance of adaptability, keeping faith in our abilities, and maintaining courage no matter how precarious our situations may seem at times. Ask nuthatch for help when connecting with nature spirits. Also, call on this bird for help in bringing abundance into your life. It is a bird of the mind that encourages us to manifest our ideas but also reminds us to stay grounded no matter how high we fly.

Follow this little bird's direction for sharpening your intuition. It can also serve as a guide for deepening spirituality, especially when seeking inner truth and higher wisdom. Perhaps like Odin, you may receive something profound. Nuthatch brings us a different perspective of the world and our lives. Most importantly, we can discover that we can move in any direction our path calls.

Make Connection

To connect with nuthatch energy, lie on your couch with your feet and legs up on the back and your head dangling over the edge of the seat so you are basically upside down. As an alternative, lie on your back across your bed with your head over the edge. If neither position is comfortable or safe for you, simply lie on your back. Close your eyes and visualize nuthatch guiding you carefully headfirst down a tree. Feel its energy keeping your feet steady and secure. As you follow, it leads you around the tree trunk and then back up to the branches where you hang upside down together. Listen carefully for any message it may send you.

Associations

Element(s): Air

Trees: Hickory, maple, oak, pine, spruce

Flower: Sunflower

Bird Identification

RED-BREASTED NUTHATCH (*SITTA CANADENSIS*)

Size: 4 to 5 inches

Wingspan: 7 to 8 inches

Comparative size: Sparrow

Description: Stocky body; very short neck; short tail; long bill; short, broad wings

Male: Black cap and eye line; white eyebrows; blue-gray back with rusty underparts

Female: Head and markings duller colors; lighter underparts

Range: From the southeastern Alaskan coast, across Canada, and throughout the United States

Habitat: Mainly coniferous forests and mountains

Eggs: White, creamy, or pinkish white and speckled with reddish brown

WHITE-BREASTED NUTHATCH (*SITTA CAROLINENSIS*)

Size: 5 to 6 inches

Wingspan: 8 to 10 inches

Comparative size: Sparrow

Description: Small body; large head; very short neck; short tail; long, narrow bill; gray-blue back; white face, throat, and chest; chestnut-brown lower belly and under tail

Male: Dark crown and nape; reddish-brown rump and flanks

Female: Gray or dull black crown and nape

Range: Parts of southern Canada, throughout most of the United States, and into parts of Mexico and Central America

Habitat: Deciduous and mixed forests, woodland edges, and residential areas

Eggs: Creamy white to pinkish-white speckled with reddish brown, gray, or purple

Collective noun(s): A jar of nuthatches

Oriole:
Baltimore Oriole, Bullock's Oriole

Baltimore Oriole (Icterus galbula)

While orioles do not figure in legends and folklore, these birds are skilled weavers and have much to share and teach us. Although not related to the orioles of Europe, the North American birds were given the same common name because of their similarity in appearance.

The name *oriole* comes from the Latin *aureolus*, which means "golden" and refers to their stunning yellow or orange coloration.[102] The Baltimore oriole was so named to honor George Calvert, Lord Baltimore (c. 1580–1632), investor and founder of the Maryland colony, whose coat-of-arms matched this bird's black and orange colors.

The two species of orioles included in this book interbreed where their ranges overlap on the Great Plains. The calls of both orioles are very similar, but the song of the Baltimore is more melodic. Although both male and female Bullock's orioles sing, they have slightly different songs. For a time, the Baltimores and Bullock's were considered one species and called the northern oriole. However, they have been returned to their former statuses.

---

102. Fraser and Gray, *Australian Bird Names*, 230.

Orioles are known for their intricately woven, pouch-like nests, which hang underneath branches. This skill strongly echoes the Bird Goddess as giver of crafts as well as all the later goddesses associated with spinning and weaving.

Magical Workings

Vivid plumage has made oriole a symbol of cheerfulness and energy as well as springtime. With its bright colors balanced by black, this bird brings stability to home, marriage, and relationships.

Just as the fate goddesses are associated with spinning and weaving, oriole can be an aid in developing skills for divination and prophecy. Call on it to help you weave your path and manifest what you seek. It is also an aid for spellwork. Oriole is instrumental for connecting with the fairy realm and tree spirits. Place an offering for fairies or tree spirits at the base of a tree, especially if it holds an oriole nest. Also, leave some seeds for the bird.

Make Connection

To connect with oriole energy, gather two candles, one orange and one black; orange and black yarn or ribbon; and a small basket. Sit quietly in front of your altar for a moment or two, and then light the candles. Slowly wind the orange and black yarn or ribbon around the outside of the basket. When you have finished, hold the basket as you say: *"Oriole bird of black and gold, bring your presence to this basket I hold."* Bring the image of an oriole into your mind. Nothing may happen the first few times you try this, but when oriole becomes present in your life you will be able to visualize small whitish-blue or gray eggs in the basket.

Associations

Element(s): Air, fire
Goddesses: Athena, the Fates, Freya, Frigg, Minerva, the Norns
Solar system: Sun
Trees: Elm, maple, cottonwood
Magical beings: Elves, fairies, tree spirits

Bird Identification

Baltimore Oriole (*Icterus galbula*)

Size: 7 to 8 inches

Wingspan: 9 to 12 inches

Comparative size: Sparrow to robin

Description: Thick neck; long, black legs; black, pointed bill with thick base; orange outer tail feathers

Male: Mostly bright orange; black head and upper back; black wings with one white bar

Female: Yellow-orange breast; gray head and back; two white wing bars

Range: Eastern United States and southern Canada to the Rocky Mountains, down to Texas and parts of Central America

Habitat: Open woods and forest edges, orchards, parks, and backyards

Eggs: Pale gray or blue-white with brown, black, or lavender blotches

Bullock's Oriole (*Icterus bullockii*)

Size: 7 to 8 inches

Wingspan: 9 to 12 inches

Comparative size: Sparrow to robin

Description: Long tail; dark gray, pointed bill; long, grayish legs; one or two wing bars

Male: Black back, nape, and crown; other parts of head and underparts orange-yellow; black eye line, chin, and center of throat; orange-yellow or yellow rump; yellow tail tipped with black and black middle feather; black wings edged white; white wing patch

Female: Pale gray-brown to yellowish upperparts with dark streaking; yellowish to green-gray underparts with paler belly; some black on throat; gray-brown wings with one or two wing bars

Range: From the West Coast of the United States, through the Rockies and the westernmost plains states, into Mexico and parts of Central America

Habitat: Open woodlands, riverbank stands of trees, and parkland

Eggs: Pale blue or grayish white splotched with purplish-brown lines

Collective noun(s): A pitch or a split of orioles

Osprey

Osprey (Pandion haliaetus)

The common name *osprey* comes from the medieval Latin *avis prede*, which means "bird of prey."[103] Ospreys are large birds that have the distinction of being the only raptor that dives into the water to catch fish instead of plucking them from the surface. This trait earned these birds the nickname of Fish Hawk. Although they dive feet-first, they often completely submerge several feet down. Amazingly, from under water they are strong enough to lift themselves and their prey into the air. The osprey's unusual outer toe and barbs on the pads of its feet allow the bird to hang on to its slippery catch during this challenging maneuver.

The species name, *haliaetus*, means "sea hawk."[104] Aristotle described and referred to ospreys as eagles and for centuries they were considered as such. In Nova Scotia, they are still sometimes called sea eagles. Although the osprey was originally classified as a hawk, it is neither a hawk nor an eagle. It now has its own family and genus, Pandionidae and *Pandion*, respectively. These names were loosely derived from a king in Greek mythology, Pandion, whose story has numerous versions. Although his two daughters were turned into a swallow and a nightingale, their suitor was a hawk.

---

103. David Brodsky, *Spanish Vocabulary: An Etymological Approach* (Austin, TX: University of Texas Press, 2008), 117.

104. Wells, *100 Birds and How They Got Their Names*, 159.

During the Middle Ages, ospreys were thought to have magical powers. According to sixteenth-century folklore, they were said to put a spell on fish because they caught them so easily. In English folklore, seeing an osprey meant good luck; however, only hearing its call meant bad luck. Other legends said that the osprey had two different feet: one with talons to catch prey, the other webbed like a goose for swimming.

This bird came close to extinction but their numbers rebounded after the ban on the pesticide DDT. They are now one of the most widespread birds of prey and can be found on every continent except Antarctica. When soaring, the osprey's wings form a distinctive *M* shape.

Magical Workings

Osprey is a bird of action and freedom, and it can help us find the particular path that is most suitable to our talents and interests. Encouraging insight, it dares us not only to follow an idea but to take the plunge and follow the beat of a different drum. Osprey helps us learn to trust where our curiosity may lead. Call on its support when developing divination skills.

Place an image of this bird on your altar to foster courage and confidence during challenging times. As a bird of abundance, osprey can be called upon to give spells of prosperity a boost. It is also a bird of good luck, and if you see one, make a wish.

Make Connection

Connect with osprey energy by visualizing that you are standing on a platform above a wide bay. Slowly bring your elbows out to the sides at or higher than shoulder height and let your hands hang down as you create the letter *M* with your arms. Imagine that you step from the platform and fly over the water. Feel the wind and smell the salt air as you glide effortlessly. When osprey makes its presence known, you may feel slightly lifted during this exercise.

Associations

Element(s): Air, water

Solar system: Moon

Bird Identification

OSPREY (*PANDION HALIAETUS*)

Size: 21 to 23 inches

Wingspan: 59 to 71 inches

Comparative size: Red-tailed hawk

Description: Slender body; long, narrow wings; long legs; brown upperparts and white underparts; white head with a broad brown stripe through the eye and on side of face

Range: Throughout most of Alaska, Canada, and the United States into Mexico, and Central and South America

Habitat: Salt marshes, rivers, ponds, reservoirs, estuaries, seacoasts, and coral reefs

Eggs: Creamy to pinkish cinnamon with reddish-brown spots

Collective noun(s): A duet of osprey

Ostrich

Ostrich (**Struthio camelus**)

The ostrich is the largest and heaviest bird in the world. Its scientific name comes from the Greek *strouthos*, meaning "bird," and *kamelos*, "camel." [105] As its name suggests, the ostrich was known as the camel bird. This is because of its long neck and prominent camel-like eyes that are fringed with sweeping eyelashes. Like camels, this bird gets along fine in high temperatures and can go without water for extended periods of time.

The biggest myth about the ostrich is that it buries its head in the sand to avoid danger. This is a misconception of a defensive behavior that is used especially in its nesting area when it lies down with its head and neck along the ground to be less visible. Despite its size, this maneuver, along with its coloring, actually allows it to blend in with the surroundings. At other times when threatened, the ostrich will run away or stand and fight. With long legs and sharp claws, it can kill a human or a lion. Speaking of lions, the male ostrich has a warning call that has been likened to the sound of a lion, although it's not a roar.

Weighing around three hundred pounds would require monumental wings to get this bird off the ground. Instead, the ostrich uses its rather small wings as rudders to aid in changing direction while running. This bird can sprint up to thirty-eight miles per

---

105. Fraser and Gray, *Australian Bird Names*, 2.

hour.[106] Because it is flightless, the ostrich has no need for typical flight feathers, which are asymmetrical and heavier on one side than the other. Instead, it has fluffy plumes, which give it a shaggy appearance. The ancient Egyptians regarded these symmetrical, balanced feathers as a symbol of truth. Maat, the goddess of justice, was usually depicted wearing an ostrich plume headdress.

Ostrich feathers were a prized commodity for thousands of years. Plumes adorned the helmets of medieval knights, women's fashions, and the robes of royalty. The craze for ostrich plumes almost led to this bird's demise in the early nineteenth century.[107] At that point, ostriches began to be raised on farms where their feathers could be plucked without having to hunt and kill the birds.

Since ancient times, ostrich eggshells have been prized and were a commodity for trade around the Mediterranean. Over time, ostrich shell becomes hard and shiny and looks almost like ivory. Ostrich eggshells have been found in Mesopotamian and Etruscan tombs as well as burials in Egypt and other areas of Africa. In Egypt, they were also fashioned into drinking cups and perfume containers.

Magical Workings

Ostrich's long association with truth makes it an ideal aid in divination practices. Call on this bird to guide you to the right interpretation of messages during any type of reading. When seeking justice in legal matters, place an ostrich plume on your altar as you state how you would like events to unfold. Ostrich is a bird of practicality and can help you as long as your desired outcome is based in reality. Also call on it for courage and protection. For grounding and centering your energy after ritual, visualize ostrich stretched along the desert sand.

Make Connection

Place a picture of ostrich on your altar and gaze at it as you bend your elbows and tuck your thumbs under your arms. Move around the room as you slowly and gracefully raise and lower your elbows out to the sides as though your arms are the small wings of ostrich. Hold your head high and visualize yourself as this bird with majestic plumes. Your

---

106. Edgar Williams, *Ostrich* (London: Reaktion Books, 2013), 39.
107. Nozedar, *The Secret Language of Birds*, 257.

feathers and eggshells are prized items for their beauty, but you know it is also because they hold the energy of knowledge and truth. Dwell in the thought of being able to produce such exquisite objects. When you find the truth in this, ostrich may speak to you.

Associations

Element(s): Air, fire

Goddess: Maat

Bird Identification

OSTRICH (*STRUTHIO CAMELUS*)

Size: 6 to 8 feet tall

Wingspan: 5 to 6 feet

Comparative size: Larger than a human

Description: Long legs; long, thin neck; small head; large, rounded body; light fuzz on neck and legs; large plumes on body and wings give a shaggy appearance

Male: Black body; buff to white tail-feather tips; white on wings; neck, head, and legs whitish or pink

Female: Medium brown-gray body; light brown neck, head, and legs

Range: Central Africa and parts of southwestern Africa; also raised in farms around the world

Habitat: Desert and savanna areas; semiarid plains

Eggs: Whitish-buff sometimes with light brown markings; average 5 to 6 inches long and weigh approximately 3 pounds

Owl:
Barn Owl, Great Horned Owl, Long-Eared Owl, Snowy Owl

Snowy Owl (**Bubo scandiacus**)

As we have seen, the association of the owl with the Goddess is ancient and enduring. Dating to approximately 13,000 BCE, a depiction of her as a snowy owl was found on a wall in the Trois Frères cave in southwestern France.[108] This image marks the earliest image of a bird of an identifiable species.

Throughout Old Europe, images of owl eyes were believed to carry the Goddess's sacred power. The Egyptian owl hieroglyph represented the letter *M* and was a symbol of wisdom and goddess-related knowledge. In Greece, the owl goddess became Athena, who was associated with wisdom and considered lucky especially to soldiers.

The Romans believed the owl to be an ally of Hecate and associated it with shape-shifting witches. They also considered the owl an omen of death, initiating an association that has lasted for millennia. In later folklore of many cultures, owls were associated with sorcery and witchcraft, and to see or hear one was an omen of death. The barn owl often appears ghostly pale when seen at night. This, and the fact that owls fly almost in silence

---

108. Armstrong, *The Life and Lore of the Bird in Nature, Art, Myth and Literature*, 200.

because of the fluffy edges of their wings, has fueled its association with death and sorcery.

Despite the negativity, owls maintained their status as protectors. In medieval Europe, a dead owl nailed to a barn was believed to protect the structure against storms and lightning. In China, owl-shaped ornaments hung on a house were thought to protect it against fire.

The name *owl* is said to come from the Latin *ulula*, meaning "owl." [109] Most owls are in the family Strigidae, which comes from the Latin *strix*, meaning "screech." [110] The great horned owl is the quintessential owl of storybooks and the most common one in North America. It is also the most dangerous predator for crows. With extremely acute hearing, the long-eared owl can grab its prey in complete darkness. The male's barking calls can be heard up to a mile away. Unlike other owls, the snowy owl is a day bird.

Magical Workings

Owl is an aid for dream work, all forms of prophecy, and deciphering omens. It supports the development of psychic abilities, especially clairaudience and clairvoyance. This bird is also a guide for astral travel and shamanic work as well as otherworld or underworld journeys. Owl can help you find the bridge between the seen and unseen worlds.

Call on owl for support and protection during magic work as it serves as a guardian. As befits this bird, call on owl when you seek higher wisdom or secret knowledge. It provides insight and clarity when searching for truth.

While owl is associated with death, it is also linked with rebirth and renewal. Invite owl to your Samhain and Imbolc rituals as you enter and return from the dark of the year. Also, place an owl figurine or picture on your altar to honor loved ones when they return to the Goddess.

Make Connection

To connect with owl energy, sit outside at dusk. Be very still and listen as darkness enfolds you. Visualize yourself as an owl sitting on a tree branch as you absorb the sounds of the night. Imagine that you take flight. Feel your body lift from the branch and your wings carry you silently across an open field to another tree. Bring into your mind the sound of an owl and very softly call "*who*" three times. Don't be surprised at what you may hear in return.

---

109. Cynthia Berger, *Owls: Wild Guide* (Mechanicsburg, PA: Stackpole Books, 2005), 27.
110. Ibid., 95.

Associations

Zodiac: Aries, Capricorn

Element(s): Air, water

Time of day: Dusk

Sabbat(s): Imbolc, Litha, Samhain, Yule

Goddesses: Artemis, Athena, Cailleach, Hecate, Lakshmi, Minerva, Persephone

Gods: Ares, Asclepius, Hades, Indra

Solar system: Moon

Trees: Beech, cottonwood, juniper, pine

Bird Identification

BARN OWL (*TYTO ALBA*)

Size: 12 to 16 inches

Wingspan: 39 to 49 inches

Comparative size: Pigeon to crow

Description: Long, rounded wings; short tail; long legs; rounded head; ear tufts; dark eyes; buff and gray mix on head, back, and upper wings; white face, underparts, and under wings

Female: More reddish and heavily spotted breast

Range: Throughout most of the United States except for parts of the upper plains states, the Appalachians, and New England; down through Mexico, Central America, and South America

Habitat: Grasslands, marshes, woodlots, ranch land, brushy fields, suburbs, and cities

Eggs: Dull white

GREAT HORNED OWL (*BUBO VIRGINIANUS*)

Size: 18 to 25 inches

Wingspan: 39 to 57 inches

Comparative size: Crow to red-tailed hawk

Description: Thick body; broad, rounded wings; large, yellow eyes; two prominent feathered tufts on the head; overall pale to sooty gray-brown mottling; reddish-brown face; white patch on throat

Range: Across North America up to the northern tree line, south through Mexico, and parts of Central and South America

Habitat: Woodlands, deserts, wetlands, grasslands, suburbs, and cities

Eggs: Dull white, almost spherical

Long-Eared Owl (*Asio otus*)

Size 14 to 16 inches

Wingspan: 35 to 39 inches

Comparative size: Pigeon to crow

Description: Slender body; squarish head; buff or orange face; two vertical white or buff lines between the eyes; yellow eyes; long, black ear tufts with buff or orange fringes

Range: From the southern Yukon and Northwest Territories across Canada to Newfoundland and south throughout the lower forty-eight states, except for Florida and parts of the southern Atlantic and Gulf Coasts

Habitat: A combination of grass or open country and tall shrubs or trees

Eggs: White

Snowy Owl (*Bubo scandiacus*)

Size: 20 to 28 inches

Wingspan: 49 to 57 inches

Comparative size: Red-tailed hawk to goose

Description: Bulky body; dense feathering on the legs; mostly white with salt-and-pepper black or brown markings on body and wings; yellow eyes

Male: Becomes whiter with age

Range: The Canadian Arctic and from Alberta across Canada to Newfoundland and the northern United States and south to Oklahoma and the Mid-Atlantic

Habitat: Lake and ocean shorelines; fields and other open areas

Eggs: White

Collective noun(s): A bazaar, an eyrie, a looming, a parliament, or a wisdom of owls, as well as an ululation of screech owls

Parrot and Parakeet:
African Gray Parrot, Yellow-Headed Parrot, American Parakeet

American Parakeet (**Melopsittacus undulatus**)

The yellow-headed parrot has been popular as a pet for several hundred years. Known as the popinjay in England until the sixteenth century, the name *parrot* was influenced by the French and Spanish names of *perroquet* and *papagayo*, respectively.[111] The African gray parrot is considered one of the most intelligent birds. Research has shown that it has the reasoning capability of a three-year-old human. In addition to learning words and phrases, the African gray can imitate individual people's voices and mimic a wide range of sounds, such as a telephone ringing.

The ancient Egyptians revered parrots, depicting them in hieroglyphics and mummifying them for placement in tombs. These colorful birds were mentioned in the writings of India and Persia dating back three thousand years.[112] Kama, a Hindu god of love, was usually depicted riding a parrot, which linked this bird with symbols of fertility. The fact that parrots can talk contributed to their status as intermediates between people and

---

111. Brodsky, *Spanish Vocabulary*, 320.
112. Rachael Hanel, *Parrots* (Mankato, MN: Creative Education, 2009), 29.

deities. It also gave them an association with prophecy, one of which was the ability to predict rain. In most cultures, to kill a parrot was considered unlucky.

Keeping a parrot became a symbol of wealth to the Romans, who introduced these birds throughout their empire. People around the world have used parrot feathers in rituals. In the sixteenth and seventeenth centuries, the feathers and birds became prized trade items. A pirate with a parrot is not just a caricature. Pirates were fond of unusual pets and often kept parrots for show as well as to supply the booming market for these birds.

In parts of Florida and southern California, feral parrots thrive in the wild. Likewise, feral flocks of parakeets can be found in the wild in Florida. The name *parakeet* comes from the Spanish *periquito*, the diminutive of *papagayo*, "parrot." [113] The only parrot native to North America was the Carolina parakeet (*Conuropsis carolinensis*), which is now extinct. Seeing them in 1774, French explorer Antoine du Pratz called them *papagai à tête aurore*, "parrots with dawn-tinted heads." [114]

The familiar pet parakeet originated in Australia. British sailors who had been down under told stories about the little green birds, and in 1840, explorer John Gould (1804–1881) was the first to take a pair back to England. [115] The name *budgerigar* was adapted from what British sailors thought they were called in Australia. Although the etymology is still disputed, one version is that the Aboriginal *betchery-gah* meant "good to eat." [116]

At one time in Italy, parakeets were used for divination. With potential answers written on slips of paper, the person asking a question would have the bird choose one of the papers. Like their larger cousins, parakeets can be trained to mimic sounds.

Magical Workings

Parrot is a bird of abundance echoing the fertility of its rich tropical origins. Call on parrot to grace your altar at Ostara and Beltane as well as Mabon. It can also give a boost to your creativity. Parakeet is an especially good aid for boosting love spells. Call on it for support when engaging in divination. Both birds are associated with communication and prophecy, and they can be your guides for interpreting messages and omens.

---

113. Brodsky, *Spanish Vocabulary*, 320.

114. Wells, *100 Birds and How They Got Their Names*, 170.

115. Julia Barnes, *Pet Parakeets* (Lydney, England: Westline Publishing, 2006), 7.

116. Ibid., 6.

Make Connection

To connect with parrot or parakeet energy, go for a walk in a park or to a playground where there is plenty of activity. Both of these birds are outgoing, social, and playful. Close your eyes and listen, but don't tune in to specific words or conversation. When the human noise begins to sound like raucous parrots or parakeets, the bird's energy will have touched you. After this, you will be able to make contact whenever needed by recalling their sounds.

Associations

PARROT

Zodiac: Gemini

Element(s): Fire

Sabbat(s): Beltane, Mabon, Ostara

Goddess: Devi

Gods: Indra, Kama

Solar system: Sun

PARAKEET

Element(s): Air

Bird Identification

AFRICAN GRAY PARROT (*PSITTACUS ERITHACUS*)

Also known as: Congo African gray parrot

Size: 12 to 14 inches

Wingspan: 18 to 20 inches

Comparative size: Pigeon

Description: Light to medium gray all over; white mask on face; black beak; silvery-yellow eyes; bright red tail

Range: West and Central Africa

Habitat: Moist lowland forests and adjacent open land

Eggs: Off-white to buff

YELLOW-HEADED PARROT (*AMAZONA ORATRIX*)

Also known as: Yellow-headed Amazon

Size: 13 to 15 inches

Wingspan: 16 to 19 inches

Comparative size: Pigeon to crow

Description: Body and wings mostly green; yellow head; red patch on wings; dark blue tips on flight feathers; yellow tips on tail feathers and red marks on the base of the outer tail; hooked beak; two toes point forward and two backward

Range: Mexico and parts of Central America

Habitat: Tropical and subtropical forests, mangrove swamps, savannah, and coastal scrub

Eggs: Glossy white

AMERICAN PARAKEET (*MELOPSITTACUS UNDULATUS*)

Also known as: Budgerigar, budgie

Size: 5 to 7 inches

Wingspan: 10 to 14 inches

Comparative size: Sparrow

Description: Slender body; rounded head; hooked beak; long, tapering tail; long flight feathers; black markings on the nape, back, and wings; bred for a range of colors including greens, blues, whites, yellows, and grays

Male: Blue or bluish-purple cere (bare skin above the beak)

Female: Tan, pink, or brown cere

Range: Central and Southern Australia

Habitat: Grasslands and woods

Eggs: White

Collective noun(s): A chattering or a flock of parakeets, and a flock, a pandemonium, or a prattle of parrots

Partridge:
Gray Partridge

Gray Partridge (Perdix perdix)

Partridges flourished in the hedgerows of England, where in Old English they were called *pertriche*.[117] Later, they were simply referred to as partridge until the red-legged partridge (*Alectoris rufa*), also known as the French partridge, was introduced into the British Isles. After that, the less colorful English bird was given the prefix of gray. The gray partridge was introduced into North America from Europe during the late 1790s.[118]

The scientific name, *Perdix*, comes from Greek mythology. The story concerns Daedalus, the craftsman who created the labyrinth on Crete. He was extremely jealous of his talented nephew Perdix and tried to kill him by pushing him from a tower in one of Athena's temples. Seeing Perdix fall, the goddess rescued him by changing him into a partridge so he could flutter safely to the ground. In folklore, this is said to be the reason why partridges do not fly very high and build their nests low to the ground. Also according to Greek myth, the partridge was associated with fecundity, love, and beauty, and the goddess Aphrodite.

The "partridge in a pear tree" of Christmas song fame is thought to have resulted from a misunderstanding of the French name for partridge, *Perdreau*, which is pronounced "pair-

---

117. Wells, *100 Birds and How They Got Their Names*, 171.

118. Kenn Kaufman, *Lives of North American Birds* (New York: Houghton Mifflin, 1996), 14.

dree." [119] Of course, it could also refer to the French partridge, which perches off the ground and frequently in trees. Pliny wrote of the partridge as a lustful bird, so perhaps giving or receiving the gift of a partridge in a pear tree (the pear is also a symbol of fertility) carried a strong message.

In medieval Europe, the partridge was a symbol of true love. However, these birds were also considered secretive and deceitful because they hide their nests and sometimes feign injury. This seemingly disparate symbolism actually fits together when considered in a different way. The partridge hides its nest to keep the eggs safe, and feigns a broken wing to draw a predator away from it. Because of this, the partridge represents unconditional mother love. This also harkens back to the partridge's ancient association with the Goddess as the nourishing protector.

Magical Workings

For Imbolc and Beltane celebrations, include a picture or figurine of a partridge (perhaps a pear, too) on your altar to represent quickening of life and the fertility of the Goddess. Because of a long association with fertility and lust, partridge is a bird to call on for sex magic and love spells.

It can also aid in divination to help you find your true love. Most of all, partridge is a symbol of motherly love, devotion, and dedication. Place a picture, figurine, or stuffed toy of this bird in your child's room to symbolize your love for him/her. In addition, call on partridge when honoring your mother as well as for help in sorting out the complexities of a mother/child relationship.

Make Connection

To connect with partridge energy, go to a grassy field, meadow, or your own backyard. Take a blanket and lie on your stomach on the ground. Prop your chin on your hands if the grass is short, or prop yourself up on your elbows so the top of the grass is at eye-level. With a soft gaze, look across the top of the grass. If weather doesn't permit or if it is winter, simply lie on the floor in your house. Imagine that you are a partridge walking through the grass, and then visualize settling onto your nest. When you feel a sense of calm security enfold you as you rest in seclusion, partridge may reach out to you.

---

119. Mark Lawson-Jones, *Why was the Partridge in the Pear Tree?: The History of Christmas Carols* (Stroud, England: The History Press, 2011), 58.

Associations

Element(s): Air, earth

Sabbat(s): Beltane, Imbolc

Goddesses: Aphrodite, Athena, Venus

Bird Identification

GRAY PARTRIDGE (*PERDIX PERDIX*)

Also known as: Hungarian partridge

Size: 11 to 13 inches

Wingspan: 21 to 22 inches

Comparative size: Pigeon

Description: Small, stocky, chicken-like body; short neck; reddish face and throat; grayish-brown back and chest; chestnut-colored bars on flanks; gray bill and legs; short, rounded wings; short, rust-colored tail

Male: A dark patch on lower breast

Female: Paler coloration; no lower breast patch

Range: Along the US-Canadian border, mainly in western and upper plains states as well as northern New York State

Habitat: Flat agricultural land and grassland areas with hedgerows or other bushy cover

Eggs: Olive green

Collective noun(s): A bevy, a brace, a covey, or a warren of partridges

Peacock:
Blue Peafowl

Blue Peafowl (Pavo cristatus)

While most of us will only see a peacock in a zoo, I have included it in this book because it is legendary and powerful, and it can be an aid for magic work. This bird is more accurately called a peafowl; the male is a peacock and the female is a peahen. People have been enamored of these magnificently colorful birds and have kept them as prized possessions for thousands of years. In India, peacocks were often kept in temple compounds and sometimes immortalized in temple carvings. This bird is not just a pretty face for ornamentation; peacocks are adept at killing snakes, including cobras.

According to Greek historian Diodorus Siculus (90–30 BCE), these birds were kept in Babylon, where they were considered symbols of royalty. The peacock was also the emblem of the monarchy in Burma and Persia. This bird's calls are extremely loud and often considered harsh and unpleasant shrieking. An Indian saying noted that the peafowl has "an angel's feathers and a devil's voice." [120]

It may be surprising to learn that the male peacock has a short tail. What we usually consider its tail is called a train. Its real tail is underneath the train, which the bird usually drags on the ground behind it. The train feathers are almost four feet long and last from June to December. They are discarded in January and new ones grow in time for

---

120. Armstrong, *The Life and Lore of the Bird in Nature, Art, Myth and Literature*, 140.

the next breeding season. Despite this bird's dazzling feathers, their coloration actually allows them to meld into a jungle and disappear.

Peacocks were regarded as a vehicle for deities in India. The goddess Sarasvati was usually depicted on a peacock and the god Brahma on a peacock or swan. Skanda, a Hindu war god, is depicted riding a peacock at the Angkor Wat temple complex in Cambodia. In Greek myth, the peacock was Hera's bird. With its all-seeing "eyes" (referring to the pattern on its train feathers), it kept watch for her husband's infidelities.

Images of peacocks in the Middle East often show them flanking the tree of life. In China, where these birds were a symbol of peace and prosperity, peacock feathers were worn at official functions. In European folklore, a peacock feather in the house of a spinster was said to jinx her chances for getting married.

Magical Workings

Although this bird epitomizes dignity and pride, it is tempered with honesty and harmony. Peacock can help you muster confidence and find your true power. As expected, peacock is associated with beauty and attraction, and it can be called upon to boost love spells. It is also an aid for manifesting abundance and prosperity.

As mentioned, this bird can seemingly disappear into a forest. Call on peacock for protection, especially when you need to fade into your surroundings and pass under the radar of a potential threat. Peacock provides support for psychic abilities, especially when making connections with past-life memories. Turn to this bird when you seek wisdom that will bring renewal and a fresh start.

Make Connection

To connect with the energy of peacock, close your eyes and visualize a shimmering, iridescent blue color surrounding you. As it draws inward, it forms a train of long feathers behind you. Feel the weight and beauty of your colorful train as you lift and open it into a wide semicircle that arches behind you. Stand tall and proud as you experience the splendor of peacock. You may feel his grounded presence through a slight tug on your "train."

Associations

Zodiac: Aquarius, Leo
Element(s): Air, fire

Goddesses: Devi, Hera, Hestia, Iris, Juno, Sarasvati

Gods: Amun, Brahma, Hermes, Horus, Pan, Shiva, Skanda, Zeus

Solar system: Moon, Sun

Moon phase: Full

Bird Identification

BLUE PEAFOWL (*PAVO CRISTATUS*)

Size: 32 to 42 inches (does not include the male's train)

Wingspan: 47 to 118 inches

Comparative size: Goose

Description: Grayish-brown legs with spurs; stiff, short tail

Male: Bright iridescent blue head, neck, and breast; white patches above and below the eyes; head crest of upright, blue-tipped feathers; grayish-brown back and wings with brown barring; multicolored train in iridescent gold, brown, green, and black with ocelli (eye spots)

Female: Brown head, nape, and back; whitish face and throat; white belly; metallic green upper breast

Range: Sri Lanka, India, Pakistan, Kashmir, Nepal, and Ceylon

Habitat: Bushland and open forest

Eggs: Glossy and brownish

Collective noun(s): A muster or a pride of peafowl as well as an ostentation of peacocks

Pelican:
American White Pelican, Brown Pelican

Brown Pelican (Pelecanus occidentalis)

The white pelican's species name, *erythrorhynchos*, is Greek meaning "red-billed."[121] It is one of North America's largest birds. While white pelicans cooperate by herding fish into areas where they can be easily caught, their brown cousins are the only pelicans to plunge-dive headfirst from high flight. Although awkward when walking on land, pelicans are graceful in the air. They are particularly known for having a stretchy throat pouch that is used for scooping up fish.

The name pelican comes from *pelecanus* and *pelekan,* the Latin and Greek names for this bird, respectively.[122] At one time, both the pelican and the albatross were known as *alcatraz.* Even though the name *albatross* evolved from this, it was more suited to the pelican. *Alcatraz* stems from the Arabic word for pelican, *al-qadous,* which was derived from the Greek word *kados.*[123] *Kados* was the name for the leather scoops on ancient water wheels, which were said to resemble the pelican's pouch.

121. Edward C. Beedy and Edward R. Pandolfino. *Birds of the Sierra Nevada: Their Natural History, Status, and Distribution* (Berkeley, CA: University of California Press, 2013), 90.

122. Sandrock and Prior, *The Scientific Nomenclature of Birds in the Upper Midwest*, 103.

123. Carl Safina, *Eye of the Albatross: Visions of Hope and Survival* (New York: Henry Holt, 2002), 25.

The pelican is second only to the dove in Christian funerary art, which is why it can be found on gravestones. This bird became a symbol of self-sacrifice and resurrection due to a lack of knowledge concerning pelican physiology and habits. A pelican feeding its fledglings from its throat pouch was misinterpreted as the bird feeding its body to its young. Stylistically in medieval art, the pelican was commonly depicted more like a phoenix.

During the Middle Ages, the pelican was an esoteric symbol in alchemy. Not only was it the name of a particular type of distillation vessel, the pelican also represented the Philosopher's Stone, the legendary element that could transmute base metals to gold as well as produce an elixir of life. Because of this, the pelican was regarded as a bird of great power.

Magical Workings

This rather gawky-looking bird shows us that all is not what it may seem. Ungainly when walking, pelican is a masterful high flier that gracefully soars across the sky. Representing wisdom and spiritual growth, it can be called upon for support in the pursuit of knowledge. Also call on the power of this bird to aid in personal and spiritual transformation.

Pelican is an aid for boosting spells to manifest abundance as long as your prosperity and good fortune are shared in the spirit of generosity and kindness. Pelican can help you meet challenges head-on, rise above problems, and recover from loss.

Make Connection

To connect with pelican energy, you will need two small containers and any type of water source, such as a pool, a pond, or the ocean. Alternatively, a sink or a bathtub can be used indoors. Close your eyes for a moment and bring the image of a pelican into your mind's eye. When you can clearly picture the bird, scoop water into one container and then slowly pour it out as you scoop water into the second one. Do this until you get into a gentle rhythm like a water wheel, and then say: *"Pelican, pelecanus, bird of abundance and alchemy; Let your wisdom enfold me like a gentle rhapsody."* Repeat the incantation twice more as you reach out with your energy and visualize a pelican soaring gracefully above you. You will feel an energy shift when this bird makes contact.

Associations

Element(s): Air, water

Bird Identification

AMERICAN WHITE PELICAN (*PELECANUS ERYTHRORHYNCHOS*)

Size: 50 to 65 inches

Wingspan: 96 to 114 inches

Comparative size: Very large

Description: White body; long, broad white wings with black trailing edge; long pinkish to pale-orange bill with hooked tip; extensible throat pouch; short legs and tail; webbed feet

Range: From Saskatchewan to Manitoba in Canada, south through most of the western United States to the Midwest, along the lower California coast, and along the Gulf Coast to Florida; also most of Mexico

Habitat: Shallow coastal bays, inlets, and estuaries as well as inland lakes, rivers, and marshes

Eggs: Dull white

BROWN PELICAN (*PELECANUS OCCIDENTALIS*)

Size: 39 to 54 inches

Wingspan: 78 to 79 inches

Comparative size: Goose to very large

Description: Stocky, gray-brown body with silvery streaks; yellowish face and white head; white neck with dark brown neck stripe; neck is dark brown during breeding season; long bill with extensible throat pouch; long, broad wings gray with streaks

Range: Southern areas on the West Coast; East Coast from Virginia to Florida; parts of the Gulf Coast, and small areas of coastal Mexico and Central America

Habitat: Estuaries and coastal marine habitats; rarely seen inland

Eggs: Chalky white

Collective noun(s): A flock, a pod, a pouch, or a squadron of pelicans, as well as a rookery of white pelicans

Penguin:
Blue Penguin, Emperor Penguin

Emperor Penguin (Aptenodytes forsteri)

Even though most of us will only see them in zoos, penguins have become endearing icons because of their portrayal in popular films. With wings that have become flippers for swimming, penguins are aquatic, flightless birds that spend only about half of their time on land. Their tuxedo-like color pattern functions as camouflage in the water. From above they are not easy to spot against the dark ocean, and from below their light color blends with the ice and sky.

The common name *penguin* comes from the Latin *pinguis*, meaning "fat," which is appropriate as they have a good layer of fat for warmth.[124] In the 1800s, European sailors called them pin-wings.[125] The most plausible explanation for this name is that pin-wing is short for pinioned wing. Pinioning a bird involves the removal of the wing joint farthest from a bird's body to render it flightless.

The emperor penguin was discovered by naturalist Johann Reinhold Forster, who was a member of Captain Cook's expedition to Antarctica in the 1770s.[126] Its species name

---

124. Fraser and Gray, *Australian Bird Names*, 54.

125. Armstrong, *The Life and Lore of the Bird in Nature, Art, Myth and Literature*, 178.

126. Fraser and Gray, *Australian Bird Names*, 55.

forsteri was designated in honor of Forster. The genus name *Aptenodytes* comes from Greek and means "flightless diver."[127]

The emperor is the largest of the penguin species. They can dive deeper than any other bird, down to 1,850 feet, and stay underwater up to twenty minutes.[128] Like the loon, penguins have solid bones, which makes them less buoyant in the water and enhances their diving abilities. Emperor penguins also use a technique called "porpoising," leaping out of the water like porpoises so they can breathe without slowing down.

The blue penguin is also known as the fairy penguin. It is the smallest of the penguin species, and one of the few to be found north of the Antarctic Ocean. These birds forage at sea during the day and return to their nest sites at nightfall. Because they move about on land after dark, they are not often seen. This penguin's scientific name, *Eudyptula minor,* means "good little diver."[129] During the winter when they are not tending young, these penguins may spend several days at a time at sea.

Magical Workings

Penguin spends a lot of time in winter twilight, thus being familiar with that otherworldly betwixt-and-between state. Call on penguin as a shamanic guide to underworld journeys, astral travel, and dream work. With the moon providing the brightest light for several months, penguin gains the wisdom of Luna and passes it along to those it guides.

Able to hold on in the harsh Antarctic winter, penguin teaches us how to be strong and to adapt to any situation. Invite penguin into your rituals to help build community and cooperation.

Make Connection

To connect with penguin energy, close your eyes and imagine a cold and vast white landscape of snow and ice. Slowly sway side to side and then imitate the walk of a penguin. Giggle a little if you feel silly, but shift your attention to an image of a penguin in your mind. Visualize the twilight skies of seasonal change and the sound of the ocean. Keep a slow, deliberate pace until you get a sense of this bird's calm, steady rhythm and then listen for it to call you.

---

127. Fraser and Gray, *Australian Bird Names,* 54.
128. Tim Birkhead, Jo Wimpenny, and Bob Montgomerie, *Ten Thousand Birds: Ornithology since Darwin* (Princeton, NJ: Princeton University Press, 2014), 208.
129. Margaret Mittlebach and Michael Crewdson. *Carnivorous Nights: On the Trail of the Tasmanian Tiger* (New York: Villard Books, 2006), 149.

Association

Solar system: Moon

Bird Identification

BLUE PENGUIN (*EUDYPTULA MINOR*)

Also known as: Little penguin, fairy penguin

Size: 14 to 16 inches

Comparative size: Pigeon to crow

Description: Blue-gray back and head; white front; gray sides of face; blackish-gray bill; white chin and throat; pinkish-white feet and legs

Male: Slightly heavier body; larger bill

Range: New Zealand, Tasmania, and parts of southern Australia

Habitat: Rocky islands

Eggs: White

EMPEROR PENGUIN (*APTENODYTES FORSTERI*)

Size: 39 to 47 inches

Comparative size: Goose to very large

Description: Black back; white front; bright yellow patches on neck and ears; orange-yellow stripe the length of black beak; webbed, black feet

Range: On and around the Antarctic continent

Habitat: Antarctic ice and surrounding waters

Eggs: White

Collective noun(s): A colony, a crèche, a huddle, a march, a parcel, or a rookery of penguins

Pheasant:
Ring-Necked Pheasant

Ring-Necked Pheasant (Phasianus colchicus)

In ancient China, the pheasant was considered an imperial bird associated with the sun, thunder, and wealth. It was also a symbol of cosmic harmony. Regarded as an emissary of Amaterasu in Japan, this bird was a symbol of mother-love and protection.

The pheasant was introduced into Europe in the early fourth century BCE.[130] Because the peacock came from the East and was associated with immortality, the same connection was applied to the less flamboyant but exotic-looking pheasant. In Greek mythology, Jason and the Argonauts were said to have brought back several pheasants from their expedition to find the golden fleece.

The Romans, who enjoyed dining on them at lavish banquets, domesticated pheasants. Although the Romans were responsible for transporting many plants, birds, and animals into the British Isles, it is thought that the Normans introduced pheasants. Over time in England and Europe, pheasants escaped or were released and became wild birds. As such, they symbolized the power of nature and beauty.

In England, King Henry VIII began the practice of raising pheasants in captivity to be released on his estates for hunting. Not only were these highly-prized game birds popular in the dining halls of manor houses, they also served as graceful motifs in tapestries

---

130. Werness, *The Continuum Encyclopedia of Animal Symbolism in Art*, 325.

throughout Europe during the 1500s.[131] Along with peafowl and swans, pheasants were part of the menagerie of exotic animals at the Tower of London. They were introduced into North America in the 1880s.[132]

Pheasants usually walk or run and only occasionally resort to flying. The male's loud two-note call can be heard up to a mile away. My house in England was in the country-side, where pheasants frequently visited the backyard. One year, a group became regular guests at breakfast time, gradually coming closer when I put out food for them. I felt privileged and blessed when the male eventually took food from my hand.

Magical Workings

As a solar bird, pheasant represents warmth, fertility, and prosperity. Its coloring echoes the ripening bounty of fields and gardens. Bring it into your Lughnasadh and Mabon rituals to help you celebrate the abundance of the harvest and give thanks. Call on this bird to boost spells for love, protection, and good luck. Dressed in beautiful colors, pheasant can also teach the finer points of attraction. As a personal guide bird, it provides support when confidence and determination are needed. If you feel that the stars are not aligned for you, ask pheasant to bring a little cosmic harmony to Earth to help you.

Make Connection

To connect with pheasant energy, place a picture of this bird on your altar and light a dark green candle around which you have painted a white ring. Sit tall with your back straight as you gaze at the image of the stately pheasant for several minutes, and then close your eyes. Imagine that you are standing in a grassy field at the edge of a wooded area. It is autumn and the world is ablaze in many shades of yellows, reds, golds, and browns. Visualize a pheasant slowly moving toward you as you offer the gift of food. It may stop and simply observe you, but if you are ready for contact, it will take the food.

Associations

Element(s): Earth, fire

Sabbat(s): Lughnasadh, Mabon

Goddess: Amaterasu

---

131. Armstrong, *The Life and Lore of the Bird in Nature, Art, Myth and Literature*, 204.

132. Wells, *100 Birds and How They Got Their Names*, 189.

Solar system: Sun

Ogham: Beith

Bird Identification

RING-NECKED PHEASANT (*PHASIANUS COLCHICUS*)

Also known as: Common pheasant

Size: 20 to 28 inches

Wingspan: 22 to 34 inches

Comparative size: Red-tailed hawk to goose

Description: Chicken-like; small head; long neck; plump body; long, pointed tail

Male: Red eye patches; iridescent green neck with wide white ring; mottled brown and iridescent russet body; long coppery tail with thin, black bars

Female: Mottled sandy brown; buff or cinnamon underparts; black spotting on sides; tail not as long as the male

Range: From New England across the northern United States and southern Canada, throughout the plains states, and areas of the West Coast

Habitat: Farmland, pastures, grassy areas, and woodland edges

Eggs: Olive-brown to blue-gray

Collective noun(s): In general, a brace, a drove, or a nest of pheasants; when on the ground they are called a covey, a nide, or a nye of pheasants; and when flushed out of the underbrush, a bouquet of pheasants

Pigeon:
Rock Pigeon

Rock Pigeon (Columba livia)

Whether revered or reviled, pigeons are one of the most familiar and abundant birds in the world. Although they are mainly urban creatures, pigeons are highly adaptive and can easily live in the wild. These birds have been known by the name of *pigeon* since the fifteenth century in England. The name was derived from the Old French *pijon*, which originally referred to a young dove.[133]

Pigeons are one of the earliest-known birds to have been domesticated. This is believed to have occurred in the Mediterranean region five thousand to ten thousand years ago.[134] In myth and affection, doves and pigeons were interchangeable throughout the Middle East. In addition, the ancient Semitic people regarded both of these birds with reverence. Along with turtledoves (*Streptopelia turtur*), pigeons were sacrificed and their blood used for the ritual cleansing of leprosy.

Aristotle wrote about pigeon sport in Athens, where these birds were used to carry messages. It was a practice Julius Caesar used to convey information to his Roman troops. Pigeons served in this capacity up through World War II.

---

133. Fraser and Gray, *Australian Bird Names*, 21.
134. Richard F. Johnston and Marián Janiga. *Feral Pigeons* (New York: Oxford University Press, 1995), 6.

Raised for food in Egypt, the Romans also enjoyed dining on fat chicks, which are called squabs. Structures called *columbaria* by the Romans were dovecote towers that housed doves and pigeons. These were attached to residential buildings and date from the early first century CE.[135] Throughout Europe during the Middle Ages, pigeons were meals for upper-class tables. In France, only aristocrats kept pigeons, which is why having a *pigeonnier* (French for "dovecote") was forbidden during the revolution in 1789.[136]

Like many birds, the pigeon has a checkered history concerning good and bad luck. In Polish folklore, a pigeon in the house meant bad luck. In England, a white pigeon alighting near a house or coming to a window was a sign that someone would die. Although it was mostly considered a bird of death in England, the pigeon was also thought to bring good luck. To dream of a pigeon meant that love was on its way. The pigeon was considered a sacred bird in Russia, where it was consecrated to Perun, the god of thunder.

French colonists introduced pigeons into North America in the seventeenth century.[137] These domestic birds escaped into the wild and flourished. Racing pigeons is a sport that dates back centuries. Birds of various owners are collected and driven a certain distance, released, and timed for how long it takes them to fly to their home roosts. My father-in-law was an avid pigeon racer, and I have to admit that it was impressive to see his birds come back after being released almost two hundred miles away.

Magical Workings

Although this bird has been associated with death, pigeon is more appropriate for communication between the worlds. It serves to interpret messages and omens and can be a guide in many forms of divination. Connected strongly with fertility, it can be called on for support in matters of family and home. Also call on pigeon to boost spells for luck and love, and to help foster peace and security in your life. If asked, this bird will show you how to adapt to the changes (big or small) in your life.

Make Connection

To connect with pigeon energy, visualize that you are sitting on an urban rooftop, looking down at the hustle and bustle below. Imagine all the noises and activity of a busy city, and then shift your focus to the sky, where you can see several pigeons flying. Visualize

135. Clive Roots, *Domestication* (Westport, CT: Greenwood Press, 2007), 173.

136. Wells, *100 Birds and How They Got Their Names*, 193.

137. Roots, *Domestication*, 173.

yourself lifting into the air, moving from the humdrum distractions of the human world to soar above the city. Pigeon will make its presence known by flying beside you and guiding you around the aerial cityscape.

Associations

Element(s): Air
God: Perun

Bird Identification

ROCK PIGEON (*COLUMBA LIVIA*)

Also known as: Rock dove, feral pigeon

Size: 12 to 14 inches

Wingspan: 29 to 26 inches

Description: Stocky body; small head; short legs; broad, pointed wings; wide, rounded tail; plumage is highly variable, most common is a dark iridescent head; bluish-gray body and wings; two dark, wide wing bars; gray tail with dark tip; pigeons can also be all white, black, reddish-brown, or speckled

Range: From southern Alaska, along the Pacific coast, across southern Canada and throughout the United States, Mexico, Central America, and South America

Habitat: Urban and suburban areas, farmland, and rocky cliffs

Eggs: White

Collective noun(s): A flight, a flock, a kit, or a loft of pigeons

Quail:
California Quail, Northern Bobwhite

California Quail (Callipepla californica)

Quail is a collective name for several genera of birds in the Odontophoridae family. Since ancient times, quail have been popular game birds. They are built better for running than flying, which has made them fairly easy to snare with nets. The ancient Egyptians employed this method for catching them and depicted this activity in wall paintings. The bobwhite is so named because the male's whistling call seems to be saying "bob-white."

In both Greek and Hindu mythology, the quail symbolized spring and revival. In Greece, this bird also represented the heat of passion and was used as a gift from one lover to another. According to one Greek legend, Zeus turned his lover Leto into a quail so she could fly away from his wife, Hera. Leto flew to the Island of Delos where she gave birth to Artemis and Apollo.

The Romans were also fond of quail and kept them for meat and eggs. Quail fighting, similar to cockfighting, was introduced into Europe from China and became popular with the Romans. As a result, these courageous little fighters became an emblem of Roman military valor. Although Shakespeare mentioned quail fighting, it was not a sport that caught on in England. European Gypsies considered the quail a bird of the devil because of its ability to fight. In addition, they associated it with witchcraft and sorcery.

The quail was also considered a protector. In German folklore, keeping one in the house was believed to protect the building from lightning. Additionally, the quail was considered a bird of prophecy. In Germany and other parts of Europe, the number of times a quail call was heard could predict the amount of money crops would bring in the marketplace. Also, hearing a quail early in the morning meant that it would rain.

Magical Workings

Whenever you are in need of courage and protection, this small bird packs a punch and can help you find your power to meet whatever challenge comes your way. Quail can warn you of potential danger as well as provide a heads-up for challenges that do not present a threat.

Quail can serve as a guardian during shamanic work and astral travel. As a master of camouflage, it can show you the intricacies of shape-shifting. The softer side of quail is its association with fertility and passion. Call on this bird to enhance spellwork, especially when it relates to love, harmony, and protection. Quail also helps to stoke the fires of creativity; keep a picture or figurine of it on your desk or in your workshop.

Make Connection

To connect with quail energy, sit in front of your altar and whistle the "bob-white" call three times. It is a simple two-note call in which the second is higher. Close your eyes and visualize a plump little quail on the ground circling around your feet. In a whispered voice, ask for its attention. It will stop and look up at you when you are ready for the connection. Quail is a cautious bird and wants to be sure of sharing its power with humans when they are prepared for it.

Associations

Element(s): Air, earth, fire
Goddess: Artemis
God: Apollo

Bird Identification

California Quail (*Callipepla californica*)
Also known as: Valley quail
Size: 9 to 11 inches

Wingspan: 12 to 14 inches

Comparative size: Robin

Description: Plump body; small head and bill; short neck; short, broad wings; long, square tail; comma-shaped topknot of feathers on the forehead; striking white and chestnut pattern on the breast and belly

Male: Gray and brown; black face outlined with bold white stripes; longer topknot than female

Female: More plain brown than the male; no facial markings

Range: From the northwestern United States to Idaho, through California, and south through the Baja Peninsula

Habitat: Coastal sagebrush, chaparral, forest foothills, suburban backyards and parks

Eggs: White or cream-colored with variable brown markings

Northern Bobwhite (*Colinus virginianus*)

Size: 8 to 11 inches

Wingspan: 12 to 14 inches

Comparative size: Robin

Description: Chunky, brown body with a patchy pattern; pale, streaked underparts; brown top of head; white face with dark streak from eye to neck; short, pointed beak

Range: From Mid-Atlantic states south to Florida, through the western plains states to areas of the Rocky Mountain foothills, and into parts of Mexico; also a small area of the Pacific Northwest

Habitat: Brushy pastures, open pine forests, and farmland

Eggs: Creamy white

Collective noun(s): A battery, a drift, a flock, or a flush of quail, as well as a covey or a bevy of Bobwhites

Raven:
Common Raven

Common Raven (Corvus corax)

Along with crows, the Celts associated ravens with goddesses of war who appeared over and around battlefields. In England, gravestones were often referred to as raven stones because of this bird's association with death. In Ireland, the gift of prophecy or second sight was called raven's knowledge. Considered the only bird that could understand and interpret omens, it was an important creature of prophecy for the Romans. To the Greeks and Romans, a raven's sound, the number of times it was heard, the direction from which it came, and the time of day that it was heard each had a specific meaning.

Despite the fact that they are black, the Greeks and Chinese considered ravens solar birds. In Swedish folklore, ravens were thought to be the spirits of the dead. Norse god Odin kept two of these birds, which represented thought and memory. In addition, his daughters, the Valkyries, often shape-shifted into ravens. The Vikings used depictions of ravens on the sails of their ships as homage to Odin and as a token of good luck. Likewise, it was good luck to see a raven at the start of a hunting trip in Scotland.

During the Middle Ages ravens were associated with witchcraft and black magic, and they were believed to be able to cast evil spells. It was also believed that witches and devils could shape-shift into ravens, as did the *dubh sidhe*, "dark fairies." As a part of English mythology, ravens have been the most famous residents at the Tower of London since

1078.[138] According to legend, if these birds leave the Tower, the British monarchy will fall. It is also legend that when King Arthur returns, he will be in the form of a raven.

The raven's species name comes from the Greek *korax*, meaning "croaker," and its common name is from Old Norse *hrafn*, "to clear one's throat." [139] In addition to gruff sounds, ravens have thirty to forty different calls and use body language. They can mimic other birds and human speech, too. Ravens are highly intelligent, make and use tools, and can solve complex problems. However, a raven's life is not all work and no play. Like crows, ravens play with each other as well as with other birds and animals. Ravens may also have a sense of humor, as they have been observed flying upside down.

Magical Workings

Raven is a bird of omens and prophecy, and in most places where this bird resides it has been believed to possess supernatural powers. Call on it to interpret messages in your divination practice or to help you develop clairvoyant skills. This bird supports shamanic work by bringing clarity to the visions you receive. Call on raven for your magic work, especially to manifest important changes. Also call on it to connect with the energy and magic of the Crone.

Use an image or figurine of raven on your altar at Samhain for aid in honoring and connecting with ancestors. It is a willing and wise guide in the otherworld who will act as a guardian to you. As a bird of battlefields, ask for raven's protection if you are serving in the military. Raven can help bolster courage and is a bird of healing.

Make Connection

To connect with raven energy, go to a graveyard just before dark. As the sun sets, whisper three times: *"Corvus corax, dark as night, come to me in fading light. With the gift of second sight, bring your magic on this night."* Stand in silence for a few minutes. It will make its presence known by the rustle of wings. Like most birds, raven will make contact when it deems you to be ready. When you return home, light a black candle on your altar to honor it.

Associations

Zodiac: Gemini, Libra, Scorpio

---

138. Nozedar, *The Secret Language of Birds*, 337.
139. Wells, *100 Birds and How They Got Their Names*, 204.

Element(s): Air, earth, water

Sabbat(s): Samhain, Yule

Goddesses: Amaterasu, Athena, Badb, Danu, Epona, Freya, Macha, Maeve, the Morrigan, Nantosuelta, Rhiannon, Tiamat

Gods: Apollo, Asclepius, Bran, Cú Chulainn, Lugh, Mars, Mithras, Odin, Saturn

Tree: Aspen

Solar system: Saturn, Sun, Venus

Bird Identification

COMMON RAVEN (*CORVUS CORAX*)

Size: 22 to 25 inches

Wingspan: 45 to 46 inches

Comparative size: Red-tailed hawk

Description: Glossy black all over; black beak, legs, and eyes; downward-curved upper bill; thick neck with shaggy throat feathers; long, broad wings; long, wedge-shaped tail

Range: Alaska, across northern Canada, down through the western United States and into Mexico; also the Great Lakes region, northern New England, and the Appalachians

Habitat: Wooded areas with open spaces, grasslands, sagebrush, seacoasts, and residential areas

Eggs: Green, olive, or blue with dark greenish, olive, or purple-brown mottling

Collective noun(s): An aerie, a conspiracy, a storytelling, or an unkindness of ravens

Roadrunner:
Greater Roadrunner

Greater Roadrunner (Geococcyx californianus)

The word *roadrunner* usually brings to mind the trials and tribulations of poor Wile E. Coyote as he was continually outwitted by one of these birds. The truth is, coyotes are a threat but roadrunners are managing to survive because they are the wily ones. In fact, roadrunners are fearless little creatures that kill and eat scorpions and snakes and even rattlesnakes. One of the biggest myths, which is not true, involves the roadrunner trapping a sleeping snake with pieces of cactus. However, it is the roadrunner's zigzag motions and quick footwork that allows it to get close enough to grab the snake and thrash it around to disable it.

Part of the cartoon portrayal of the roadrunner that is somewhat accurate is how it leans forward almost parallel to the ground as it runs with its tail streaming behind. Using its tail for balance and as a rudder, the roadrunner can reach speeds of up to fifteen miles per hour. Although they are sometimes seen perching on fence posts or higher objects, roadrunners prefer running to flying. Because of this, the white crescent shape on its wings is rarely seen. When roadrunners fly, it is usually a ground-hugging endeavor.

The name *roadrunner* comes from this bird's habit of running across and along roads. A member of the cuckoo family, its genus name, *Geococcyx,* means "ground cuckoo."[140]

---

140. Wells, *100 Birds and How They Got Their Names,* 211.

In Mexico, roadrunners are affectionately called *paisano*, "fellow countryman," and sometimes domesticated and kept around a home or a farm to get rid of mice.[141] The greater roadrunner has a slightly smaller cousin, the lesser roadrunner (*Geococcyx velox*) that lives only in Mexico and in parts of Central America.

The roadrunner has a distinctive X-shaped footprint, which is created because two of its toes point forward and two backward. This makes it difficult to know which direction the bird was heading. The Pueblo people used the roadrunner footprint as a symbol to confuse and ward off evil.

The first time I saw a roadrunner in the wild I thought it was a scruffy, scrawny chicken. It took me a moment to figure out what it was as it scampered around my feet and looked up at me expectantly. This wily bird knew that guests at the sprawling hotel complex I was staying in could be charmed into giving it food.

Magical Workings

Sometimes it is difficult to get the comic image of roadrunner out of our minds to work with this bird seriously; however, if you can do this you will find a powerful little ally. It reveals the importance of adaptability and can be a guide when quick-witted decisions must be made. Roadrunner can also aid in discerning the right opportunities to grasp when they come your way. Call on roadrunner for spells or charms that bolster courage. Place an image of roadrunner on your esbat altar; with a hidden crescent shape on its wings, its special energy can enhance your ritual.

Make Connection

To connect with roadrunner energy, use its X-shaped footprint, which is also a symbol of the Goddess's life-giving aspect. Draw an *X* on a number of index cards or small pieces of paper. Place a picture of roadrunner on your altar and light a brown candle. In front of your altar, lay out the cards in a circle that is large enough for you to sit inside. Gaze at the picture of roadrunner for a few minutes, and then close your eyes. Visualize the bird running in a circle around you. It's okay to giggle if you think you hear a soft "beep beep" sound; however, a faint swishing noise or breeze will confirm roadrunner's presence.

---

141. Robert Hendrickson, *The Facts on File Dictionary of American Regionalisms: Local Expressions from Coast to Coast* (New York: Facts on File, 2000), 532.

Association
Element: Earth

Bird Identification
GREATER ROADRUNNER (*GEOCOCCYX CALIFORNIANUS*)

Also known as: Chaparral cock

Size: 20 to 24 inches

Wingspan: 19 inches

Comparative size: Red-tailed hawk

Description: Pheasant-like with a long, straight tail; bushy blue-black crest; dark streaking on upperparts, wings, and chest; buff underparts; short, rounded wings

Male: Patch of blue and red skin on sides of head near eyes

Range: From California throughout the Southwest to Kansas, and south through most of Mexico

Habitat: Grasslands, desert, brushy chaparral, open woodland, and suburban areas

Eggs: Chalky white sometimes stained with brown or gray

Collective noun(s): A marathon of roadrunners

Robin:
American Robin

American Robin (Turdus migratorius)

Early settlers to North America gave this bird its common name because it had a red breast like the European robin (*Erithacus rubecula*), with which they were familiar back home. However, the American robin is more closely related to the European blackbird (*Turdus merula*) than its Old World namesake. Although robins are considered harbingers of spring, many do not migrate. Because they spend more time roosting in trees than on the ground in the winter, they are not as conspicuous. Robins have distinctive movements on the ground: either hopping or stop-and-go running.

According to folklore, robins were said to present themselves at funerals to sing last rites. It was also believed that if robins found an unburied human corpse they would cover it with moss or leaves. As a result, this bird became associated with lost loved ones and the afterlife. Folklore also explained that this bird's red breast resulted from singeing its feathers when descending into hell to either bring fire back for humans or take water to lost souls.

Associated with storms, the robin was sacred to Thor and was nicknamed the storm cloud bird. English legend noted that fairies were afraid of robins because they could not shape-shift into its form. For the most part, the robin was regarded as a bird of good fortune and to kill one would bring bad luck. It was thought that if you made a wish before the first robin you saw in the spring flew away, your wish would come true. In addition, a light snowfall in the spring is called a robin snow.

The robin was considered a bird of prophecy, heralding the return of spring and approaching rain. My grandmother used to say that when a robin sang a particular song, rain was on the way. Sometimes the weather prophecy was determined by the bird's location (on a barn or in a bush) when it was heard. The robin was considered oracular in other ways, too. If one flew into a house, a death in the family could be expected. Also, if an unmarried woman saw a robin on Valentine's Day, she would marry a sailor.

Despite its connections with spring, the robin is also associated with winter, Yule, oak trees, and the wren. Representing the light and dark halves of the year, the oak king and holly king trade places at Yule. The wren is considered the bird of the holly king; the red-breasted robin, representing the returning sun, is the oak king's bird. In folklore, the robin killed the wren at winter solstice to initiate the return of spring.

Magical Workings

Robin is a bird of renewal, growth, and change. As a symbol of spring and quickening, it adds energy to Imbolc rituals as well as both summer and winter solstices. Represent robin on your altar with images or figurines, or with several small blue gemstones to represent its eggs.

This bird can boost spells for luck and aid in making your wishes come true. To invite joy into your life, get up at dawn and listen for robin's song, or place a picture of one on your windowsill and bring its song into your mind.

As a bird of comfort and affection, robin can help ease grief when a loved one passes beyond the veil. Robin can also help interpret messages from the otherworld as well as bring clarity to obscure omens.

Make Connection

To connect with robin energy, put on a red shirt and a dark gray or brown sweater or jacket. Get up while it is still dark and listen to the dawn chorus. If you don't hear a robin, bring the sound of its song into your mind. Visualize yourself sitting on a tree branch, singing and greeting the day. Most of all, listen, and it will make its presence known.

Associations

Zodiac: Aries, Taurus
Element(s): Air, fire
Sabbat(s): Imbolc, Litha, Yule
Gods: Belenus, Jupiter, Thor
Tree: Oak

Bird Identification

American Robin (*Turdus migratorius*)

Size: 8 to 11 inches
Wingspan: 12 to 16 inches
Description: Large, rounded body; long legs; long tail; reddish bill and legs
Male: Dark gray-brown upperparts; almost black head; white around the eyes; underparts orange to brick-red; throat whitish with dark streaks; lower belly white
Female: Similar to male but duller colors
Range: From Alaska throughout the United States, most of Canada, and Mexico
Habitat: Residential areas and parks, urban areas, forests, and open country
Eggs: Light blue or bluish-green

Collective noun(s): A blush or a riot of robins

Sandpiper and Plover:
Least Sandpiper, Spotted Sandpiper, Killdeer

Least Sandpiper (Calidris minutilla)

Busy little shorebirds tend to congregate together and are notoriously difficult to identify. As a result, when you see a group of sandpipers, you may also be watching plovers. These birds are similar in appearance—tan on top and light underneath. The easiest clue is that sandpipers have long, thin bills and smallish eyes, and plovers have short bills and large eyes. While plovers are shore birds, they also search for food in open meadows.

The spotted sandpiper is, well, spotted, making it easy to identify in a mixed group of birds, but only during the mating season. However, it has a distinctive teeter when it walks, bobbing its tail up and down. Small sandpipers are known as peeps and the least sandpiper is the smallest of the small. The killdeer plover is easy to identify because of the two dark bands across its breast.

Although these birds are related to the legendary lapwing (*Vanellus vanellus*), the plover is a closer cousin than the sandpiper. The lapwing's association with magic has carried over to its American cousins. According to Danish folklore, the souls of old maids turned into lapwings and the souls of bachelors into sandpipers.

Sandpipers were named *pipers* for their piping call when danger is sensed. The name *plover* comes from the Latin *pluvia*, meaning "rain."[142] Plovers were looked to for weather divination, and in Germany they were called rain pipers. The plover family, Charadriidae,

---

142. Wells, *100 Birds and How They Got Their Names*, 196.

was named for a mythical medieval bird that was said to have the power to discern if a sick person would live or die.

The killdeer was named for the sound it makes, which can be fairly loud. This bird calls when circling in the air and is often heard after dark. In folklore, the cry of the killdeer was said to call up the wind, and several flying overhead singing was a sign of strong wind. Other weather lore says that there is usually one more late-winter storm after the killdeer returns for the season. It was also believed that if you robbed a killdeer's nest and ate the eggs, you would break your arm.

Magical Workings

Sandpiper and plover are liminal birds, spending most of their time at the water's edge, a place that passes back and forth between water and land. Call on these birds to aid you in reaching that in-between state of being during rituals or spellwork. Associated with abundance, sandpiper can help draw prosperity and close relationships into your life. Plover is a bird of guidance that can aid in any type of travel as well as divination.

Make Connection

Place a picture of a sandpiper or a plover on your altar. Gaze at it for a few moments as you fix the image in your mind. Close your eyes and whisper three times: *"Betwixt and between, so much more can be seen. On shore or field, knowledge reveal."* Continue to hold the image in your mind, and when you are able to visualize a group of sandpipers and/or plovers darting around your feet, you will be ready to work with them.

Associations

Element(s): Earth, water

Bird Identification

Sandpipers

Least Sandpiper (*Calidris minutilla*)

Size: 5 to 6 inches

Wingspan: 10 to 11 inches

Comparative size: Sparrow

Description: Round body; short, pointed wings; black bill; brown upperparts; white underparts; yellow-green legs; whitish rump visible in flight

Range: Throughout Alaska, most of Canada, the United States, Mexico, and Central America as well as parts of South America

Habitat: Mudflats of beaches and estuaries

Eggs: Pale yellowish-brown, with brown spots or blotches

SPOTTED SANDPIPER (*ACTITIS MACULARIUS*)

Size: 7 to 8 inches

Wingspan: 14 to 16 inches

Comparative size: Sparrow to robin

Description: Body tapers to a long tail; white, rounded breast; grayish-brown back; pale yellow bill; has the appearance of leaning forward; in breeding season, dark spots on breast; orange bill; dark brown back; in flight a thin, white stripe along wing can be seen

Range: Throughout most of Alaska and Canada, all of the United States and Mexico, and most of South America

Habitat: Stream banks, rivers, ponds, lakes, and beaches

Eggs: Off-white, pinkish, or pale green speckled with brown

PLOVER

KILLDEER (*CHARADRIUS VOCIFERUS*)

Size: 8 to 11 inches

Wingspan: 18 to 19 inches

Comparative size: Robin

Description: Slender and lanky body; long, pointed tail; long wings; large, round head; large eyes; short bill; brownish-tan upperparts; white underparts; two black breast bands; brown face with black and white patches; orange-buff rump

Range: From British Columbia east to southern Quebec and the Maritimes, throughout the United States, Mexico, and Central America

Habitat: Sandbars, mudflats, pastures, fields, lawns, golf courses, and parking lots

Eggs: Buff-colored and heavily marked with blackish-brown

Collective noun(s): A congregation or a trip of plovers

Seagull:
Herring Gull, Ring-Billed Gull

Ring-Billed Gull (Larus delawarensis)

With their wheeling and whirling flight, seagulls are masters of the wind. The herring gull is the quintessential seagull and one of the most familiar on the East Coast. Their family name comes from the Greek *laros,* meaning "seabird."[143] The name *gull* came into use in the middle of the fifteenth century, and it is thought to have come from the Cornish *gullen* or the Welsh *gwylan,* which mean "throat" and "wailing," respectively.[144] Before that time, these birds were known as mews because of their crying sounds.

Since medieval times, gulls were believed to be the souls of people drowned at sea. These birds were thought to possess prophetic powers and anyone who made a living on the sea used them for guidance. Sailors kept an eye on seagulls for indications of weather changes, and fishermen observed them to find schools of fish. According to folklore, a seagull spotted far inland meant rain or a storm at sea. Also, if a seagull landed on a ship, the voyage would be a good one.

There were negative connotations about seagulls, as well. Three or more gulls flying overhead was an omen of death, or if a seagull flew against the window of a sailor's house

---

143. Wells, *100 Birds and How They Got Their Names*, 101.

144. Philip Durkin, *Borrowed Words: A History of Loanwords in English* (New York: Oxford University Press, 2014), 92; Nozedar, *The Secret Language of Birds*, 387.

while he was away it meant that he was in danger. In Greek legend, the sea nymph Ino, who was also known as the goddess Leucothea, could shape-shift into a seagull. In addition to the dove, the seagull was one of Aphrodite's symbols.

Seagulls are highly intelligent birds. Herring gulls have been known to bait fish by floating bits of food on the surface of the water to bring them into reach.

Magical Workings

Most often associated with freedom, seagull is a mystical traveler of the realms. It is instrumental as a guide and guardian when journeying or traveling on terra firma. Call on seagull to communicate with deities and spirits. Place an image or figurine of this bird on your Samhain altar to aid your contact with loved ones at this sabbat or any time someone passes.

Seagull can provide clarity to messages and omens, especially those that seem particularly obscure at first. Known as an opportunist, it can help you discern your best prospects and live up to your true potential. Also call on seagull for spells to draw abundance into your life.

Make Connection

To connect with seagull energy, go to an ocean, a lake, or a waterway where there are gulls, or use an ocean sound recording that includes seagulls. If you are at the seaside or other body of water, watch the seagulls. If you are listening to a recording, visualize them. Listen to the rhythm of the water as you follow the birds' flight. Allow your spirit to soar and whirl over the water with these masters of the wind. One will stay close to you to indicate its presence in your life.

Associations

Zodiac: Cancer

Element(s): Air, water

Sabbat(s): Samhain

Goddesses: Aphrodite, Cliodna, Dôn, Leucothea

Gods: Manannan, Njord

Ogham: Fearn

Magical beings: Fairies

Bird Identification

HERRING GULL (*LARUS ARGENTATUS*)

Size: 22 to 26 inches

Wingspan: 54 to 57 inches

Comparative size: Red-tailed hawk to goose

Description: White head; hefty yellow bill with red spot; broad wings with black tips; light gray back; white underparts; dull pink legs; brownish streaks on the head and neck during winter

Range: From Alaska across northern Canada to the Maritime Provinces and throughout the United States and parts of coastal Mexico

Habitat: Fresh and saltwater shore lines, open ocean, lakes, rivers, estuaries, and urban areas

Eggs: Light olive, buff, or greenish with darker splotches or speckling

RING-BILLED GULL (*LARUS DELAWARENSIS*)

Size: 17 to 21 inches

Wingspan: 41 to 46 inches

Comparative size: Crow to red-tailed hawk

Description: Slim yellow bill with black ring; square-tipped tail; white head, neck, underparts, and tail; gray back and wings; wingtips black with large, white spots; yellow feet and legs

Range: Throughout most of Canada and the lower forty-eight United States as well as Mexico

Habitat: Fresh and saltwater, open country, and urban areas

Eggs: Pale olive gray with dark brown speckles

Collective noun(s): A colony, a flock, a flotilla, a gullery, or a squabble of gulls

Sparrow:
House Sparrow, Song Sparrow

House Sparrow (**Passer domesticus**)

Despite its name, the house sparrow is not related to other North American sparrows. Originating in the Mediterranean region and India, this bird spread as civilizations expanded. With good intentions, farmers imported the house sparrow into North America to help control crop-threatening insects.

Although sparrows devour a high volume of insects, they themselves have been considered pests. Sparrow pots were used in seventeenth-century England to deal with this bird's booming population.[145] These small clay pots were hung on the walls of houses to provide attractive nesting sites for sparrows. The young birds were removed before they fledged and often ended up in pies to supplement a farm family's diet. Sparrows were also considered pests in Central Europe, where charms were used to keep them away from grain stores.

Quite the opposite was true with the ancient Romans, who considered sparrows an asset to farmers. In fact, sparrows were regarded as household spirits and a symbol of protection. To the Greeks, the sparrow was regarded as a bird of love. In her "Hymn to Aphrodite," Greek poet Sappho (c. 610–570 BCE) described the goddess's chariot as

---

145. J. Denis Summers-Smith, *In Search of Sparrows* (London: T & AD Poyser, 1992), 31.

being drawn by sparrows. Aristotle represented sparrows as a symbol of promiscuity, and their eggs were thought to be an aphrodisiac.

In British folklore, it was believed that ancestors could return as sparrows despite this bird having personified the lower classes during the Middle Ages. In addition, sparrows were thought to carry the souls of the dead.

This bird's common name can be traced back to the Old English *sparwa* or *spearwa*, with "sparrow" finally appearing in the fourteenth century.[146] The bird's French name, *moineau*, was derived from *moine*, meaning "monk," because of the bird's drab coloring and the appearance of wearing a hood.[147] In the early American colonies, English settlers referred to many types of small brown birds as sparrows.

Magical Workings

This unassuming little bird is instrumental in activating energy for manifesting dreams and desires. Sparrow's association with love can be called upon for spells of attraction and fidelity as well as sex magic. Place an image or figurine of sparrow on your Ostara altar to symbolize fertility and the fecundity of spring. Sparrow is also an aid for grounding energy after ritual and magic work.

Despite its size, sparrow teaches us about assertiveness and can aid in providing protection. Invite this bird into your home to foster happiness. It is also an aid for attracting luck.

Make Connection

To connect with sparrow energy, put on a brown hoodie or use a brown blanket or bath towel to cover your head and shoulders. Squat down on the floor and make yourself as small as you can. Visualize pulling your aura close to your body. Slowly look around you and try to sense what it feels like to be a little bird. Be aware of your feet on the floor, and when you feel grounded and sure of yourself, be attentive for any messages sparrow may send.

Associations

Zodiac: Libra, Virgo

Element(s): Air, earth

---

146. Fraser and Gray, *Australian Bird Names*, 284.

147. Wells, *100 Birds and How They Got Their Names*, 231.

Sabbat(s): Ostara
Goddesses: Aphrodite, Venus
Solar system: Moon, Sun

Bird Identification

HOUSE SPARROW (*PASSER DOMESTICUS*)

Size: 6 to 6½ inches

Wingspan: 7 to 9 inches

Description: Stout, chunky body; full chest; large, rounded head; stubby, pointed bill

Male: Gray crown; white cheeks; black bib; bill black in summer, yellow in winter; sides of head, back, and wings brown with black patterning; buff to gray underparts

Female: Light brown crown; back and wings light brown with darker patterning; broad, buff eye line; buff-brown underparts

Range: Most of Canada, throughout the lower forty-eight United States, Mexico, Central America, and parts of South America

Habitat: Residential areas, parks, urban areas, open country, and grassland

Eggs: White to greenish or bluish white, spotted gray or brown

SONG SPARROW (*MELOSPIZA MELODIA*)

Size: 4½ to 6½ inches

Wingspan: 7 to 9 inches

Description: Short bill; rounded head; long, rounded tail; broad wings; upperparts streaked russet and gray; white chest and flanks with thick streaks; color and streaking varies by region

Range: From southern coastal Alaska, across Canada, throughout the United States into northern Mexico

Habitat: Nearly any open habitat from fields, backyards, and forest edges

Eggs: Blue, blue-green, or gray-green spotted with brown, red-brown, or lilac

Collective noun(s): A crew, a flutter, a host, or a quarrel of sparrows

Starling:
European Starling

European Starling (Sturnus vulgaris)

The starling's common name is derived from the Anglo-Saxon name for this bird, *staer*, which means "little star." [148] It is thought that the starling was so named either because of its star-shaped silhouette in flight or because of its speckled, starry-like winter plumage.

Starlings are not native to North America. In the early 1890s, one hundred of them were imported and released in New York City's Central Park by Shakespeare enthusiasts who thought that all of the birds mentioned by the great bard should live in the New World.[149] Being adaptable birds, starlings rapidly increased their numbers and came to be considered pests. Back in England on August 12, 1949, so many roosted on the hands of Big Ben that they managed to stop the clock.[150]

The starling's nearest relatives, the mynah birds, are well known for imitating human speech. Like its cousin, the starling can mimic humans, dogs, and even car sounds. They can also imitate the songs of up to twenty different birds. Pliny noted that he knew of one

---

148. Erickson, *For the Birds*, 141.

149. Leslie Day, *Field Guide to the Natural World of New York City* (Baltimore: Johns Hopkins University Press, 2007), 228.

150. Wells, *100 Birds and How They Got Their Names*, 236.

such talented starling that spoke both Latin and Greek. Mozart kept a starling as a pet and trained it to whistle parts of his compositions.

The Gaelic name for starling is *druid*. They are also called *druid-bhreac*, "speckled druid"; *druideag*, "little druid"; and black star.[151] In Celtic legend, Branwen rescued a starling from the clutches of the kitchen cat and taught it to speak. She also used it like a pigeon to carry messages to her brother Bran.

According to folklore in regions where starlings migrate, if they arrive in their winter areas early, the season will be severe. Starlings are strong fliers, reaching up to forty-eight miles an hour. They are also very noisy. These birds travel in large groups that often include blackbirds and grackles. Although a very common bird, starlings are masters of aerobatic displays. When I was a child, I enjoyed watching an enormous flock of starlings as they wheeled in unison over the woods behind our house. The evening display of flowing patterns seemed to ebb and flow like ocean waves.

Magical Workings

Starling is a master of adaptation and a model for developing new skills. While it can be called upon when aggression is needed, starling shows us that confrontational situations are best handled through peaceful negotiation. Call on starling for guidance in such situations.

Starling is a bird of empowerment that fosters confidence and a sense of worth. Ask for starling's inspiration to help stoke the embers of your imagination. Also, place a picture of it in your work area to help stoke your creative expression. In addition, this bird helps to foster communication that strengthens relationships and draws community together.

Make Connection

To connect with starling energy, go outside on a clear night and gaze at the stars. Use your imagination to see the stars as the speckled plumage of starlings and visualize their shapes moving against the night sky. As you begin to pick out more starlings among the stars, imagine them moving in great morphing shapes back and forth across the sky. Feel the flow of their flight and their connection with each other as you recite three times:

---

151. Alexander Robert Forbes, *Gaelic Names of Beasts (Mammalia), Birds, Fishes, Insects, Reptiles, Etc.* (Edinburgh, Scotland: Oliver and Boyd, 1905), 335.

"Birds of the stars, dark as night, may I join you in your flight." When they deem you ready, you will feel yourself draw into their murmuration (group).

Associations
Element(s): Air
Ogham: Tinne

Bird Identification
EUROPEAN STARLING (*STURNUS VULGARIS*)

Size: 8 to 9 inches

Wingspan: 12 to 15½ inches

Comparative size: Robin

Description: Stocky body; short tail; long and slender yellow beak; short, triangular wings; appears black all over at a distance but is purplish-green iridescent in summer, brown with white spots in winter

Range: From a small area of southwestern Alaska, across most of Canada, and south throughout the United States, and parts of northern Mexico

Habitat: Cities, suburban areas, farmlands, and ranches

Eggs: Bluish or greenish white

Collective noun(s): A chattering, a cloud, a filth, a murmuration, or a roost of starlings

Stork:
Wood Stork

Wood Stork (Mycteria americana)

People of the Baltic region considered the stork a hearth deity that protected their homes from fire and thunderstorms and that safeguarded their families. Throughout other parts of Europe, storks became a symbol of wealth and their nests were a welcome sight on housetops to garner good luck. It became common practice to place cartwheels, baskets, or platforms on house roofs to encourage nesting. Storks return year after year to the same nest, and it was a bad omen for the homeowner if they did not. I saw many stork nests and platforms on roofs in Germany and the Alsace region of France when I lived in Europe.

As an emblem of paternal care, the Roman *Lex Ciconia*, "stork law," required citizens to take care of their elderly relatives.[152] In addition, the stork was portrayed on Roman coins dating from approximately 77 to 43 BCE.[153] To the Greeks, the stork was an archetypal symbol of mother and provider. Because of their return in the spring, storks were a symbol of fertility, which is no surprise since they are still used today when celebrating pregnancy and birth. However, the link between storks and human babies is a very old and widespread notion.

---

152. Tate, *Flights of Fancy*, 132.
153. Arnott, *Birds in the Ancient World from A to Z*, 247.

The ancient Vedic myths of India told of babies being formed in the *śaiśava*, "baby pool," which was said to be located in a bend of the River Ganges.[154] When a baby was ready, a stork would retrieve it and carry the infant to its human mother. In addition, it was believed in Egypt and Europe that unborn souls waited in watery, marshy areas, which are stork habitats.

Stories of storks bringing babies were especially prevalent in Germany, Holland, and Denmark. An old German name for stork, *Adebar* or *Odebaro,* may have meant "soul-bringer"; however, it has also been interpreted as "luck-bringer" and "child-bringer." [155] And, of course, there's Hans Christian Andersen's story "The Storks," which told how human babies waited in a state of dreaming in a pond in Egypt until a stork brought them to families.

The only stork native to North America was originally called a wood ibis because of its slightly downward-curving bill. The stork's common name comes from the Old English word *stearc,* meaning "stiff," in reference to the appearance of the bird's posture.[156] The way to tell a stork from a heron is that the stork flies with its neck extended while herons tuck their necks back into an S-shape during flight.

While storks can hiss, croak, and whistle, they most often rattle their bills to make sound. Because of this, they became associated with sorcery.

Magical Workings

Rightfully so, stork is associated with fertility, pregnancy, and childbirth. Call on it to aid you in these aspects of your life. Use an image or figurine of stork on your altar for a child-naming or dedication ritual, or to express your devotion to your child. Stork boosts protection spells, especially those intended for children.

As a symbol of spring, include stork on your Ostara altar to celebrate the rebirth and renewal of nature. In addition, this bird supports transitions for any type of new beginning in your life. It is also instrumental in boosting spells to attract luck, opportunities, and wealth. As a bird of watery habitats, stork is associated with and supports the emotions. It also stirs the waters of creativity. Additionally, stork can be called upon for help in contacting spirits.

---

154. E. J. Michael Witzel, *The Origins of the World's Mythologies* (New York: Oxford University Press, 2012), 173.

155. Anatoly Liberman, *An Analytic Dictionary of the English Etymology: An Introduction* (Minneapolis, MN: University of Minnesota Press, 2008), 72.

156. Tate, *Flights of Fancy*, 133.

Make Connections

To connect with stork energy, visualize yourself in a dreaming pool of warm, soothing water. Fronds of long grass move gently, enveloping your body in a soft blanket of green. Through the water you can see a large bird peering down at you with loving eyes. It gently gathers the grass around you and lifts you from the water. The next thing you are aware of is being snuggled and warm in your bed. When stork is ready to make connection, it will bend toward you and gently touch you with its beak.

Associations

Zodiac: Pisces

Element(s): Air, water

Sabbat(s): Ostara

Goddesses: Hera, Juno, Venus

God: Hermes

Magical beings: Fairies

Bird Identification

WOOD STORK (*MYCTERIA AMERICANA*)

Size: 35 to 45 inches

Wingspan: 59 to 69 inches

Comparative size: Goose

Description: White overall; white wings with black flight feathers; black tail; long, thick, down-curved bill; bare, gray or brownish head and neck; long, gray legs

Range: Coastal South Carolina, south throughout Florida and the Gulf Coast to Texas, as well as coastal Mexico, Central America, and many parts of South America

Habitat: On or near the coast and marshy wetlands

Eggs: White

Collective noun(s): A clatter, a flock, a mustering, or a silence of storks

Swallow and Swift:
Barn Swallow, Chimney Swift, White-Throated Swift

Barn Swallow (Hirundo rustica)

Although swallows and swifts come from different families, they have a great deal in common and their energy is similar, which is why I have presented them together. First, it is important to know their basic differences for identification. Swallows have deeply forked tails and a slight bend in their wings during flight. Swifts have long, crescent-shaped wings when seen in flight. While you may see swallows sitting on wires or fences, swifts cannot do this because their feet are so tiny. However, they have no trouble clinging to vertical surfaces.

The swallow was one of the birds often used to represent the Egyptian ba (soul), and it was believed that deceased people could return as swallows. The bird was also depicted riding in the prow of Ra's solar boat, and Isis was said to change into a swallow at night. Because swallows and swifts nest in or near houses, the Romans considered them sacred to household deities. Always on the move, swifts can sleep on the wing during long migratory flights. They have been regarded as very mysterious because they seem to disappear so suddenly in the autumn.

Folklore has treated these birds differently, with the swift a negative omen and the swallow a positive one. It was considered good luck to have a swallow build its nest on your house. However, if a swift came all the way down a chimney and into a house, it was regarded as a sure sign that someone in the family would soon die. Despite being a bad omen, the swift, along with the swallow, was associated with the return of spring and increasing light.

Magical Workings

Swallow and swift are birds of the home, nesting under our roofs and in our chimneys. Light a candle in their honor for bringing security, warmth, and protection to your shared abode. Represent both or either of these birds on your Ostara altar to welcome the return of spring and the renewal of the green world.

Call on swallow to boost spells relating to love, fertility, and family. Swallow also brings powerful energy for manifesting what you desire and for reversing spells. Swift is an aid for inviting opportunities into your life as well as seeing the ones that may already be at hand. Swallow and swift foster healing energy and can be called upon to grace circle gatherings for this purpose. Both birds support divination practices; however, swift is especially adept at boosting psychic abilities and prophecy skills.

Make Connection

To connect with the energy of swallow and swift, go outside at dusk, gaze up at the sky, and with your arms out to the sides turn in circles. Visualize whirling and circling above the trees and rooftops with speed and agility. Stop spinning but continue to hold your arms out to the sides. If you feel dizzy, sit on the ground but keep your arms up. Close your eyes and imagine a flight of swallows or a flock of swifts above you. When they begin to fly lower around you, encircling you with their light, they are ready to connect with you.

Associations

SWALLOW
Element(s): Fire
Sabbat(s): Mabon, Ostara
Goddesses: Aphrodite, Inanna, Isis, Venus
God: Ra
Solar system: Sun

SWIFT

Element(s): Air, water

Sabbat(s): Ostara

Goddesses: The Muses

Solar system: Moon

Moon phases: Waxing or Waning Crescent

Bird Identification

BARN SWALLOW (*HIRUNDO RUSTICA*)

Size: 6 to 7½ inches

Wingspan: 11 to 12½ inches

Comparative size: Sparrow

Description: Overall cone shape; slightly flattened head; long, pointed wings; long outer feathers on tail; steely blue back, wings, and tail; buff to reddish underparts; blue crown and face; cinnamon-colored forehead and throat

Range: From southern coastal Alaska to Newfoundland and south throughout the United States, Mexico, Central America, and South America

Habitat: Open agricultural fields, suburban areas, marshes, and lake or pond shores

Eggs: Creamy or pinkish white, with brown, lavender, or gray spots

CHIMNEY SWIFT (*CHAETURA PELAGICA*)

Size: 4½ to 6 inches

Wingspan: 10 to 12 inches

Comparative size: Sparrow

Description: Slender, spindle-shaped body; long, narrow, curved wings; round head; short neck; short, tapered tail; short, wide bill; dark gray-brown all over; slightly paler throat; sometimes appears black

Range: From southeastern Saskatchewan across southern Canada to Nova Scotia and south through the plains states to the East Coast, along the Gulf Coast into Mexico and parts of South America

Habitat: Forests, open country, and towns

Eggs: White

WHITE-THROATED SWIFT (*AERONAUTES SAXATALIS*)

Size: 6 to 7 inches

Wingspan: 13 to 14 inches

Comparative size: Sparrow

Description: Cylindrical body; black back, wings, and tail; white throat, belly, and flanks; long, pointed, swept-back wings

Range: From British Columbia through the Rocky Mountains, California, the Southwest, and parts of Mexico and Central America

Habitat: Arid mountains and rocky areas

Eggs: White

Collective noun(s): A flight or a kettle of swallows and a flock or a swoop of swifts

Swan:
Mute Swan, Trumpeter Swan, Tundra Swan

Mute Swan (Cygnus olor)

Around the world and throughout time, the swan has been considered a bird of extreme beauty, spirituality, and power. The mute swan can be distinguished from other species by the way it holds its neck in a graceful curve; other swans hold their necks up straight. Romantic as it is, the myth that the mute swan only finds its voice just before death is not true. Although it is not as vocal as other swans, it does make noise throughout its life. The trumpeter swan was so named because of its resounding calls.

Legends of swan maidens can be found from the Babylonians and the Egyptians to the Norse and the Celts. Swans were almost universally believed to shape-shift into human form. Celtic lore sometimes portrayed them as fairies in disguise. Swans figured largely in the stories of Llyr, Angus, and many other Celtic gods. In Norse myth, swans embodied the Valkyries, who were regarded as symbols of beauty and mystery, and their feathers were considered magical. They could also shape-shift into ravens. Shamans in various traditions were said to wear cloaks of swan feathers.

Swans were believed to move between the physical and spiritual worlds, and were closely associated with the soul. In many cultures, the swan was associated with music, poetry, and love. In Finnish myth, a swan singing a haunting melody circled the island of the dead. Although associated with death and the otherworld, the swan also embodied the solar principle of light and fecundity. On Scotland's Hebrides islands, to hear a swan on Friday means good luck.

The genus name *Cygnus* is Latin, meaning "swan." Male swans are called cobs, females are called pens, and baby swans are cygnets.[157]

Magical Workings

The otherworldly beauty of swan has linked it with death and the afterlife. It can help you find a connection with those you love who have passed beyond the veil. Swan is also instrumental for understanding the symbolism of dreams and remembering past lives. Long associated with shamanic work, this bird can guide you through other realms and support your vision quests. Swan aids divination as well as interpreting messages and omens. It can also help build your clairvoyant skills.

Closely aligned with spirituality, swan can light the way to show where your path lies. It can help you awaken to your power and cultivate intuition. Call on swan to boost love spells and to break enchantments. With its help, you can foster change and manifest what you desire. A bird of transformation, swan provides support during life's transitions. Place an image of swan on your Imbolc and Mabon altars to symbolize these seasonal changes.

Make Connection

To connect with swan energy, visualize one moving majestically across a still pond. Having transformed from an ugly duckling, its enigmatic beauty fosters enchantment and mystery. Knowing that beauty is only skin deep, swan holds grace, love, and compassion in high regard. Keep your heart open and your intentions selfless to invite swan's contact, which will bring a deep, meaningful sense of love.

From June to October the Cygnus constellation is easily visible in the northern hemisphere. The brightest stars in this constellation form a cross shape. About an hour after sunset, look straight up to the brightest star overhead. That star marks the tail of the swan; the lower part of the cross is its long neck and head. Visualize the swan and then close your eyes to feel the peace and power of this great bird.

---

157. Wells, *100 Birds and How They Got Their Names*, 242.

Associations

Zodiac: Libra, Pisces

Element(s): Air, earth, water

Sabbat(s): Imbolc, Mabon, Samhain

Goddesses: Aphrodite, Brigid, the Muses, Nemesis, Sarasvati, Venus

Gods: Angus, Apollo, Brahma, Cú Chulainn, Lir/Llyr, Midir, Njord, Zeus

Solar system: Sun, Venus

Ogham: Eadha, Gort

Magical beings: Elves, fairies

Bird Identification

MUTE SWAN (CYGNUS OLOR)

Also known as: Domestic swan, wild swan

Size: 50 to 60 inches

Wingspan: 82 to 94 inches

Comparative size: Very large

Description: All-white body and wings; orange bill with black knob at base; legs and feet range from black to grayish-pink

Range: Small areas from the Mid-Atlantic states through the Midwest

Habitat: Ponds, rivers, bogs, coastal lagoons, and bays

Eggs: Blue-green when first laid, turning white, and then brown with staining

TRUMPETER SWAN (CYGNUS BUCCINATOR)

Size: 54 to 62 inches

Wingspan: 75 to 80 inches

Comparative size: Very large

Description: All-white body and wings; long, straight neck; black bill and face; black legs and feet

Range: Small areas of southern Alaska, British Columbia, Alberta, Oregon, Idaho, Montana, and Wyoming

Habitat: Marshes, lakes, or rivers with dense vegetation

Eggs: Creamy white

TUNDRA SWAN (*CYGNUS COLUMBIANUS*)

Also known as: Whistling swan

Size: 47 to 58 inches

Wingspan: 66 inches

Comparative size: Very large

Description: All-white body and wings; black bill, usually with yellow patch in front of each eye; black legs and feet

Range: Arctic coasts of Alaska and Canada, along corridors to the Mid-Atlantic coast and the West Coast; occasionally on the Great Lakes

Habitat: Tundra, marshy lakes, and bays

Eggs: Creamy white

Collective noun(s): A bevy, a lamentation, a regatta, or a wedge of swans

Turkey:
Wild Turkey

Wild Turkey (Meleagris gallopavo)

Although we most often think of turkeys in relation to Thanksgiving dinner, the Pueblo people of the Southwest kept flocks of turkeys mainly for their feathers, which were used for ritual and adornment. Native Americans generally regarded the turkey as a symbol of wisdom and a guide to the afterlife. These birds were also considered a symbol of male virility and female fecundity.

Instead of the eagle, Benjamin Franklin proposed the turkey as the national bird because of its intelligence and regal display of feathers. We may question Franklin's assessment of intelligence because of the bird's current reputation as being dim-witted. However, this notion stems from the early nineteenth century when turkeys were easy to hunt and considered stupid for being inattentive to sounds.[158] They have since learned to be wary of humans.

Called the king of the game birds, turkeys were often described as majestic and noble. If you encounter a wild turkey, you will understand this sentiment because of this bird's stately presence. In the sixteenth century, wild turkeys were introduced into Europe,

---

158. Angus K. Gillespie and Jay Mechling, eds. *American Wildlife in Symbol and Story* (Knoxville, TN: University of Tennessee Press, 1987), 24.

where they were kept as ornamental birds in parks and large gardens along with pheasants and peacocks.[159]

This bird's name has nothing to do with the country of Turkey. According to speculation, the name *turkey* came from the Hindi word *toka*, meaning "peacock" or "big hen."[160] In fact, the word *turkey* was in use in England before this bird arrived in the British Isles. Prior to the sixteenth century, the word *turkey* had the meaning of "strange" or "exotic," and it is thought to have referred to guinea fowl.[161]

While the turkey was associated with Thanksgiving prior to President Lincoln's declaration of a national feast day, it did not become the pièce de résistance until domestic turkey farms were established in the early twentieth century.[162] While the domesticated bird cannot fly, the wild turkey flies up into trees to roost.

According to folklore, a turkey gobbling at you while a guest at someone's home meant you were a welcomed visitor. Turkeys were considered weather birds and associated with rain because of their restlessness before storms. And, of course, ending up with the largest half of a turkey wishbone after the Thanksgiving meal is a sign of good luck. A female turkey is called a hen, a male is a gobbler or a tom, and babies are called poults.[163]

Magical Workings

Place a picture or a figurine of turkey on your Mabon altar to represent abundance and shared blessings. Call on turkey when a loved one passes to serve as a guide for them. Also bury an intact wishbone in the ground to honor the person who has died and to mark their passage into rebirth. Use a feather in spells related to fertility and sexuality, or place one under your bed to emphasize your intent. In addition, a feather or a figurine can be placed on your altar to express gratitude.

Make Connection

Begin with a piece of paper, the bigger the better, to fashion a fan. Place it on a flat surface, and then fold one short end back about an inch or so. Flip the paper over and make

---

159. Nozedar, *The Secret Language of Birds*, 273.

160. Andrew F. Smith, *The Turkey: An American Story* (Urbana, IL: University of Illinois Press, 2006), 26.

161. Ibid., 27.

162. Gillespie and Mechling, *American Wildlife in Symbol and Story*, 31.

163. Fraser and Gray, *Australian Bird Names*, 7.

another fold. Continue until you reach the other end of the paper. This will serve as your fantail. Hold it with both hands behind your back, and then slowly walk around the room lifting a knee up high for each step. Visualize a majestic turkey, the king (or queen) of game birds who was an equal to the peacock in Europe for its nobility. Reach out with your energy and ask turkey to join you. Listen for subtle noises and perhaps a very faint "gobble" for a sign of this bird's presence.

Associations
Element(s): Earth
Sabbat(s): Mabon

Bird Identification
WILD TURKEY (*MELEAGRIS GALLOPAVO*)

Size: 43 to 47 inches

Wingspan: 49 to 56 inches

Comparative Size: Goose to very large

Description: Plump body; long legs; bare head and neck; overall dark patterns with iridescent bronze sheen; bands of buff or rusty brown on rump and tail feathers; wide, rounded tail

Male: Bright red neck and wattles on throat; blue on face; spurs on feet; long "beard" on breast

Female: Brownish head and neck; small, reddish wattle

Range: Most of southern United States from Arizona east, and north to New England

Habitat: Forests especially with nut trees, and field edges; woodsy suburban and urban areas

Eggs: Pale yellowish-tan with reddish-brown or pinkish spots

Collective noun(s): A flock or a rafter of turkeys

Vulture:
Black Vulture, Turkey Vulture

Turkey Vulture (Cathartes aura)

Associated with death and renewal for thousands of years, it has only been in more re-cent centuries that vultures have acquired a sinister connotation. While their common name comes from the Latin *vuellere*, "to tear," the vulture's family name, Cathartidae, comes from the Greek *kathartes*, meaning "a cleanser."[164] Cleansing and purification were considered part of the cycle of renewal and transformation. Not equipped for kill-ing, vultures are recyclers relying on nature to provide for them.

In addition to ridding the world of dead carcasses, vultures were believed to conduct souls to the next world. According to the Egyptian Book of the Dead, a vulture goddess guarded the first gate to the underworld. In addition, the Egyptian goddess Nekhbet was often depicted as a vulture or wearing a vulture headdress, as was the goddess Mut. Both goddesses were called upon to ease childbirth. Also, Mut's name meant "mother."[165]

To the Greeks, the vulture was a symbol of the duality and unity of heaven and earth, the spiritual and material. Both the Greeks and Romans used the vulture's flight pattern for augury. Worldwide, the vulture has been regarded as a bird of mystery and power. Vulture feathers were used as amulets and considered a powerful totem to the Pueblo

---

164. Fraser and Gray, *Australian Bird Names*, 258.
165. Pat Remler, *Egyptian Mythology A to Z, Third Edition* (New York: Chelsea House, 2010), 126.

people of the American Southwest. In South America, the Maya regarded vultures as solar birds and associated them with the cosmos and the cycles of life.

Vultures are graceful flyers as they circle high on thermals, which they have the unique ability to see. Black vultures and turkey vultures often soar together and can be distinguished in flight: the black vulture uses strong wing beats followed by short glides, whereas the turkey vulture rolls and sways from side to side. On the ground, black vultures look compact compared to the lanky turkey vultures.

Magical Workings

This powerful bird is a guardian of the mysteries that turn the cycle of life, death, and rebirth. Call on vulture to guide a loved one over the threshold into the afterlife toward eventual renewal and transformation. Vulture's compassionate nature provides comfort to those who remain in this world.

Long regarded as a symbol of mother goddesses, this bird shows us how to nurture others as well as ourselves. Call on it to aid in childbirth for strength and protection as you welcome a new person into this world. Vulture fosters loyalty and trust in families, and can be especially helpful when resolving problems. It supports all forms of divination and aids in the development of psychic skills. Call on vulture to guide you in shamanic work and spiritual growth.

Make Connection

To connect with vulture energy, drape a red cloth or blanket around your shoulders and across your arms so you can hold one end in each hand. Open your arms wide, creating large wings, as you visualize yourself in the ancient vulture shrine room at Çatalhüyük. With vulture you stand at the threshold between life and death, and life renewed. Along with the frightening power of vulture, you will also find compassion and gentleness. Vulture will reveal both sides of itself when you are ready.

Associations

Zodiac: Scorpio
Element(s): Air, earth, water
Sabbat(s): Imbolc, Samhain
Goddesses: Artemis, Hathor, Isis, Mut, Nekhbet, Nephthys, Tiamat
Gods: Apollo, Ares, Cronus, Mars, Saturn, Zeus

Bird Identification

BLACK VULTURE (*CORAGYPS ATRATUS*)

Size: 23 to 27 inches

Wingspan: 54 to 59 inches

Comparative size: Red-tailed hawk to goose

Description: Overall almost uniformly black; small, bare, grayish head; narrow, hooked bill; broad, rounded wings; short, rounded tail; white patch near wingtips

Range: From the Mid-Atlantic south to Florida and west to Missouri, south and west through part of Texas, most of Mexico, Central America, and South America

Habitat: Open areas with nearby forests

Eggs: Pale green or bluish white with a few large, brown blotches

TURKEY VULTURE (*CATHARTES AURA*)

Also known as: Turkey buzzard

Size: 25 to 32 inches

Wingspan: 67 to 70 inches

Comparative size: Goose

Description: Long, broad wings; long tail; small, bare, red head; pale bill; dark brown all over; trailing edge and wingtips slightly lighter

Range: From southern British Columbia east to southern Maine and south throughout the United States, Mexico, Central America, and South America

Habitat: Open areas such as roadsides, suburbs, fields, and woodlands

Eggs: White slightly tinged with gray, blue, or green, along with dark brown spots

Collective noun(s): A colony, a committee, a looming, or a wake of vultures

Waxwing:
Bohemian Waxwing, Cedar Waxwing

Bohemian Waxwing (Bombycilla garrulus)

Sleek and silky, waxwings look like they just fluttered out of a painting. These birds are well known for traveling in large flocks that swoop into fruit trees. Sitting in a row, small groups share food by passing fruit down the line until one eats it. Because of their sudden erratic appearance in the autumn, these birds gained a reputation for being harbingers of war, pestilence, and other disasters.

During the Middle Ages, their appearance was an omen of the plague. To German speakers, they were known as *sterbe-vogel*, "death birds," because huge flocks would swoop in and devour vast amounts of fruit before it could be harvested.[166] In Irish folklore, the waxwing was regarded as a harbinger of the banshee who would wail when death was nigh. In addition, the red spots of color on some of the wing feathers were called "drops of hellfire."[167] To others, the red drops looked more like sealing wax, which is the source of the bird's common name, waxwing.

The perception of waxwings changed by the fifteenth century thanks in large part to artists who appreciated their beauty. Despite the fact that cedar waxwings trill and whistle more than produce a song, they became associated with angelic music. As far as prophecy

---

166. Armstrong, *The Life and Lore of the Bird in Nature, Art, Myth and Literature*, 61.
167. Murphy-Hiscock, *Birds: A Spiritual Field Guide*, 203.

was concerned, a large flock of waxwings in the autumn simply came to mean that the approaching winter would bring very cold weather. The waxwing also became a sign of good luck if it visited your property.

The genus name, *Bombycilla*, is Latin for "silk tail," in reference to the silklike ribbon of color on their tails.[168] Because it seemed to travel in nomadic winter flocks, the Bohemian waxwing was so named in reference to an unconventional or gypsy-like lifestyle.

Magical Workings

The eye mask on the face of waxwing has linked it with shamanism and the ability to transverse the realms. Call on this bird for support in journeying, astral travel, or any practice that involves a shift in consciousness. Also ask for its help in contacting the angelic or fairy realms. Keep an image of waxwing nearby when engaging in divination or any form of prophecy to foster clarity. It can also give your good luck spells a boost.

Although this bird was linked with death and negativity in the past, its nature is anything but destructive. Waxwing can bring a gentleness to Samhain rituals or anytime you bid a loved one farewell. It can also help you through the changes that follow a death. A bird of community, waxwing fosters harmony through group effort and sharing.

Make Connection

To connect with waxwing energy, gather a red candle, yellow ribbon, a heat-resistant plate, and a cup of berries or small pieces of fruit. As you sit in front of your altar, cut several short lengths of the yellow ribbon and place them on the plate. Light the candle and gaze at it as you visualize a crab apple or other tree ladened with fruit. Carefully tip the candle, allowing several drops of wax to fall on the ribbon. Set the candle down and gaze at the flame as you say: "*Waxwing, waxwing, silky and sleek; Blessed be and merry meet.*"

Continue with your visualization and see the tree with a flock of waxwings passing fruit to each other. Slowly and one by one eat the fruit you have placed on your altar. When you are finished, blow out the candle, close your eyes, and hold the image of waxwing in your mind. Let the image fade, but if it remains longer than expected, waxwing may be present.

Associations

Element(s): Air, fire

Sabbat(s): Samhain

---

168. Sandrock and Prior, *The Scientific Nomenclature of Birds in the Upper Midwest*, 24.

Trees: Cherry, crab apple, hackberry

Magical beings: Fairies

Bird Identification

BOHEMIAN WAXWING (*BOMBYCILLA GARRULUS*)

Also known as: Black-throated waxwing, silktail

Size: 7 to 8 inches

Wingspan: 12 to 13 inches

Comparative size: Sparrow to robin

Description: Sleek body; mostly light brownish gray; darker wings; head crest often lies flat; black eye mask and throat; white wing patches; white and yellow edging on wings; yellow, square-tipped tail; yellow to rusty color under tail

Range: From Alaska east through Canada to Newfoundland and northern New England, around the Great Lakes; and from Wisconsin south to Colorado to the West Coast

Habitat: Open forests, parks, and suburban and urban areas wherever fruit is found

Eggs: Pale blue-gray with black spots

CEDAR WAXWING (*BOMBYCILLA CEDRORUM*)

Also known as: Cedar bird, cherry bird

Size: 6 to 8 inches

Wingspan: 9 to 12 inches

Comparative size: Sparrow to robin

Description: Sleek, brownish-gray body; rusty-orange breast fades into yellow belly; head crest often lies flat; black eye mask bordered by white stripe; broad, pointed wings; red tips on inner wing feathers; short, yellow or reddish, square-tipped tail

Range: From Pacific coast in Canada east to Newfoundland and south throughout the United States, Mexico, Central America, and a small part of South America

Habitat: Open woodlands, orchards, and residential areas

Eggs: Pale blue or blue-gray eggs, often with black or gray spots

Collective noun(s): A museum of waxwings

Woodpecker:
Downy Woodpecker, Northern Flicker

Downy Woodpecker (Picoides pubescens)

Wherever woodpeckers live, they have been considered magical birds with powers of prophecy. They were believed to be able to forecast weather, and in many countries they were known as rain birds. In his play *The Birds*, Greek writer Aristophanes (c. 450–388 BCE) told a story of how Zeus became the god of thunder after stealing the woodpecker's scepter. From ancient Greece to the Teutonic tribes of Germany and the Pueblo people of North America, these birds were associated with thunder and lightning. In addition, woodpeckers were thought to have the ability to avert lightning, and their feathers were used for protection against it.

In Norse legend, the woodpecker's association with thunder and lightning made it a bird of Thor. According to Etruscan legend, red-headed woodpeckers were actually red-cap fairies. In both Greece and Rome, woodpeckers were considered omens of good luck. According to Roman myth, Circe, a goddess of magic, turned King Picus, a seer and the son of Saturn, into a woodpecker. In addition, Pan was said to have been hatched from a woodpecker's egg.

The woodpecker's drumming sound is not produced while feeding instead the noise substitutes for a call or a song. This drumming noise gave rise to an association with shamans and the ability to communicate with deities. According to folklore, these birds were believed to have access to a magical herb called springwort, which was said to grow where humans could not find it. Springwort was believed to provide woodpeckers with the mystical ability to open secret places and to locate hidden treasure.

Woodpeckers use their stiff tails as props for support and balance as they move around on trees. Although the northern flicker can climb tree trunks like other wood-peckers, it usually gets its food on the ground. There are two colorations of northern flickers: The one called yellow-shafted lives east of the Rocky Mountains, and the red-shafted lives in the westernmost states.

Magical Workings

Woodpecker is a bird of activation. It stimulates cycles, growth, and the mind. Shamanic work with this bird can awaken hidden knowledge and reveal the truth that you seek. Woodpecker is a guide for travelers in the mundane world and in other realms. It also provides protection and security, allowing you the freedom to fully experience your adventures.

Call on woodpecker for support in all forms of divination, and to aid in understanding any messages or prophecy you receive. It can also give your magic a boost especially spells for luck. If fertility is an issue, keep pictures or figurines of woodpecker on your altar, in your bedroom, and various places around your home to enhance your intention.

Make Connection

To connect with woodpecker energy, use two percussion sticks, drumsticks, or two pieces of wood to clap together. Find a rhythm that you can sustain, close your eyes, and focus on the sound. If you feel a shift in consciousness, allow it to occur and bring the image of a woodpecker into your mind. Wait to see if it will interact with you. If it does, let woodpecker guide you.

Associations

Zodiac: Aries

Element(s): Air, earth, fire

Gods: Ares, Buddha, Jupiter, Mars, Pan, Silvanus, Zeus

Tree: Oak

Flower: Peony

Solar system: Mars

Bird Identification

DOWNY WOODPECKER (*PICOIDES PUBESCENS*)

Size: 5½ to 7 inches

Wingspan: 10 to 12 inches

Comparative size: Sparrow

Description: Straight, chisel-shaped bill; blocky head; wide shoulders; straight-backed posture; upperparts checkered black and white; black wings with white spots; face streaked black and white; outer tail feathers white with a few black spots

Male: Red patch on back of head

Range: From Alaska across Canada to Labrador, south throughout the United States except a few parts of the Southwest and Texas

Habitat: Open woodlands, orchards, city parks, and backyards

Eggs: White

NORTHERN FLICKER (*COLAPTES AURATUS*)

Size: 10 to 14 inches

Wingspan: 16 to 20 inches

Comparative size: Robin to pigeon

Description: Rounded head; slightly down-curved bill; long, flared tail tapers to a point; brown overall with patterns of black spots, bars, and crescents; white rump patch

Yellow-shafted: Yellow wing linings; red patch on nape. Male: Black mustache

Red-shafted: Reddish to salmon-pink wing linings. Male: Red mustache

Range: From Alaska east to Newfoundland and south throughout the United States except southern Arizona; also in parts of Mexico and Central America

Habitat: Parks, large gardens, open country with trees, swamps, and marsh edges

Eggs: White

Collective noun(s): A descent of woodpeckers

Wren:
House Wren

House Wren (Troglodytes aedon)

Believed to have great magical power, the wren was considered a *magus avium*, "sorcerer bird." [169] A wren feather was believed to be powerful enough to be used as an amulet to protect against magic spells. This bird's feathers were also used as charms against shipwrecks on the Isle of Man, where it was believed that a sea sprite could conjure storms and then fly away as a wren.

The wren was closely associated with the Druids and said to be used for divination. The Welsh word *dryw* means both "wren" and "druid." [170] This association may have made the bird a target for a practice in the British Isles and parts of France called the Hunting of the Wren. It was considered unlucky to kill a wren except between Yule and New Year's Day. Later the hunt was centered on December 26 and said to rid the world of evil forces because the wren was thought to have a drop of the devil's blood in its veins. Killing this Druid bird was symbolic of ousting Pagan beliefs and practices. Also in the early Christian times of Ireland, wrens were believed to be witches. Although

---

169. Elizabeth Atwood Lawrence, *Hunting the Wren: Transformation of Bird to Symbol* (Knoxville, TN: University of Tennessee Press, 1997), 159.

170. Nozedar, *The Secret Language of Birds*, 150.

killing a wren for this annual hunt became illegal, the tradition continued with a token object in place of the bird.

It wasn't only the Druids who believed in the wren's oracular powers; in Rome this bird was said to have predicted the murder of Julius Caesar. As an omen, it was considered unlucky to see a wren at a wedding in Greece. A tale attributed to the Greek writer Aesop (620–564 BCE) tells how the wren outwitted the eagle to become the king of birds. A great avian assembly decided that the one who could fly highest would be their sovereign. From the get-go, the eagle looked like a sure winner until at the height of his flight, a tiny wren that had hidden in the eagle's feathers popped out and climbed higher in the sky.

Another legend about the wren, which is included in the entry on robin, concerns the symbolism of the wren and the robin representing the holly king and oak king, respectively. Unlike that tale of struggle, other folklore portrayed these two birds as mates: the female Jenny Wren to the male Robin Redbreast.

The wren's species name, *aedon*, is derived from the Greek words for "nightingale" and "songstress." [171] Songstress is an appropriate name since the wren sings all year rather than only during the mating season as most birds do. Wrens also sing their trilling melodies in duets and tend to be very loud at dawn. They are most often heard and not seen even though they live in close proximity to people.

Magical Workings

A renowned bird of magic, wren can help us explore and find our powers. Call on it for aid in developing magical and divination skills. When seeking interpretation of messages received through prophecy or any type of omen, hold an image of wren between your hands and let it speak through your intuition. Also do this before a divination session for aid in activating and opening the channels of communication. In addition, wren is instrumental in connecting with spirits.

This small creature shows us that no matter our beginnings, we can overcome our fears and achieve monumental things. Wren shows us that adaptability, resourcefulness, and endurance are key to attaining our goals as long as we remain grounded and true to our values. Honor it at Yule and especially on December 26 by placing its image or a figurine on your altar along with a sprig of holly.

---

171. Sandrock and Prior, *The Scientific Nomenclature of Birds in the Upper Midwest*, 146.

Make Connection

To connect with wren energy, dress in colors appropriate to a park, woods, or other land-scape near you. If possible, choose a place with tangled bushes or vines—places that wrens prefer—and sit nearby. Close your eyes and visualize this tiny bird sitting close by in the bushes. When the image becomes clear in your mind's eye, whisper three times: *"Magus avium, sorcerer bird; Hidden from view and only heard. From you there is much to learn; I hope your trust, I will earn."* Wren may choose to respond in your visualization or later in a dream.

Associations

Element(s): Air, earth, fire

Sabbat(s): Litha, Yule

Gods: Jupiter, Saturn, Taliesin, Thor

Trees: Holly, oak

Solar system: Saturn, Sun

Ogham: Duir

Bird Identification

HOUSE WREN (*TROGLODYTES AEDON*)

Size: 4½ to 5 inches

Wingspan: 6 to 6½ inches

Comparative size: Sparrow

Description: Small head, short neck, and plump body gives the appearance of a ball of feathers; long, curved beak; short wings; short tail usually held cocked; brown all over with dark patterning; paler brown underneath; pale eyebrow

Range: From British Columbia across Canada to New Brunswick, throughout the United States, Mexico, and Central and South Americas

Habitat: Open forests, farmland, residential areas, and city parks; especially in tangled bushes, thickets, and hedgerows

Eggs: White with brown marks

Collective noun(s): A chime of wrens

Summary

As we have seen, the Neolithic people of Old Europe had a rich Goddess-worshipping culture that celebrated and honored the cyclical turning of the wheel of life. The earliest deity was the Bird Goddess, whose veneration lasted almost twenty thousand years. In her aspects as life-giver and sustainer, death-wielder and regeneratrix, and transformer and energy of spirit, she encompasses the greatest mysteries of our world. Throughout all her forms, she is Mother. She gives us life, takes us back at death, and through her spirit our spirits are kept and then rekindled to start a new cycle.

As we explored each aspect of the Goddess, we learned how to incorporate her symbols into our twenty-first-century lives to enrich our spiritual paths. Beyond the suggestions in this book, you may find other ways and places where her symbols will have meaning for you. As we use these symbols, they become sacred again. Reaching back through time we can touch the lives of those who have gone before us so very long ago and keep the ember of their spirits alive. As we do this, we take our places along the strands in the great web of life.

Through the Goddess we have learned how her birds can keep us in touch with the natural world and its seasonal markers. We can enjoy these amazing creatures that live everywhere. Getting to know our local birds helps us stay in tune with the rhythm of the natural world. Birds can enhance our celebrations of sabbats and esbats and help us understand deities who came after the Bird Goddess.

Because everyone's experience is different, you may find it important to develop your own ways to connect with the energy of particular birds. Your guide bird may even assist you in this. Birds have a great deal to teach and share. Working with them helps awaken our intuition and aids in tapping into the subtle energies around us. Information comes softly like the whispering flutter of wings as the Bird Goddess speaks.

Appendix A
Chronology

Following are the approximate dates for the ages and civilizations mentioned in this book.

Approximate dates for ages:

2,000,000 to 10,000 BCE — Paleolithic (Old Stone Age)

10,000 to 5500 BCE — Mesolithic (Middle Stone Age)

5500 to 2500 BCE — Neolithic (New Stone Age) (Neolithic and Copper Age usually grouped together)

3000 to 1200 BCE — Bronze Age

1400 to 800 BCE — Iron Age

Approximate dates for civilizations:

7000 to 4000 BCE — Old Europe

4000 to 2000 BCE — Sumerian

3500 to 30 BCE — Egyptian

3000 to 1000 BCE — Minoan

1800 to 600 BCE — Babylonian

1600 to 1400 BCE — Mycenaean

800 to 200 BCE — Etruscan

800 to 146 BCE — Greek

323 to 146 BCE — Greek Hellenistic Period

31 BCE to 476 CE — Roman

Appendix B
Sabbats and Deities

For convenience, the following list of sabbats and deities provides the birds associated with them. The deities include a few major heroes and heroines.

Sabbats

Yule: Cardinal, eagle, goose (snow), kingfisher, owl, raven, robin, wren

Imbolc: Flamingo, owl, partridge, robin, swan, vulture

Ostara: Cormorant, crane, cuckoo, hawk, lark, meadowlark, parrot, sparrow, stork, swallow, swift

Beltane: Parrot, partridge

Litha: Cuckoo, eagle, falcon, finch, flamingo, hummingbird, lark, kingfisher, owl, robin, wren

Lughnasadh: Cock, pheasant

Mabon: Crane, goose, hawk, parrot, pheasant, swallow, swan, turkey

Samhain: Blackbird, chicken (hen and cock), cormorant, egret, gull, jay, magpie, owl, raven, swan, vulture, waxwing

Goddesses

Amaterasu: Chicken/cock, crow, pheasant, raven

Aphrodite: Bluebird, dove, goose, magpie, partridge, seagull, sparrow, swallow, swan

Artemis: Chicken/cock, crane, hawk, owl, quail, vulture

Astarte: Dove

Atargatis/Derceto: Dove

Athena: Blackbird, crane, crow, cuckoo, dove, nighthawk, oriole, owl, partridge, raven

Badb: Crane, crow, raven

Bertha: Blackbird, goose

Brigid: Chicken/cock, swan

Cailleach: Crane, crow, owl

Cerridwen: Chicken/hen, hawk

Circe: Hawk

Cliodna: Seagull

Danu: Hawk, raven

Demeter: Dove

Devi: Parrot, peacock

Dôn: Seagull

Epona: Raven

The Fates: Blackbird, nighthawk, oriole

Freya: Blackbird, dove, falcon, goose, nighthawk, oriole, raven

Frigg: Blackbird, falcon, nighthawk, oriole

Gaia: Jay

Hathor: Vulture

Hecate: Owl

Hera: Crane, cuckoo, dove, goose, hawk, peacock, stork

Hestia: Peacock

Holda/Holle: Blackbird, dove

Inanna: Dove, swallow

Iris: Peacock

Ishtar: Dove

Isis: Blackbird, dove, eagle, goose, hawk, ibis, swallow, vulture

Juno: Cuckoo, goose, peacock, stork

Justitia/Iustitia: Eagle

Lakshmi: Owl

Leucothea: Seagull

Lilith: Nightjar

Maat: Ibis, ostrich

Macha: Crow, raven

Maeve: Crow, raven

Maia: Dove

Minerva: Blackbird, flamingo, nighthawk, oriole, owl

The Morrigan: Crane, crow, raven

The Muses: Swift, swan

Mut: Vulture

Nantosuelta: Dove, raven

Neith: Blackbird

Nekhbet: Vulture

Nemesis: Swan

Nephthys: Falcon, hawk, vulture

The Norns: Blackbird, nighthawk, oriole

Persephone: Owl

Rhea: Dove

Rhiannon: Blackbird, crow, raven

Sarasvati: Peacock, swan

Sequana: Dove, duck

Tanit: Bluebird

Tiamat: Raven, vulture

Venus: Dove, partridge, sparrow, stork, swallow, swan

Gods

Agni: Cuckoo, eagle

Amun: Goose, heron, peacock

Angus: Swan

Apollo: Chicken/cock, crane, crow, dove, hawk, quail, raven, swan, vulture

Ares: Chicken/cock, eagle, owl, vulture, woodpecker

Asclepius: Cock, crow, owl, raven

Attis: Chicken/cock

Bacchus: Magpie

Belenus: Eagle, robin

Benu: Crane
Brahma: Goose, peacock, swan
Bran: Raven
Buddha: Crow, woodpecker
Cronus: Vulture
Cú Chulainn: Raven, swan
The Dagda: Crane, hawk
Esus: Egret
Geb: Goose
Hades: Owl
Helios: Chicken/cock
Hephaestus: Crane
Hermes: Chicken/cock, crane, hawk, ibis, peacock, stork
Horus: Falcon, goose, peacock
Hypnos: Nightjar
Indra: Eagle, owl, parrot
Jove: Chicken/cock
Jupiter: Eagle, robin, woodpecker, wren
Kama: Parrot
Khonsu: Falcon
Lemminkäinen: Cuckoo
Lir/Llyr: Swan
Loki: Crow, falcon, hawk
Lugh: Chicken/cock, crane, crow, cuckoo, eagle, raven
Manannan: Crane, seagull
Mars: Chicken/cock, jay, raven, vulture, woodpecker
Mercury: Chicken/cock, crow, hawk
Midir: Crane, swan
Mithras: Chicken/cock, crow, raven
Njord: Seagull, swan
Odin: Eagle, goose, raven
Osiris: Chicken/cock, goose
Pan: Cuckoo, eagle, peacock, woodpecker

Perun: Pigeon

Ra: Falcon, goose, hawk, swallow

Saturn: Crow, raven, vulture, wren

Shiva: Peacock

Silvanus: Woodpecker

Skanda: Chicken/cock, peacock

Taliesin: Wren

Thor: Cuckoo, robin, wren

Thoth: Ibis

Vishnu: Eagle, goose

Woden: Falcon

Zeus: Chicken/cock, cuckoo, dove, eagle (golden), peacock, swan, vulture, woodpecker

Bibliography

Books:

Aburrow, Yvonne. *Auguries and Omens: The Magical Lore of Birds*. Milverton, England: Capall Bann, 1994.

Ackerman, Diane. *The Rarest of the Rare: Vanishing Animals, Timeless Worlds*. New York: Vintage Books, 1995.

Adamson, Melitta Weiss. *Food in Medieval Times*. Westport, CT: Greenwood Press, 2004.

Alban, Gillian M. E. *Melusine the Serpent Goddess in A. S. Byatt's* Possession *and in Mythology*. Lanham, MD: Lexington Books, 2003.

Alcock, Joan P. *Food in the Ancient World*. Westport, CT: Greenwood Press, 2006.

Alderfer, Jonathan, ed. *National Geographic Complete Birds of North America*. Washington, DC: National Geographic Society, 2006.

——— . *National Geographic Bird-watcher's Bible: A Complete Treasury*. Washington, DC: National Geographic Society, 2012.

Allan, Tony, and Sara Maitland. *Ancient Greece and Rome: Myths and Beliefs*. New York: Rosen, 2012.

Andrews, Carol. *Amulets of Ancient Egypt*. Austin, TX: University of Texas Press, 1994.

Andrews, Sarah, and Josephine Quintero. *Lonely Planet Canary Islands*. Oakland, CA: Lonely Planet, 2007.

Andrews, Tamra. *A Dictionary of Nature Myths: Legends of the Earth, Sea, and Sky*. New York: Oxford University Press, 2000.

Andrews, Ted. *Animal Speak: The Spiritual and Magical Power of Creatures Great and Small*. St. Paul, MN: Llewellyn Publications, 2004.

Anonymous. *The Poetic Edda. Translated by Carolyne Larrington*. New York: Oxford University Press, 2014.

Anonymous. *The Upanishads. Translated by Juan Mascaró*. New York: Penguin Putnam, 1965.

Armstrong, Edward A. *The Life and Lore of the Bird: In Nature, Art, Myth and Literature*. New York: Crown Publishers, 1975.

Armstrong, Marian, ed. *Wildlife and Plants, Volume 6*. Tarrytown, New York: Marshall Cavendish, 2007.

Arnold, Caroline. *Stone Age Farmers Beside the Sea: Scotland's Prehistoric Village of Skara Brae*. New York: Clarion Books, 1997.

Arnott, W. Geoffrey. *Birds in the Ancient World from A to Z*. New York: Routledge, 2007.

Baring, Anne, and Jules Cashford. *The Myth of the Goddess: Evolution of an Image*. New York: Penguin Putnam, 1993.

Barnes, Julia. *Pet Parakeets*. Lydney, England: Westline Publishing, 2006.

Battistini, Matilde. *Symbols and Allegories in Art*. Los Angeles: Getty Publications, 2005.

Beath, Mary. *Hiking Alone: Trails Out, Trails Home*. Albuquerque, NM: University of New Mexico Press, 2008.

Becker, Udo, ed. *The Continuum Encyclopedia of Symbols*. New York: The Continuum International Publishing Group, 2000.

Beedy, Edward C., and Edward R. Pandolfino. *Birds of the Sierra Nevada: Their Natural History, Status, and Distribution*. Berkeley, CA: University of California Press, 2013.

Beletsky, Les. *Australia: The East*. Northampton, MA: Interlink Publishing, 2007.

———. *Birds of the World*. Baltimore: The Johns Hopkins University Press, 2006.

Berger, Cynthia. *Owls: Wild Guide*. Mechanicsburg, PA: Stackpole Books, 2005.

Bird, David M. *The Bird Almanac: A Guide to Essential Facts and Figures of the World's Birds*. Buffalo, NY: Firefly Books, 2004.

Birkhead, Tim, Jo Wimpenny, and Bob Montgomerie. *Ten Thousand Birds: Ornithology since Darwin*. Princeton, NJ: Princeton University Press, 2014.

Boatright, Mody C., Wilson M. Hudson, and Allen Maxwell, eds. *The Best of Texas Folk and Folklore, 1916–1954*. Denton, TX: University of North Texas Press, 1998.

Briggs, Constance Victoria. *The Encyclopedia of God: An A–Z Guide to Thoughts, Ideas, and Beliefs about God*. Charlottesville, VA: Hampton Roads, 2003.

——— . *Encyclopedia of the Unseen World*. San Francisco: Red Wheel/Weiser, 2010.

Brodsky, David. *Spanish Vocabulary: An Etymological Approach*. Austin, TX: University of Texas Press, 2008.

Browne, Ray B., and Pat Browne, eds. *The Guide to United States Popular Culture*. Madison, WI: The University of Wisconsin Press, 2001.

Bull, John, and John Farrand, Jr. *National Audubon Society Field Guide to North American Birds, Eastern Region*. New York: Alfred A. Knopf, 1995.

Burton, John A. *Birds of the Tropics*. London: Orbis Publishing, 1973.

Campbell, Joseph, with Bill Moyers. *The Power of Myth*. New York: Doubleday, 1988.

Carroll, William, ed. *Superstitions: 10,000 You Really Need*. San Marcos, CA: Coda Publications, 1998.

Chevalier, Jean, and Alain Gheerbrant. *A Dictionary of Symbols. Translated by John Buchanan-Brown*. New York: Penguin Books, 1996.

Christ, Carol P. *Rebirth of the Goddess: Finding Meaning in Feminist Spirituality*. New York: Routledge, 1997.

Cirlot, Juan E. *A Dictionary of Symbols*. Translated by Jack Sage. Mineola, NY: Dover Publications, 2002.

Cobham, David. *A Sparrowhawk's Lament: How British Breeding Birds of Prey Are Faring*. Princeton, NJ: Princeton University Press, 2014.

Coe, James. *Eastern Birds: A Guide to Field Identification*. New York: St. Martin's Press, 2001.

Colles, Abraham. *"A Witches' Ladder," The Folk-lore Journal*, Volume 5; Volume 19, 1–5. London: The Folklore Society of Great Britain, 1887.

Conway, D. J. *By Oak, Ash and Thorn: Modern Celtic Shamanism*. St. Paul, MN: Llewellyn Publications, 1995.

Corrick, James A. *Uniquely Arizona*. Chicago: Heinemann Library, 2004.

Cunningham, Scott. *Divination for Beginners: Reading the Past, Present and Future*. St. Paul, MN: Llewellyn Publications, 2004.

Dalal, Roshen. *The Religions of India: A Concise Guide to Nine Major Faiths*. New York: Penguin, 2014.

Daniels, Cora Linn, and C. M. Stevans, eds. *Encyclopedia of Superstitions, Folklore, and the Occult Sciences of the World*, Volume 3. Honolulu: University Press of the Pacific, 2003.

Davidson, Hilda R. Ellis. *Myths and Symbol in Pagan Europe: Early Scandinavian and Celtic Religions*. Syracuse, NY: Syracuse University Press, 1988.

Dawe, Neil, and Karen Dawe. *The Bird Book*. New York: Workman Publishing, 1988.

Day, Leslie. *Field Guide to the Natural World of New York City*. Baltimore: Johns Hopkins University Press, 2007.

de Grummond, Nancy Thomson. *Etruscan Myth, Sacred History, and Legend*. Philadelphia: University of Pennsylvania Museum of Archeology and Anthropology, 2006.

de Kay, James E. *Zoology of New York, Part II, Birds*. Albany, NY: The New York Assembly, 1844.

Dennis, Geoffrey W., Rabbi. *The Encyclopedia of Jewish Myth, Magic and Mysticism*. Woodbury, MN: Llewellyn, 2007.

Doniger, Wendy, ed. *"Earth Mother," Merriam-Webster's Encyclopedia of World Religions*. Springfield, MA: Merriam-Webster, 1999.

Doughty, Robin W. *The Mockingbird*. Austin, TX: University of Texas Press, 1988.

Duncan, Francis Martin. *Cassell's Natural History*. New York: Cassell and Company, 1913.

Duriš, Jaroslav Spirhanzl, and Edmund Burke. *Spotting Birds: A Pocket Guide to Bird Watching*. London: Hamlyn, 1990.

Durkin, Philip. *Borrowed Words: A History of Loanwords in English*. New York: Oxford University Press, 2014.

Eason, Cassandra. *Fabulous Creatures, Mythical Monsters, and Animal Power Symbols: A Handbook*. Westport, CT: Greenwood Press, 2008.

Eastman, John. *The Eastman Guide to Birds: Natural History Accounts for 150 North American Species*. Mechanicsburg, PA: Stackpole Books, 2012.

Eisler, Riane. *The Chalice and the Blade: Our History, Our Future*. New York: HarperCollins, 1995.

Eliade, Mircea. *Images and Symbols: Studies in Religious Symbolism*. Translated by Philip Mairet. Princeton, NJ: Princeton University Press, 1991.

Elliott, Lang. *Know Your Bird Sounds: Songs and Calls of Yard, Garden, and City Birds,* Volume 1. Mechanicsburg, PA: Stackpole Books, 2004.

Emerson, Ellen Russell. *Nature and Human Nature.* New York: Houghton, Mifflin and Company, 1902.

Erickson, Laura. *For the Birds: An Uncommon Guide.* Duluth, MN: Pfeifer-Hamilton, 1994.

———. *101 Ways to Help Birds.* Mechanicsburg, PA: Stackpole Books, 2006.

Farrand, John. *Eastern Birds: An Audubon Handbook.* New York: McGraw-Hill, 1988.

Ferguson, Diana. *The Magickal Year.* London: Batsford, 1996.

Fontana, David. *The Secret Language of Symbols: A Visual Key to Symbols and Their Meanings.* San Francisco: Chronicle Books, 2003.

Forbes, Alexander Robert. *Gaelic Names of Beasts (Mammalia), Birds, Fishes, Insects, Reptiles, Etc.* Edinburgh, Scotland: Oliver and Boyd, 1905.

Fraser, Ian, and Jeannie Gray. *Australian Bird Names: A Complete Guide.* Collingwood, Australia: CSIRO Publishing, 2013.

Fundaburk, Emma Lila, and Mary Douglass Fundaburk Foreman, eds. *Sun Circles and Human Hands: The Southeastern Indians Art and Industries.* Tuscaloosa, AL: University of Alabama Press, 2008.

Furtman, Michael. *Ruffed Grouse: Woodland Drummer.* Mechanicsburg, PA: Stackpole Books, 1999.

———. *Why Birds Do That: 40 Distinctive Bird Behaviors Explained and Photographed.* Minocqua, WI: Willow Creek Press, 2004.

Gessner, David. *Return of the Osprey: A Season of Flight and Wonder.* Chapel Hill, NC: Algonquin Books of Chapel Hill, 2001.

Gibson, Claire. *Goddess Symbols: Universal Signs of the Divine Female.* New York: Barnes & Noble Books, 1998.

Gill, Frank B. *Ornithology, Third Edition.* New York: W. H. Freeman and Company, 2007.

Gillespie, Angus K., and Jay Mechling, eds. *American Wildlife in Symbol and Story.* Knoxville, TN: University of Tennessee Press, 1987.

Gimbutas, Marija. *The Goddesses and Gods of Old Europe: Myths and Cult Images.* Berkeley, CA: University of California Press. 1982.

———. *The Civilization of the Goddess: The World of Old Europe.* San Francisco: HarperSanFrancisco, 1991.

Gimbutas, Marija. *The Language of the Goddess*. San Francisco: HarperSanFrancisco, 1991.

——— . *The Living Goddesses*. Berkeley, CA: University of California Press, 2001.

Green, Miranda. *Symbol and Image in Celtic Religious Art*. New York: Routledge, 1992.

——— . *Animals in Celtic Life and Myth*. New York: Routledge, 2002.

Goldman, Phyllis B., ed. *Monkeyshines on Mexico: Land of Legends!* Greensboro, NC: North Carolina Learning Institute for Fitness and Education, 1995.

Hagen, Rose-Marie, and Rainer Hagen. *What Great Paintings Say,* Volume 1. Los Angeles: Taschen America, 2003.

Hall, James. *Dictionary of Subjects and Symbols in Art*. Boulder, CO: Westview Press, 2008.

Hanel, Rachael. *Parrots*. Mankato, MN: Creative Education, 2009.

Hardwick, Charles. *Giants, Fairies and Boggarts: In Northern England*. Auckland, New Zealand: The Floating Press, 2012.

Harris, Tim, ed. *National Geographic Complete Birds of the World*. Washington, DC: National Geographic Society, 2009.

Hendrickson, Robert. *The Facts on File Dictionary of American Regionalisms: Local Expressions from Coast to Coast*. New York: Facts on File, 2000.

Hill, Caroline, and Ina Stradins, eds. *American Museum of Natural History Birds of North America Eastern Region*. New York: Dorling Kindersley, Limited, 2011.

Hoffman, Susanna, and Victoria Wise. *Bold: A Cookbook of Big Flavors*. New York: Workman Publishing, 2013.

Hudson, W. H. *Birds in Town & Village*. Whitefish, MT: Kessinger Publishing, 2004.

Husain, Shahrukh. *The Goddess: Power, Sexuality, and the Feminine Divine*. Ann Arbor, MI: University of Michigan Press, 2003.

Impelluso, Lucia. *Nature and Its Symbols*. Translated by Stephen Sartarelli. Los Angeles: Getty Publications, 2004.

Jacobs, Joseph, ed. *Folklore,* Volume 12. Memphis, TN: General Books, 2012.

Johnson, Buffie. *Lady of the Beasts: The Goddess and Her Sacred Animals*. Rochester, VT: Inner Traditions International, 1994.

Johnston, Richard F., and Marián Janiga. *Feral Pigeons*. New York: Oxford University Press, 1995.

Jordan, E. Bernard. *The Laws of Thinking: 20 Secrets to Using the Divine Power of Your Mind to Manifest Prosperity.* Carlsbad, CA: Hay House, 2006.

Jung, Carl Gustav. *Man and His Symbols.* New York: Dell Publishing, 1968.

Kaplan, Gisela, and Lesley J. Rogers. *Birds: Their Habits and Skills.* Crows Nest, Australia: Allen & Unwin, 2001.

Kaufman, Kenn. *Lives of North American Birds.* New York: Houghton Mifflin, 1996.

———. *Field Guide to Birds of North America.* New York: Houghton Mifflin, 2000.

Keister, Douglas. *Stories in Stone: A Field Guide to Cemetery Symbolism and Iconography.* Layton, UT: Gibbs Smith, 2004.

Kenner, T. A. *Symbols and Their Hidden Meaning.* London: Carlton Publishing Group, 2007.

Kerényi, Carl. *Dionysos: Archetypal Image of Indestructible Life.* Translated by Ralph Manheim. Princeton, NJ: Princeton University Press, 1976.

Kinch, John A. *A Journey for All Seasons: A Cross-country Celebration of the Natural World.* New York: The Lyons Press, 2000.

King, Scott Alexander. *Animal Dreaming: The Symbolic and Spiritual Language of the Australasian Animals.* Glen Waverley, Australia: Blue Angel Gallery, 2007.

Koch, John T. *Celtic Culture: A Historical Encyclopedia,* Volumes 1-5. Santa Barbara, CA: ABC-CLIO, 2006.

Knight, Sirona. *Celtic Traditions: Druids, Faeries, and Wiccan Rituals.* New York: Citadel Press, 2000.

Kroodsma, Donald. *The Singing Life of Birds: The Art and Science of Listening to Birdsong.* New York: Houghton Mifflin, 2005.

Lachman, Larry, Diane Grindol, and Frank Kocher. *Birds Off the Perch: Therapy and Training for Your Pet Bird.* New York: Fireside, 2003.

Lack, Peter. *The Atlas of Wintering Birds in Britain and Ireland.* London: T & AD Poyser, 2011.

Lamb, Sydney M., and E. Douglas Mitchell. *Sprung from Some Common Source: Investigations into the Prehistory of Languages.* Stanford, CA: Stanford University Press, 1991.

Larson, Jeanette, and Adrienne Yorinks. *Hummingbirds: Facts and Folklore from the Americas.* Watertown, MA: Charlesbridge, 2011.

Lawrence, Elizabeth Atwood. *Hunting the Wren: Transformation of Bird to Symbol.* Knoxville, TN: University of Tennessee Press, 1997.

Lawson-Jones, Mark. *Why was the Partridge in the Pear Tree?: The History of Christmas Carols*. Stroud, England: The History Press, 2011.

Le Blanc, Charles, and Susan Blader, eds. *Chinese Ideas About Nature and Society: Studies in Honour of Derk Bodde*. Hong Kong: Hong Kong University Press, 1987.

Leland, Charles G. *Gypsy Sorcery and Fortune Telling*. Altenmünster, Germany: Jazzybee Verlag Jürgen Beck, 2012.

Lerro, Bruce. *From Earth Spirits to Sky Gods: The Socioecological Origins of Monotheism, Individualism, and Hyper-Abstract Reasoning, From the Stone Age to the Axial Iron Age*. Lanham, MD: Lexington Books, 2000.

Liberman, Anatoly. *An Analytic Dictionary of the English Etymology: An Introduction*. Minneapolis, MN: University of Minnesota Press, 2008.

Lindsey, Terence. *Albatrosses*. Collingwood, Australia: CSIRO Publishing, 2008.

Littleton, C. Scott, ed. *Gods, Goddesses, and Mythology*, Volume 2. Tarrytown, NY: Marshall Cavendish, 2005.

Ludwig, Allan I. *Graven Images: New England Stone Carving and its Symbols 1650–1815*. Middletown, CT: Wesleyan University Press, 1999.

Lutwack, Leonard. *Birds in Literature*. Gainesville, FL: University Press of Florida, 1994.

MacKillop, James. *Myths and Legends of the Celts*. New York: Penguin, 2006.

MacLeod, Sharon Paice. *Celtic Myth and Religion: A Study of Traditional Belief, with Newly Translated Prayers, Poems, and Songs*. Jefferson, NC: McFarland & Company, 2012.

Marinatos, Nannó. *The Goddess and the Warrior: The Naked Goddess and Mistress of Animals in Early Greek Religion*. New York: Routledge, 2005.

Marshack, Alexander. *The Roots of Civilization: The Cognitive Beginnings of Man's First Art, Symbol and Notation*. Wakefield, RI: Moyer Bell, 1991.

Martimort, A. G., I. H. Dalmais, and P. Jounel, eds. *The Liturgy and Time: The Church at Prayer: An Introduction to the Liturgy, Volume IV*. Collegeville, MN: Liturgical Press, 1986.

Martin, Deborah L. *Best-Ever Backyard Birding Tips: Hundreds of Easy Ways to Attract the Birds You Love to Watch*. New York: Rodale, 2008.

Marvelly, Paula. *Women of Wisdom: A Journey of Enlightenment by Women of Vision Through the Ages*. London: Watkins Publishing, 2005.

Maxon, Martha Anne. *The Real Roadrunner*. Norman, OK: Oklahoma University Press, 2005.

McDermott, Bridget. *Decoding Egyptian Hieroglyphs: How to Read the Secret Language of the Pharaohs.* San Francisco: Chronicle Books, 2001.

McIntosh, Jane. *Handbook to Life in Prehistoric Europe.* New York: Oxford University Press, 2006.

McPhee, John. *The Survival of the Bark Canoe.* New York: Farrar, Straus and Giroux, 1982.

Milne, Lorus, and Margery Milne. *North American Birds.* Englewood Cliffs, NJ: Prentice-Hall, 1969.

Mittelbach, Margaret, and Michael Crewdson. *Carnivorous Nights: On the Trail of the Tasmanian Tiger.* New York: Villard Books, 2006.

Monaghan, Patricia. *The Encyclopedia of Celtic Mythology and Folklore.* New York: Facts on File, 2004.

Morrison, Lesley. *The Healing Wisdom of Birds: An Everyday Guide to Their Spiritual Songs and Symbolism.* Woodbury, MN: Llewellyn Publications, 2011.

Morton, Mark. *Cupboard Love 2: A Dictionary of Culinary Curiosities,* Second Revised Edition. Toronto, Canada: Insomniac Press, 2004.

Moss, Stephen. *A Bird in the Bush: A Social History of Birdwatching.* London: Aurum Press, 2004.

——— . *The Garden Bird Handbook.* London: New Holland Publishers, 2006.

Moss, Stephen, and David Cottridge. *Attracting Birds to Your Garden.* London: New Holland Publishers, 2006.

Murphy-Hiscock, Arin. *Birds: A Spiritual Field Guide.* Avon, MA: Adams Media, 2012.

Murtagh, Nyiri. *The Backyard Duck Book: For the Love of Ducks,* Revised Edition. Collingwood, Australia: CSIRO Publishing, 2012.

Nahmad, Claire. *Earth Magic: A Wisewoman's Guide to Herbal, Astrological, and Other Folk Wisdom.* Rochester, VT: Destiny Books, 1994.

Noble, Vicki. *The Double Goddess: Women Sharing Power.* Rochester, VT: Bear & Company, 2003.

Nozedar, Adele. *The Secret Language of Birds: A Treasury of Myths, Folklore and Inspirational True Stories.* London: Harper Element, 2006.

Nuttall, Mark. *Encyclopedia of the Arctic.* New York: Routledge, 2005.

Oliver, Harry. *Black Cats & Four-Leaf Clovers: The Origins of Old Wives' Tales and Superstitions in Our Everyday Lives.* New York: Perigee Books, 2010.

Osborne, June. *The Cardinal.* Austin, TX: University of Texas Press, 1992.

Pasieczny, Robert G., ed. *DK Eyewitness Travel Guide: Canary Islands.* New York: Dorling Kindersley, 2013.

Patent, Dorothy Hinshaw. *Feathers.* New York: Cobblehill Books, 1992.

Peek, Hedley, and Frederick George Aflalo. *The Encyclopedia of Sport.* London: Richard Clay and Sons, 1901.

Peterson, Roger Tory. *A Field Guide to Feeder Birds: Eastern and Central North America, Fifth Edition.* New York: Houghton Mifflin, 2002.

Pinch, Geraldine. *Handbook of Egyptian Mythology.* Santa Barbara, CA: ABC-CLIO, 2002.

Potts, Annie. *Chicken.* London, England: Reaktion Books, 2012.

Pratt, Christina. *An Encyclopedia of Shamanism,* Volume One, A–M. New York: Rosen, 2007.

Randolph, Vance. *Ozark Magic and Folklore.* Mineola, NY: Dover 1964.

Rapoza, Brian. *Birding Florida.* Guilford, CT: Morris Book, 2007.

Read, Marie. *Secret Lives of Common Birds: Enjoying Bird Behavior through the Seasons.* New York: Houghton Mifflin, 2005.

Regardie, Israel. *The Philosopher's Stone: Spiritual Alchemy, Psychology, and Ritual Magic.* Woodbury, MN: Llewellyn Publications, 2013.

Remler, Pat. *Egyptian Mythology A to Z,* Third Edition. New York: Chelsea House, 2010.

Rigoglioso, Marguerite. *The Cult of Divine Birth in Ancient Greece.* New York: Palgrave Macmillan, 2009.

Rising, James D. *A Guide to the Identification and Natural History of the Sparrows of the United States and Canada.* London: Christopher Helm, 2010.

Robins, Gay. *Women in Ancient Egypt.* Cambridge, MA: Harvard University Press, 1993.

Rolleston, T. W. *Celtic Myths and Legends.* Mineola, NY: Dover Publications, 1990.

Roots, Clive. *Flightless Birds.* Westport, CT: Greenwood Press, 2006.

——— . *Domestication.* Westport, CT: Greenwood Press, 2007.

Ross, Anne. *Pagan Celtic Britain: Studies in Iconography and Tradition.* London: Constable and Company, 1992.

Ruth, Maria Mudd. *Hawks and Falcons.* Tarrytown, NY: Marshall Cavendish, 2004.

Sacher, Jay, ed. *A Compendium of Collective Nouns: From an Armory of Aardvarks to a Zeal of Zebras.* San Francisco: Chronicle Books, 2013.

Safina, Carl. *Eye of the Albatross: Visions of Hope and Survival.* New York: Henry Holt, 2002.

Sandrock, James, and Jean C. Prior. *The Scientific Nomenclature of Birds in the Upper Midwest.* Iowa City, IA: University of Iowa Press, 2014.

Sax, Boria. *The Mythical Zoo: An Encyclopedia of Animals in World Myth, Legend, and Literature.* Santa Barbara, CA: ABC-CLIO, 2001.

Scholz, Floyd. *Birds of Prey.* Mechanicsburg, PA: Stackpole Books, 1993.

Shaheen, Naseeb. *Biblical References in Shakespeare's Plays.* Lanham, MD: Rowman & Littlefield, 2011.

Sherk, Bill. *500 Years of New Words.* Tonawanda, NY: Dundurn Press, 2004.

Shipley, Joseph T. *Dictionary of Word Origins.* Whitefish, MT: Literary Licensing, 2012.

Skafte, Diane. *Listening to the Oracle: The Ancient Art of Finding Guidance in the Signs and Symbols All Around Us.* San Francisco: HarperSanFrancisco, 1997.

Smith, Andrew F. *The Turkey: An American Story.* Urbana, IL: University of Illinois Press, 2006.

Smith, Jane S. *In Praise of Chickens: A Compendium of Wisdom Fair and Fowl.* Guilford, CT: Lyons Press, 2012.

Snell, Daniel C. *Religions of the Ancient Near East.* New York: Cambridge University Press, 2011.

Snodgrass, A. M. *The Dark Age of Greece: An Archeological Study of the Eleventh to Eighth Centuries B.C.* Edinburgh, Scotland: Edinburgh University Press, 2000.

Sorenson, Sharon. *Birds in the Yard Month by Month.* Mechanicsburg, PA: Stackpole Books, 2013.

Spence, Lewis. *An Introduction to Mythology.* New York: Cosimo, 2005.

———. *The Magic Arts in Celtic Britain.* New York: Dover Publications, 1999.

Spielvogel, Jackson J. *Western Civilization,* Sixth Edition. Independence, KY: Cengage Learning, 2005.

Stap, Don. *Birdsong.* New York: Scribner, 2005.

Stevens, Anthony. *Ariadne's Clue: A Guide to the Symbols of Humankind.* Princeton, NJ: Princeton University Press, 1998.

Stevens, Thomas. *Through Russia on a Mustang.* New York: Cassell Publishing, 1891.

Stewart, William. *Dictionary of Images and Symbols in Counseling*. London: Jessica Kingsley Publishers, 1998.

Stonham, Charles. *The Birds of the British Islands*, Volume 1. London: E. Grant Richards, 1906.

Streep, Peg. *Sanctuaries of the Goddess: The Sacred Landscapes and Objects*. Boston: Bulfinch Press, 1994.

Strong, Herbert A. *The Syrian Goddess*. Charleston, SC: BiblioBazaar, 2007.

Summers-Smith, J. Denis. *In Search of Sparrows*. London: T & AD Poyser, 1992.

Sutcliffe, Steven. *Religion: Empirical Studies*. Burlington, VT: Ashgate Publishing Company, 2004.

Swaysland, W. *Familiar Wild Birds*, Volume 4. New York: Cassell and Company, 1901.

Sykley, Julie-Anne. *The Twilight Symbols: Motifs-Meanings-Messages*. Alresford, England: Our Street Books, 2012.

Tate, Peter. *Flights of Fancy: Birds in Myth, Legend, and Superstition*. New York: Bantam Dell, 2007.

Titlow, Budd. *Bird Brains: Inside the Strange Minds of Our Fine Feathered Friends*. Guilford, CT: Lyons Press, 2013.

Tresidder, Jack. *The Complete Dictionary of Symbols*. San Francisco: Chronicle Books, 2005.

——— . *The Watkins Dictionary of Symbols*. London: Watkins Publishing, 2008.

Tveten, John L., and Gloria A. Tveten. *Our Life With Birds*. College Station, TX: Texas A&M University Press, 2004.

Tyrrell, Esther Quesada. "Jewels of the Sky," *Islands* Vol. 14, No. 6. (Nov–Dec 1994): 52–56.

van Grouw, Katrina. *The Unfeathered Bird*. Princeton, NJ: Princeton University Press, 2013.

Vollmar, Klaus. *Dream Symbols*. New York: Sterling Publishing, 1997.

Vriends, Matthew M. *Pigeons: A Complete Pet Owner's Manual*. Hauppauge, NY: Barron's Educational, 1988.

Vriends, Matthew M., and Tanya M. Heming-Vriends. *The Canary Handbook*. Hauppauge, NY: Barron's Educational, 2001.

Waldau, Paul, and Kimberley C. Patton, eds. *A Communion of Subjects: Animals in Religion, Science, and Ethics*. New York: Columbia University Press, 2006.

Walker-Meikle, Kathleen. *Medieval Pets.* Woodbridge, England: Boydell Press, 2012.

Wansbury, Andrea. *Birds: Divine Messengers: Transform your Life with their Guidance and Wisdom.* Forres, Scotland: Findhorn Press, 2006.

Wauer, Roland H. *The American Robin.* Austin, TX: University of Texas Press, 1999.

Weir Huber, Barbara. *Transforming Psyche.* Montreal, Canada: McGill-Queen's University Press, 1999.

Wells, Diana. *100 Birds and How They Got Their Names.* Chapel Hill, NC: Algonquin Books of Chapel Hill, 2002.

Werness, Hope B. *The Continuum Encyclopedia of Animal Symbolism in Art.* New York: Continuum International, 2006.

Westmoreland, Perry L. *Ancient Greek Beliefs.* San Ysidro, CA: Lee and Vance Publishing, 2007.

Wheeler, Ramona Louise. *Walk Like an Egyptian: A Modern Guide to the Religion and Philosophy of Ancient Egypt,* Third Edition. Rockville, MD: Wildside Press, 2005.

Wheye, Darryl, and Donald Kennedy. *Humans, Nature, and Birds: Science Art from Cave Walls to Computer Screens.* New Haven, CT: Yale University Press, 2008.

White, Newman Ivey, ed. *The Frank C. Brown Collection of North Carolina Folklore,* Vol. VII. Durham, NC: Duke University Press, 1977.

Wild, Dennis. *The Double-Crested Cormorant: Symbol of Ecological Conflict.* Ann Arbor, MI: University of Michigan Press, 2012.

Williams, Edgar. *Ostrich.* London: Reaktion Books, 2013.

Witzel, E. J. Michael. *The Origins of the World's Mythologies.* New York: Oxford University Press, 2012.

Yarnall, Judith. *Transformations of Circe: The History of an Enchantress.* Champaign, IL: University of Illinois Press, 1994.

Young, William. *The Fascination of Birds: From the Albatross to the Yellowthroat.* Mineola, NY: Dover Publications, 2014.

Zaczek, Iain. *Pirates: Facts, Figures and Fun.* Wisley, England: AAPPL Artists' and Photographers' Press, 2007.

Zickefoose, Julie, ed. *Natural Gardening for Birds: Simple Ways to Create a Bird Haven.* Emmaus, PA: Rodale Press, 2001.

Online Resources:

The Cornell Lab of Ornithology—Cornell University. http://www.allaboutbirds.org.

The International Osprey Foundation. "Osprey." Accessed June 20, 2014. www.ospreys
  .com/styled/index.html.

Migratory Bird Treaty Act. Accessed January 20, 2012. www.fws.gov/migratorybirds.

The National Audubon Society. www.audubon.org/field-guide.

The National Geographic Society. animals.nationalgeographic.com/animals/birds/.

New Hampshire Public Television. "American Flamingo." Accessed August 15, 2014.
  www.nhptv.org/wild/greaterflamingo.asp.

New Zealand Birds. "Collective Nouns." Accessed October 30, 2014. www.nzbirds.com/
  more/nouns.html.

Palomar Audubon Society. "Collective Nouns." Accessed April 5, 2014.
  palomaraudubon.org/collective.html.

Stromberg, Joseph. "African Grey Parrots Have the Reasoning Skills of 3-year-olds,"
  Smithsonian.com. August 8, 2012. www.smithsonianmag.com/science-nature
  /african-grey-parrots-have-the-reasoning-skills-of-3-year-olds-15955221/?no-ist.

University of Michigan Museum of Zoology. www.lsa.umich.edu/ummz/.

Index

To Write to the Author

If you wish to contact the author or would like more information about this book, please write to the author in care of Llewellyn Worldwide Ltd. and we will forward your request. Both the author and publisher appreciate hearing from you and learning of your enjoyment of this book and how it has helped you. Llewellyn Worldwide Ltd. cannot guarantee that every letter written to the author can be answered, but all will be forwarded. Please write to:

Sandra Kynes
℅ Llewellyn Worldwide
2143 Wooddale Drive
Woodbury, MN 55125-2989

Please enclose a self-addressed stamped envelope for reply,
or $1.00 to cover costs. If outside the U.S.A., enclose
an international postal reply coupon.

Many of Llewellyn's authors have websites with additional information and resources. For more information, please visit our website at http://www.llewellyn.com